T0330141

Industrial Districts

To my 'extended' family

Industrial Districts
Evolution and Competitiveness in Italian Firms

Ivana Paniccia

University of Reading, UK
Italian Energy Authority, Italy

Edward Elgar
Cheltenham, UK • Northampton, MA, USA

Published by
Edward Elgar Publishing Limited
Glensanda House
Montpellier Parade
Cheltenham
Glos GL50 1UA
UK

Edward Elgar Publishing, Inc.
136 West Street
Suite 202
Northampton
Massachusetts 01060
USA

A catalogue record for this book
is available from the British Library

Library of Congress Cataloguing in Publication Data
Paniccia, Ivana.
    Industrial Districts : evolution and competitiveness in Italian firms / Ivana Paniccia.
        p. cm.
    Includes bibliographical references and index.
    1. Industrial Districts. 2. Competition, International. 3. Industrial districts—Italy—Case studies. I. Title.

HD1393.5 .345 2002
338.6'0945—dc21   2001051132

ISBN 1 84064 684 5

Printed and bound in Great Britain by Biddles Ltd. *www.biddles.co.uk*

Contents

Figures

Tables

Acknowledgements

During my years of research on industrial districts I have met many people deeply involved in the vibrant activity of industrial districts or in their no less passionate analysis. Some of them have helped me to answer some questions, while others have more simply transmitted to me their enthusiasm for industrial districts or for research in general, and encouraged me to persist with my studies. My deepest thanks and appreciation goes to Mark Casson for his methodological teaching during my PhD course at the University of Reading and for convincing me that the 'mysteries of research are . . . in data'. I would also like to mention the following people, apologizing in advance for all those that I have forgotten: Fiorenza Belussi (University of Padua); Lucio Biggiero (University of L'Aquila); John Cantwell (University of Reading); Giancarlo Corò (Ires, Veneto); Anna Grandori (University of Modena and Bocconi University); Franco A. Grassini (Luiss University, Rome); Paolo Gurisatti (Bassano); Pasquale Lelio Iapadre (University of L'Aquila); Luciano Lecce (Cisl, Giulianova); Marisa Lucano (Cgil, Biella); Fabrizio Mele (Luiss University); Fabio Sforzi (Irpet, Florence); Carlo Vedù (Bassano, Centro Ceramica); Gianfranco Viesti (Cerpem, Bari); the Staff of Cisl of Arzignano; the Staff of Unione Industriale di Teramo and the staff of Cisl, Ufficio Studi in Florence.

Above all, I owe a profound debt to my husband, Silverio, and my 'extended' family for their unremitting encouragement and support.

Introduction and Outline

Over the last few decades, several experts in various fields and countries have interested themselves in industrial districts (henceforth: IDs), a term which, generally speaking, stands for any agglomeration of small to medium-sized firms engaged in one or a few complementary industries in a limited area.

Following their discovery by A. Marshall a century ago, IDs have flourished since the Second World War throughout Europe, and in Italy in particular, where they have become another 'made in Italy' export product. After some years of suspicion or indifference on the part of mainstream economics, IDs have attracted close attention in the academic literature, and even the economic press in Italy now acknowledges their decisive contribution to the development and performance of the country's domestic economy. The wide extension of IDs in Italy explains that country's model of specialization and its role in the international division of labour. Less numerous, but not irrelevant, are IDs in other European countries, such as Denmark (Kristensen, 1992), France (Benko et al., 1997; Camagni, 1991; OECD, 1996), Germany (Grotz and Braun, 1997; Herrigel, 1996), and Spain (Benton, 1992; OECD, 1996), while agglomerations of SMEs dependent on a few, generally transnational, leading companies may also be found in the UK (Keeble and Wilkinson, 1999). The latter cases may better be defined as 'clusters'; that is, a mix of large and small enterprises with strong local supply chains, a phenomenon also widespread in the USA (Markusen, 1996; Porter, 1990). IDs are also documented in the developing countries (Cadene and Holstrom, 1998; Di Tommaso and Rabellotti, 1999; Rabellotti, 1997).

The idea of the ID has exerted great fascination on authors belonging to various disciplines, who envisage it as an alternative to mass production, or to the market institution, as a new organizational mode or as an embedded economic system. The idea of IDs in the international debate owes much of its success to the works of Piore and Sabel (1984), Scott (1988a and 1988b) and Best (1990), who view them as an alternative to mass production. Accordingly, numerous authors have discovered an example of the post-Fordist economic paradigm in the particular way that work is organized in IDs. This view has convinced foreign scholars and governments: indeed, in the United States, the former President Clinton included the promotion of IDs in his first electoral programme.

A large body of literature has offered evidence of successful IDs in Italy and elsewhere, and of their ability to act as bulwarks against the redundancies put into effect by larger firms during the 1980s, or to sustain national competitiveness in several countries in the past decade. In the present economic and technological context, IDs may still appeal to policy makers or scholars as an organizational or local development model able to reconcile local identity or social cohesion and globalization. The competitiveness and sustainability of IDs in the face of globalization processes, however, cannot be taken for granted, especially if certain new social and economic trends are considered.

The challenge for IDs and local networks of small and medium-sized enterprises (henceforth: SMEs) to stay competitive and preserve their local 'embeddedness' is particularly important, both for the countries in which they are still a large component of the industrial structure, and for those countries anxious to promote native entrepreneurship (for example, Eastern Europe).

Notwithstanding the many studies on and different approaches to IDs, no sound theory has yet been developed. The frequently misused term of 'ID' may conceal many forms of work organization and many different socio-cultural structures. The term still suffers from semantic ambiguity. Empirically speaking, in spite of the wide variety of research carried out in various disciplines and throughout the world, a systematic and comparative study is still lacking – as also admitted by the pioneers in this field (Becattini and Rullani, 1993).

What strikes the reader of case studies on IDs is the variety of approaches used and the diversity of the phenomena examined. The resulting impression is twofold: specific and not repeatable features of specific IDs are attached to a general, though sometimes unspecified, model; general features of the model are automatically applied, with no empirical assessment, to areas which simply display a high concentration of (small) firms.

The shortcomings in the available literature reside both in the lack of comparative and historical studies and in the disregard shown for an agreed and operationalized definition of 'ID'. Comparative studies can explain the structural features common to IDs, while an evolutionary analysis makes it possible to understand their formation, change and adaptability. The available literature offers a conceptualization of IDs, rather than a theory; what we require is a more general theory of local phenomena of industrial development able to distinguish among different types of IDs. Moreover, and perhaps more crucially, a testable theory based on operational concepts is required; one able to explain how different models of IDs can be classified, how they arise, evolve and perform.

This book scrutinizes whether, under which conditions, and to what extent (all) IDs perform positively. It provides an attempt to operationalize the definition of the ID as deriving from various but often converging approaches.

Second, the book tackles the issue of the change and evolution of IDs; that is, the questions of whether, on the one hand, they can continue to be a stable model of organization able to ensure continuous growth and job opportunities for all components of local society and, on the other hand, whether they are able to evolve, innovate and adapt – preserving their 'identity' – to external changes.

A third question concerns the nature of IDs as an alternative mode of governance of interfirm linkages based on trust and cooperation. The issue of cooperation as a pervasive rule of governance in IDs or networks and of explanatory conditions for the diffusion of cooperative behaviours – if any – will be analysed in depth.

The approach adopted in this book is multidisciplinary and quantitative in that it takes account of social (institutional) and economic factors. The methodology adopted has enabled evaluation of the 'regulatory' or 'normative' value of the 'canonical' ID model (for example, G. Becattini, M. Best, M. Piore and C. Sabel) and its status as a model of growth or as a model of socio-economic or industrial organization.

The empirical data used are drawn from a comparative and quantitative study carried out by the author in the last six years on a sample of Italian IDs. The latter are initially defined as agglomerations of SMEs engaged in one or a few complementary industries in a given area. The sample covers more than 30 per cent of manufacturing employment in all Italian IDs. Data are taken both from industry and population censuses (1951 to 1996) and other official sources of statistics, and from questionnaires sent to qualified observers and institutions.

This approach differs from most other studies, which are mainly qualitative in nature and based on a single or a few case studies. Starting from these differences, the book 'lays bare' and 'destructures' the 'canonical' idea of IDs and applies different conceptual tools taken from economics and sociology. Supported by multivariate and econometric analyses, the variety resulting from empirical analysis is referred to four general types of IDs with different regulatory rules and institutions, inter-organizational relations, success (and decline) factors and development paths.

The results show that while IDs on average achieve better static or dynamic economic performance than do non-ID areas, discrepancies emerge among different types of ID, while the features of an integrated society are not apparent in all cases. Analysis based on a wide spectrum of comparable indicators and information highlights some lines of discontinuity in the socio-economic equilibrium of IDs that may impair their future competitiveness and social sustainability. A leading role for socio-economic entrepreneurs able to redirect the development of these areas is envisaged.

The book is divided into two parts. Part One examines the main issues on the ID research agenda by conducting a critical survey of studies arising from different traditions of thought in economics and sociology. Part One also explains the methodology used by the author to select a sample of IDs, to operationalize the main theoretical concepts, and to test the hypotheses. Part Two outlines the results of the empirical work conducted by the author. The structure and performance of an extended sample of Italian IDs are analysed by testing a differentiated set of hypotheses through multivariate analysis and econometrics. A final technical Appendix, in which a summary of the data and indicators at the local labour market level are given, concludes the book.

The first chapter conducts a critical survey of the concept of 'industrial district' in the economic and sociological literature. This survey starts with Marshall's seminal work and then examines various theoretical approaches, from regional economics to industrial economics or organization studies. Special attention is paid to the approach used by Becattini (1990), Best (1990), Brusco (1990), Piore (1990), Piore and Sabel (1984) and their collaborators; the pioneers of research on IDs in Italy and elsewhere. In this regard, the discussion centres on the two basic components constitutive of IDs: their population of firms and their community of people. Section 1.7 examines recent findings in the literature on networks, in order to assess whether IDs can be conceived as a form of (social) network.

Chapter 2 concentrates on methodological issues on the ID research agenda. The discussion focuses on two crucial stages of analysis, which are treated as distinct: identification and operationalization. Both concern the construction of indicators, but the aim in the former case is the geographical identification of IDs as mere concentrations of specialized SMEs, while operationalization involves the translation of the main concepts yielded by the literature into workable indicators.

The sample is selected on the basis of two general criteria. An attempt is made to dispense with generic territorial references, and to pass from mere intuition of the industrial district to its analytical localization in Italy. After discussion of the limitations and opportunities of operationalization intended to identify the determinants of ID performance, the data sources and the indicators used to approximate the notion of industrial district are illustrated. Then various sets of indicators are discussed with which to measure industrial and human agglomerations, the division of labour, the social structure, endowment of 'human and social capital', and performance. Finally, an illustration of the most efficacious techniques used to test ID performance is provided.

Part Two outlines the findings of the research. Chapter 3 comments on the results of multivariate analysis, coming up with four distinct types of IDs. The 'factors' explanatory of these resulting types are regressed on the performance indicators, which are taken to be independent variables. The types identified largely correspond to different models of labour division and network structures, interpreted according to the concepts developed by economic and organizational analysis. There then follows a review of co-operative behaviours in the areas studied, as well as an attempt to explain under what circumstances they arise and evolve. Chapter 4 discusses the effects of agglomeration on an industry's growth and looks at the evolutionary patterns of IDs. Chapter 5 discusses some general social trends in IDs that may shift their evolution towards new socio-economic equilibria, and then illustrates the features of a differentiated and 'phase-based' industrial policy for IDs coherent with the results obtained.

The final section, 'Conclusions', summarizes the main empirical and theoretical findings of the research and points out further directions for research.

PART ONE

Theoretical Foundations/Perspectives

1. A Critical Review of the Literature on Industrial Districts: in Search of a Theory

1.1. AN OVERVIEW OF THE LITERATURE

1.1.1. Is there a Model for Industrial Districts?

After more than a decade of studies on IDs carried out by different scholars in various disciplines and regions of the world, the question of what precisely is an ID remains only partly answered. Under the umbrella term ID, extensively used in various disciplinary fields, many different forms of organization of labour and many different socio-cultural fabrics are hidden.

An empirical literature on IDs, largely based on case studies, has exerted a great influence on both theory and policy, offering many rich insights on the internal structure and formation of IDs but being far from a rigorous comparative approach. On the one hand, specific and non-replicable features of single IDs have been associated to a general model – yet not always specified; on the other hand, general features of the 'model' delivered by the literature are lightly applied – without a rigorous empirical assessment – to areas showing simply a high concentration of (small) firms.

The various contributions available in the literature may be divided according to their underlying view of IDs. These different views and approaches to IDs depict a competing scenario among theories, where a non-contentious model is still far from being established. Such a variety of approaches might not be a disadvantage, as it reflects the empirical variety of IDs and may suggest a preference for an 'eclectic' approach. In this case, however, the lack of a theory may condemn the ideas of IDs to be just an empirical construct that different theoretical tools can analyse. We review the pros and cons of the different approaches, showing how only 'bricks' taken from defined models may be applicable to IDs, while no one model fits their complex nature. It is our claim that an evolutionary perspective may accommodate, under different historical or contingent circumstances, the multifaceted world of IDs.

1.1.2. Competing Models of the Industrial District

The economic rationale of IDs may be found in the notion of external economies, as pointed out by Marshall and then better refined by other scholars in economic geography and economics.

Economic geography helped to clarify how external economies and economies of agglomeration appear as the two basic pillars of the concept of IDs, affecting their static performance and growth. Geographers conceive the ID as a *model of local economic development* based on external economies. Among this group of authors, some emphasize the role of agglomeration or proximity of firms (in economic studies) and people (in urban studies) as the sole factor able to produce by itself positive effects, in terms of efficiency, growth and innovation.

More recently, theorists of technological innovation together with geographers have emphasized how the proximity of firms and households fosters spillovers of knowledge, and this explains why the growth of a localized industry (or city) and related innovation processes are faster. The combined effects of the people's and firms' agglomeration in IDs would qualify them as innovatory systems.

Most of the Italian literature, pioneered by Becattini (1990) – an Italian economist – and supported by a number of contributions (for example, Piore and Sabel, 1984 and the Gremi approach), would claim that the mere agglomeration of firms is not enough to denote an ID, but other conditions attaining to the attitudes and values of local population are also important to determine positive performance. In this view, IDs are *socio-economic systems joining together a community of people with common values or culture and economy (market)*. Most of the social features of this type of ID resemble what in sociology has been termed the 'communitarian' model. On a level of interpretation that parallels Becattini's approach, Brusco (1982, 1990) – stressing the light equilibrium between cooperation and competition in IDs – would require an extended division of labour to recognize an ID and its effects on social integration. The emphasis on intrafirm and interfirm relationships within IDs is common to Piore and Sabel, and leads them to qualify IDs as 'flexible systems of production', as well as an *alternative* to the *mass production paradigm*.

A main feature of an ID community, in Becattini's view, is cooperation. Dei Ottati (1987) – a colleague of Becattini – sustains that a necessary condition for the success of districts is cooperation. Cooperation economizes on transaction costs and fosters flexibility and innovation. Cooperation, as a rule of governance of IDs, qualifies them as *social networks* or, according to some organization theorists, as *an ideal-typical organization model between market and hierarchy*.

In addition, a long stream of authors on subjects ranging from economics to organizational studies assume cooperation as a distinctive feature of IDs that facilitates their innovativeness, flexibility and 'equity'. This view arises the question of whether cooperation – as a mechanism producing trust – is at the same time a necessary and pervasive rule of governance of IDs. A similar question concerns institutions that are conceived as an important ingredient for the efficiency or dynamism of IDs (Piore, 1990).

On a line of reasoning contrary to the one mentioned above, the way IDs' markets function may approximate to a *model of (micro) contestable market.*[1] High competition between many firms, each engaged in a different task, low barriers to entry and exit, may configure – unfavourably with the non neoclassical approach of Becattini or Brusco – a model of 'contestable' market. However, even admitting that the business structure rests on a contestable market, the reproduction of the tangible and intangible resources sustaining the district's market is affected by non-market mechanisms.

The entrenchment of resources in the local context may legitimate organizational approaches based on 'cybernetic' concepts or on a competence-based theory of the firm. Some authors have recently looked at IDs' evolutionary paths, conceiving them as 'self-organized' systems; that is, as complex social and economic systems resulting from recursive interactions between their components and autonomy with regard to their environment (Biggiero, 1999; Corò and Rullani, 1998; Dematteis, 1994). Others have suggested applying to IDs the analytical tools of the competence theory of the firm, which are therefore conceived as a repository of local (latent) capabilities (Lawson, 1998; Maskell, 1999; Maskell and Malberg, 1999). Another recent approach applies ecological theory (Hannan and Freeman, 1989) to IDs, drawing attention to exogenous mechanisms of change (Lazzeretti and Storai, 1999; Staber, 1997, 1998), whereas the cognitive perspective (Nonaka, 1994) emphasizes learning in IDs (Becattini and Rullani, 1993; Belussi and Pilotti, 2000; Pilotti, 1997).

Historians and sociologists studying Italian IDs have highlighted their historical prerequisites. Italian IDs have appeared in specific particular historical circumstances. The contributions of Paci (1982) and others suggest that north-eastern Italian IDs arose from an artisan background where a widespread system of land tenure – sharecropping – helped to train entrepreneurial skills. In other regions of Italy and the world, IDs first arose from a different entrepreneurial background and then followed distinct patterns of development (see Chapter 4). Following this stream of literature, IDs may be defined as an entrepreneurial model of development.

1.1.3.   An 'Instrumental' Definition of the Industrial District

The different conceptions of IDs – on the one hand – taken as a mere agglomeration of firms or micro contestable market and, on the other, as complex socio-economic systems, strike a balance between the various theoretical approaches to the matter at issue, with implications relevant to the method applied and results obtained.

A critical point is to understand the relationship between the empirical forms of alleged IDs and a 'normative' model of an ID. This requires the isolation of the ID's rationale; according to the approaches reviewed in the following sections, it may be found in the notion of external economies only (in economic approaches) or in other attitudes of local population (sociological theory), in the recursive properties of networks (organizational approaches) or in the mechanisms underpinning the interaction between tacit and codified knowledge. Indeed, we believe this to be the crucial question in the research agenda, as a first step in building a sound theory of IDs. An agreed and operationalized definition of IDs, as distinct from other likely forms of agglomeration, is urgently required and this study sets out to reach such a definition. For the purposes of this work, the term ID is used as a generic one to denote the agglomeration of small to medium-sized firms specialized in one or a few industries in a bounded area.

This 'agnostic' definition of ID is comprehensive enough to include areas showing different organizational arrangements and avoids qualifying the ID with precise socio-economic features (for example, horizontal and vertical networking, innovativeness, cooperation, trust, and so on), that imply different theories.

What follows is a (attempt of) critical review of the literature, which also provides basic concepts and hypotheses to be used in the empirical part of the book. Further theoretical reflections are made at the end of this book, relying also on the general implications drawn from empirical results.

1.2.   INDUSTRIAL DISTRICTS AS A MODEL OF LOCAL DEVELOPMENT: THE CONCEPT OF EXTERNAL ECONOMIES

1.2.1.   The Marshallian Discovery

The term ID has a very prestigious ancestry, deriving from Alfred Marshall. In his books *Principles of Economics* and *Industry and Trade* he used the term to describe some industrial agglomerations of small and medium-sized British enterprises in textile (Lancashire and Yorkshire) industry in the last century.

He observed that small firms could benefit from external economies by grouping together. '[External economies of scale] are those dependent on the general development of the industry [and] can often be secured by the concentration of many small businesses of a similar character in particular localities: or, as is commonly said, by the localization of industry' (Marshall, 1950, p. 266). In his view, an increase in the scale of production of any kind of goods generates both internal and external economies of scale.

In his last book, *Industry and Trade*, Marshall added some new qualifications to the concept of ID, but without a clear rigorous formalization of the notion. Notably, he introduced the notion of 'industrial atmosphere', which together with the existence of 'mutual knowledge and trust', already mentioned in *The Principles*, 'facilitates the generation of skills required by the industry, and promotes innovations and innovation diffusion among small firms within IDs'. (ibid., p. 96)

As examples of external economies, Marshall mentions the possibility of splitting the production process into specialized phases:[2] the increasing knowledge of markets accompanying the expansion of industrial output, the creation of a market for skilled labour,[3] for specialized services and for subsidiary industries,[4] and finally, the improvement of physical infrastructures such as roads and railways.[5]

The ID was originally conceived as a socio-economic mixing, where social forces cooperate with economic. Friendship linkages among local population and neighbourhood relations favour the diffusion of knowledge:

> The mysteries of the trade become no mysteries; but they are as it were in the air, children learn many of them unconsciously. Good work is rightly appreciated, inventions and improvements in machinery, in processes and the general organization of the business have their merits promptly discussed: if one man starts a new idea, it is taken up by others and combined with suggestions of their own; and thus it becomes the source of further new ideas. (Ibid., p. 271)

The economies so far described consist of the localization advantages considered from the point of view of the economy of production, but Marshall suggests considering the convenience for the customer too, by implying savings on transaction costs:

> He will go to the nearest shop for a trifling purchase: but for an important purchase he will take the trouble to visit any part of the town where he knows that there are especially good shops for his purpose. Consequently shops which deal in expensive and choice objects tend to congregate together and those which supply ordinary domestic needs do not. (Ibid., p. 273)

Marshall did not forget to warn of the diseconomies of industrial concentration as well, these consisting in the higher cost of labour of one kind of work or in the expensive cost of land. As a solution to these disadvantages, the author underlines how different industries in the same neighbourhood may offer different job occupations to the various components of the society (for example, women) or mitigate each other industry's depressions.

Scitovski (1954) described the concept of external economies as one of the most elusive in economic literature. This view is widely shared. Chipman, for example, states that they are 'an inspired idea awaiting adequate formalization' (1965, p. 740). However, Sraffa (1926) claimed that, in *The Principles*, they were the sole cause of increasing returns in a regime of competition and that they must be understood as external to the firms but internal to the industry. A long debate then followed, while more recently Krugman (1991a, 1991b, 1996) and other economists have offered a reappraisal of external economies in formal models of regional growth.

The 'new economic geography', the research programme heralded by Krugman and supported by Arthur (1994) and Venables (1996), is focused on the importance of increasing returns – as deriving from pecuniary externalities (for example, due to market size effects) and non-pecuniary externalities (due to technological factors) – in the process of spatial agglomeration, together with transport costs and factor mobility. The (mathematical) models of spatial agglomeration developed by this literature are endogenous in that they assume that once certain initial conditions (chance locational events) have been established through forward and backward linkages (Hirschman) and/or self-fulfilling prophecies based on increasing returns, situations of either convergent or divergent growth are possible. Because of the self-organized nature of the agglomeration process, several alternative equilibria are possible. Most of the research has tended to focus on models which predict divergent growth and hence the emergence of geographical clusters or industries.

This literature makes no mention of the ID phenomenon, with authors preferring instead to cite illustrative cases in the USA to support their models. However, this approach suggests consideration of the path-dependent nature of, and the importance of history in the development patterns of geographical agglomerations, like IDs are. Chapter 4 shows the difficulties of calibrating endogenous models of growth with data taken from empirical observation of IDs, and the complexity of the factors that explain the emergence and development of an ID, only retaining the metaphorical value of a self-organized perspective (see also Sections 1.7.1 and 1.9).

1.2.2.   External Economies of Scale and Economies of Agglomeration

In order to solve some ambiguity in the notion of external economies, they have been recast by some geographers. In fact, the production of external economies of scale does not necessarily require proximity of firms. As long as the industry grows, the opportunity to subdivide the productive process in different stages enlarges as well. A firm may subcontract a phase of activity to more efficient suppliers because the growth of the industry allows a subcontractor to reach its optimal scale. These advantages are produced every time a firm decides to subcontract to another one, even if they are not neighbours. We are therefore obliged to use an additional notion to cast the economies deriving from the localization of an industry in a given territory.

In regional economics handbooks (for example, Dicken and Lloyd, 1990) a distinction is usually made between *economies of localization* and *economies of urbanization*. The former are the advantages deriving from the concentration of a given industry in a territory that broadly consist of the advantages mentioned by Marshall to denote external economies. They also encompass natural factors of localization. Economies of urbanization, on the contrary, benefit all the industries located in an urban or industrial area and consist of a differentiated local labour market, specialized banks and business services, universities or research centres and public goods like roads, railways, airports, and so on.

Other geographers suggest that the advantages deriving from the concentration of firms and households in a certain area should be better termed as economies of agglomeration, as a specification of external economies of scale. In this view, it is also suggested that we can distinguish economies of agglomeration from other kinds of economies of localization, such as those deriving from low labour or raw materials costs, which are identified as natural localization factors (Asheim, 1994). External economies are common to many forms of industrial agglomerations, such as the localization model of Weber, the pole of development of Perroux (1955), the Japanese just-in-time production systems or the networks of subcontractors that can be observed in Italy (the Benetton nationwide system). These typologies do not require the territorial agglomeration of the system of firms in order to perform effectively or to grow, but are perfectly viable in 'abstract economic spaces'.

According to this line of reasoning, here briefly summarized, both external economies of scale and external economies of agglomeration contend to be the two explicit basic dimensions that depict the ID notion. External economies of scale are a necessary condition for the existence of IDs, while economies of agglomeration are a sufficient condition (Asheim, 1994).

The wide debate on local economies among regional economists, and the various types or models that it has produced, have paid scarce attention to the dynamic dimension as contrasted to the emphasis on static and tangible factors of localization. The juxtaposition of different forms of local development risks failing acknowledge how they evolve and mutate from one type to another. Chapter 4 shows how agglomeration takes a different form and gives rise to distinct development patterns in different localities. The entrepreneurship typical of small firms generally sprouts where some specific facilitating factors are at work, such as the availability of capital funds or competencies.

1.3. THE ECONOMIC SIDE OF INDUSTRIAL DISTRICTS

1.3.1. The Definition of the 'Canonical' Industrial District

Becattini, a fine scholar of Marshall who has contributed to the acquaintance of the latter's ideas to Italy, has revitalized the notion of IDs in a prolific and influential work written in the late 1970s (Becattini, 1979).

However, the Marshallian background has not played so crucial a role in Brusco who discovered the concept of IDs without referring to the Marshallian framework. Indeed, many of the features attached to modern IDs cannot be considered typical of those agglomerations of firms observed by Marshall, as will become clearer in the following sections. The same applies to the strand of literature on 'flexible specialization', which describes IDs as an example of work organization able to represent a new paradigm of post-Fordist society (Barca and Magnani, 1989; Piore and Sabel, 1984; Sabel and Zeitlin, 1982).

In an influential and collective book published in 1990 (Pyke, Becattini and Sengenberger, 1990), Becattini and – to some extent – his collaborators, together with a small group of scholars, offer a systematization of the concept of IDs with a comprehensive description of its distinctive features. The approach and concepts developed in this book,[6] together with the contributions that implicitly or explicitly assume IDs as a 'normative' model (see Chapter 2) are referred to throughout this work as the 'canonical' model. Among the contributors are Becattini himself (1979, 1987, 1989, 1990, 1997) and other scholars of his Florentine group, Piore and Sabel (1984), Piore (1990) and, to a lesser extent, Best (1990), Saxenian (1994) and Scott (1988a, 1988b). The following definition provided by Becattini, together with the distinction between 'community of people' and 'population of firms' is assumed as the 'canonical' ID: 'a socio-territorial entity which is characterized by the active presence of both a <u>community of people</u> and a <u>population of firms</u> in one naturally and historically bounded area' (Becattini,

1990, p. 39).

Although many similar others may be found in Becattini's works, this definition is employed here as a 'canvas' for the discussion of the two critical components of society and industry in IDs.

We begin by commenting on the population of firms, which is the economic component of an ID, and then move on to discuss the ID's community.

1.3.2. Becattini's Industrial District: Characteristics of the Population of Firms

1.3.2.1. The number of firms

Becattini describes the 'population of firms' as the spatial concentration of many SMEs in a bounded geographical area. Firms must be numerous, but definite statements about their precise number cannot be found in the 'canonical' literature because – to some extent – this depends on the nature of the process and on the size of market demand. However their number is certainly greater than that observed by Marshall, who described only headquarters in or on the outskirts of big towns, nothing like such an extended area as Prato or Carpi, where 8 000–9 000 firms are operating. The elusiveness of the 'canonical' literature on the number of firms leaves open the question of a viable efficient threshold – provided it is differentiated by industry – after which external economies manifest themselves.

1.3.2.2. The division of labour between firms

In addition to a large number of firms, the second character of a canonical ID is an extended division of labour. As Becattini puts it:

> Each firm tends to specialize in just one phase, or a few phases, of the production process typical of the district. The firms of the district belong mainly to the same industrial branch, but the term industrial branch must be defined in an especially broad sense as it includes upstream, downstream and ancillary industries. In this respect, Marshall talked of 'main industry' and 'auxiliary industry'; other scholars talk of filières, or of vertically integrated branches. (Becattini, 1990, p. 40)

In order for such an extended specialization to take place, the decomposability of the production process must be a prerequisite or, as Brusco makes explicit, sectors must be characterized by limited economies of vertical integration. In the same way, the deep specialization of firms is associated with a strategic, commercial and ownership independence and a technical interdependence. In this respect, it must be noted that Marshall did not observe IDs, as they have been lately conceptualized by Becattini and others, but as a dispersed hierarchy; a set of narrowly specialized and hierarchically coordinated production units (Piore, 1992). In contrast, in Becattini's view districts' ownership and management tend to coincide, and firms, particularly subcontractors, avoid dependence on one client only. However, as the factories are specialized in subsequent and complementary stages of production, they need to exchange intermediate products or materials and be coordinated in time. A coordinating specialist or function, whether this is a firm or an individual, is necessary in IDs.

1.3.2.3. Welfare effects of a 'vertical' division of labour

The way that a production process is organized has obvious implications on the degree of efficiency and the effectiveness of the industry concerned. Efficiency derives from both the principle of specialization – either in relation to human or physical assets – and from competition conditions.

The kind of specialization of firms may differ according to whether a vertical or horizontal division of labour is prevalent. Very roughly, the former coincides with specialization of firms in different tasks, while the latter concerns specialization in the same task (Leijonhufvud, 1986). Supporters of this distinction hold that the former leads to a reduction in the human-capital requirements; that is, in the craft skills or capabilities of those involved in the production process (*à la* Penrose); while the latter covers a large spectrum of activities and therefore wider capabilities. This view contrasts with the integration of conception and execution at each task stage that is implied in the idea of an extended division of labour and in some conceptualizations of the ID as a model of organization alternative to mass production, where a social rather than a detailed (*à la* Smith) labour division is achieved (Piore, 1990, 1992). According to Piore (1992), the model of division of labour between firms in IDs can be interpreted as a sequence of conceptually distinct operations having their meaning independently from other operations in the factory (or the *filière* in the district). We therefore agree that, in the canonical model, both a vertical and a horizontal division of labour compatible with the integration of conception and execution at each task stage takes place. Another qualifying feature of the 'peculiar' vertical division of labour within IDs is that the governance or the 'intelligence' of the deverticalized structure is the principal function of the final firms of the district's *filière*, or of the coordinators. Provided they are included in the same environment as the subcontracting firms, the local territory is undoubtedly the recipient of their capabilities. In other words, even if single firms do not own the overall knowledge and capabilities to govern the entire productive process, the inclusion of coordinators and local social mechanisms of sanctions and rewards ensures that these capabilities are produced and transmitted on a strictly local level.

A horizontal division of labour may be considered to have the same efficiency effects as a vertical one, since the specialization principle holds in both cases. Moreover, a multiplicity of firms performing similar tasks coincides with the parallel testing of a variety approaches that favour successful learning and innovation processes. There are further implications for effectiveness, rather than efficiency effects alone, in the vertical division of labour as well. Firstly, a vertical division of labour produces a flexible system of production, because each task can be reorganized with a different mix of specialized producers. Flexibility, in turn, has two other effects: it allows quick response to variation in degree and quantity of final demand and gives a spurt to innovative processes. Secondly, it has effects on the welfare of some of the stakeholders in the industry concerned.

In addition, the extended presence of myriad small firms produces an even model of society. Two radical academics such as Piore and Sabel (1984) saw in a flexible system of production and in IDs the realization of a democratic world. As Perrow stressed, speaking of small-firm networks:

> The heads of 1 000 firms related to furniture production will receive a great deal less in salary and benefits than the two heads of the two large firms . . . Furthermore, one of the problems of uneven development and uneven economies associated with multidivisional and giant firms is that locally generated wealth is spent or invested non-locally. (Perrow, 1992, p. 462)

Given certain conditions, a vertical division of labour is able to contain the effects of a reduction of demand. Brusco, in particular, has illustrated such an outcome:

> The impact of a fall in demand for the products of a particular firm depends on its level of vertical integration: where this is high, such a fall in demand will produce unemployment; where it is low, the workers employed in subcontracting firms will simply receive their orders from more successful competitors. (Brusco, 1982, p. 175)

Where there is an extended division of labour, the number of workers losing their job may be predicted to be lower in negative external economic circumstances.

Another welfare effect of the extended division of labour in IDs, both horizontal and vertical, concerns the spurt of entrepreneurship that is realized. As we will observe in more detail later, the low barriers to entry in IDs favour a high mobility, which ensures a stronger social cohesion in and even rewards to local population, either in terms of capabilities or capital funds.

1.3.2.4. The size of the units of production in the district

Regarding the dimension of the unit of production of each single stage, the 'canonical' literature is again not definite, but a limited range of variability is admitted. It is, however, assumed that the multiplicity of phases and fierce competition will keep optimal technical dimensions fairly small (Brusco, 1990). Strictly speaking this will not exclude even large firms, particularly if one considers that the district produces phase products for the outside world as well. Actually, the presence or the formation of large firms is not easily acknowledged by Becattini who, unlike Brusco, excludes the possibility that a structure of relationships between firms of an asymmetric nature, where some firms may have a more important role, can be labelled a ('canonical') ID:

> Coalitions and agreements of various kind between firms in the district also occur, but whenever the weight of those which take a financial form increases too much, or the growth of some firms sends it 'out of scale', as it were, we are already out of the canonical form of the Marshallian district. (Becattini, 1990, p. 41)

1.4. INDUSTRIAL DISTRICTS AS A MODEL OF MICRO CONTESTABLE MARKETS

Once one accepts that the multiplicity of phases of production and their increasing competition keeps optimal technical dimensions fairly small, firms are thus assumed to operate close to their optimal size, at least in a state of equilibrium. If we consider that a surplus is associated with the local product, we have enough elements to introduce an interpretation of the ID as a model of a micro contestable market. In fact, Becattini requires that the

> image of the district will be separated both from that of the single firms in it, and from that of the other districts . . . and that the representative commodity of each particular district be distinguishable from similar commodities by some special characteristic of its own, regarding either its average qualitative standards (raw materials, technical requirements, etc.), or some accessory conditions of the transactions (timing of the deliveries, homogeneity of the batches, etc.). (1991, p. 44)

This requisite implies that the ID's surplus is produced either by the uniqueness of its product, related to knowledge, abilities, and skills from which it derives, or from the way the productive and logistic process is organized. If these reasons are stable, over time, the ID may prove less vulnerable to external competition and become a sustainable model of development.

The uniqueness of the product must be conceived in terms of non-imitability of the product and thus of the locally rooted competencies and knowledge from which it is realized. The nature of the ID as a model of development characterized by economies of agglomeration defines the sources of competitive advantage of local firms. If the area is characterized by traditional economies of localization (for example, low labour costs), it is likely that firms will generally exhibit a cost advantage, while if the area stands out, let's say, for a century of tradition in the manufacturing of a given product, the competitive advantage will rest in product quality or differentiation with respect to other competitors.

Becattini, Best and Piore and Sabel demonstrate that the sources of IDs' surplus are not so much cost advantages – otherwise they would have qualified the ID product less expensive than those of their direct competitors – as the fact that they are rooted in some qualitative characteristic or organizational or technological factor. This legitimates the identification of these sources in local knowledge, *savoir-faire* and competencies, and in the specific pattern of labour division among production and distribution firms.

If an ID's product has a surplus, the local market of the typical good is not *contestable* by external operators. As knowledge is locally rooted or 'context specific' (see Section 1.7.2), an external competitor may have to become part of the local economic and social texture by absorbing local competencies (or by simply hiring the people who have those skills) or adopting the local organization model, in order to enter the market.

In the internal market, we expect conditions of contestability to operate. As Becattini argues, in IDs 'everyone struggles incessantly to improve his own and his family's position and nobody can rely on economic solutions which are considerably inferior to those which prevail in the markets outside the district' (Becattini, 1990, p. 45). An internal *gendarme*, different from the pure market ensures that efficiency conditions are reached by the district. The fact that each stage of production has its own price, resulting from the competition game, gives to the deverticalized structure of the district an advantage over an integrated firm, which has to simulate its internal transfer prices. In this sense, the district reaches that efficiency which is between the market and the firm according to the ideal model of the firm in Coase (1937).

However, if it is clear that the ID produces a surplus, it remains to be analysed who appropriates it. In a simplistic representation, two 'communities' or markets may be distinguished internally: the micro industry of stage producers and the micro industry of final producers. The micro industry of stage producers operates in a state of contestability. This implies that in equilibrium conditions: (a) each firm produces at the minimum average cost; (b) prices equal minimum production costs; (c) there are no technical conditions for natural monopoly; (d) the average cost function is not sub-additive; and (e) there is workable competition.

Different conditions define the micro industry of final producers. They are protected by competition threats coming from firms external to the district: firstly, because of the absolute cost advantages ensured by the contestability equilibrium established in the stage producers segment; and secondly, because of the image, or reputation, of local production, which gives a price advantage over non-local producers. Final producers, on the other hand, are exposed to potential competition coming from inside the ID: new firms that decide to enter into the commercial stage of the *filière*. Hence, even if the incumbents benefit from monopolistic advantages in setting their price on the global market, internal entrants can *hit and run* the market, thus introducing internal contestability conditions. As Capecchi puts it, 'the separation of those firms which sell their products and those which act as sub-suppliers to other firms is not rigid: a small firm can, at a given moment, be a sub-supplier and at another, a seller' (1990, p. 22).

The functioning of the double equilibrium for the two micro-industries requires them to be separated. This happens when the competencies and, more generally, the resources sustaining the competitive advantage of the final producers segment are not easily imitable or appropriable by the stage producers segment. In the reverse case, the final market segment becomes contestable and subject to hit and run competition from firms of the latter segment.

Profit accrues to the scarcest capabilities in the district, which because of their origin are the commercial ones. The existence of non-normal profits is not incompatible with the existence of efficiency conditions, provided that the market is contestable.

The correspondence of prices of intermediate and final output to their costs is one of the reasons why IDs are efficient. The fact that, at each stage of production of the *filière*, different prices can be compared (because of proximity) enables the market to reach an equilibrium price that is equal to costs. Also, client firms can easily detect unfair price strategies. The ease with which cheating strategies (that is, prices over normal costs) can be detected fosters trust among economic actors and acts as a spur for the creation of long-term relationships.

The interpretation of the ID as a micro-contestable market has never been made explicit by Becattini and other scholars who, indeed, refuse to reduce the ID to a pure market representation. Nonetheless, such an interpretation is in any case legitimate, as we have shown. In a recent contribution, Becattini (1997) asserts that the price of intermediate inputs is fixed in an administrative way as a result of negotiations between commissioning firms and subcontractors or suppliers, rather than resulting from the equilibrium between demand and supply. These agreements, documented in the case of Prato (see also Dei, 1998), allow the microindustry of stage producers to bargain a price that covers operating and investment costs. In Becattini's scenario, this price prevents some stage producers from going into bankruptcy. Does this mean that a short-term inefficiency is tolerated and sustainable in IDs because of a major efficiency in the long run? We shall attempt to formalize the equilibrium envisaged by Becattini.

The equilibrium price p for an intermediate product i in a district d ranges between the level of an external market price p_i^m, where m is the external market, and an efficient price p_i^c, where c is the level of average costs, that would result if a pure market mechanism were in force in the district.

$$p_i^c < p_i^d < p_i^m \qquad (1.1)$$

The profit of final producers is reduced by the rent assigned to stage producers, but the competitiveness of the district's market is nonetheless preserved since the final efficient prices are set at a level lower than those of competitors:

$$0 < P_f^d - p_i^d \qquad (1.2)$$

The equilibrium is sustainable if:

$$P_f^d < P_f^m. \qquad (1.3)$$

Where P_f^d is the final price in the district d, and P_f^m is the final price in the market m (practices by firms not belonging to an ID).

Similar relationships may be imagined for the equilibrium wage in the labour market. In this way, a micro-founded economic model of IDs may be built (see also Chapter 2).

The reduction of profits is accepted by final producers because they internalize a preference for local (district) stage producers, rather than external ones in their utility function. The experience of the past has released a strong awareness of higher interdependence between all components of the local society. The final producer is profoundly aware of the advantages associated with the proximity of stage producers. More precisely, s/he is convinced that unhealthy conditions in one component of local society may in the long (medium) term disadvantage him/her. Again, the functioning of the market in an ID and the behaviours of its components may only be understood by considering the district's society as a whole, as a densely interconnected society and economy that evolves by ensuring it provides the humus for the reproduction of local resources.

Formalization of market equilibrium in a canonical ID, though useful for understanding the foundations of competitiveness, fails to recognize what lies at the basis of the contributions by Becattini and other scholars of IDs. Although numerous mercantile relations arise on the basis of price mechanisms, they in reality spring from non-monetizable decision-making processes and relations which significantly affect the success or otherwise of a given productive choice. The market is not the only *medium* for the exchange of information, labour and intermediate goods.

The conditions formalized above are quite restrictive and no attempts to formalize and test the existence of such an equilibrium have been in the literature. Moreover, as mentioned above, the case of Prato only offers evidence of agreements on the administrative definition of intermediate prices.

1.5. THE SOCIAL DIMENSION OF INDUSTRIAL DISTRICTS

1.5.1. The System of Values

The most important trait of the 'community of people', as described by Becattini, is its relatively homogeneous system of values and views (same values, behaviours, expectations, language, dialect, and so on), which is an expression of an ethic of work and activity, of the family, of reciprocity, and of change (Becattini, 1990, p. 39). Undoubtedly, the cultural factors underpinning the phenomenon of the ID were already present in Marshall, but Becattini makes explicit the nature of the ID as an 'economic and social whole' and reintroduces the necessity for a multidisciplinary approach grouping together sociological, historical and economic contributions. This view finds a point of convergence with the 'milieu' approach (Aydalot, 1986) and, in particular, with the first phase of the Gremi research project, since IDs as local 'milieux' encompass not only factors related to industrial and organizational structure, but also social, cultural and institutional factors (Maillat, 1995; Saxesian, 1994).

To the extent that a population is geographically and historically bounded, face-to-face relationships are frequent and people tend to interact continually developing a shared culture and implicit rules of common behaviour (customs). In small areas where IDs are located, norms of reciprocity and trust tend to emerge (Dei Ottati, 1994). According to Marshall, 'mutual trust and knowledge' tend to be diffused. Because people know each other, economic relationships tend to be regulated by personal ties. Hiring procedure, subcontracting relationships, exchange of goods, capital equipment or finance are generally very informal and based on trust; local institutions and diffused trust supplant the need for more formal social regulatory bodies. Brusco provides a brilliant description of the informality of relationships within the firm, where there is no clear or strict distinction between the owner and the workers. In Hofstede's terminology (1991), the 'psychic distance' between the owner and the worker is very short and the former is perceived as 'one of us'. Economic or social relationships tend to be characterized by reciprocity. Because of 'closeness' of local population, the withdrawal of reciprocity acts as a sanctioning mechanism.

1.5.2. The 'Communitarian Model'

The terms further used by Becattini and other scholars to point out socio-cultural factors in IDs roughly describe what in sociology has been termed the 'communitarian' model (Toennies, 1963; Taylor, 1989). Contiguity of population makes economic as well as social relationships more frequent, thus contributing to the creation of a homogeneous recognisable community of people, which is precisely Becattini's 'community of people'.

A more formal account of this model has been provided by Lorenz (1993), who recalls the following features as distinctive of a community, as stated by Taylor:

1. common beliefs and values;
2. direct relations with each other as opposed to being directed by the state or some other bureaucratic institution;
3. many-sided relations as opposed to specialized;
4. diffused reciprocity, which represents a form of social control that substitutes the role of external institutions.

These features can be easily seen as corresponding to those used in the canonical literature on IDs, testifying that the canonical view of IDs relies strongly – although implicitly – on the communitarian model.

The static nature of the social dimension of the ID is evident in attempts to qualify the prevailing values of IDs. In this respect, Becattini (1990) asserts that only some combinations of values are admissible, while others are not. For example, he maintains that a positive attitude towards innovation is a constant feature of the ID culture. Further, in exploring the possible combinations of values compatible with an ID, he states: 'Under no circumstance . . . can the system of values be such as to discourage enterprise or the introduction of technical change' (1990, p. 39).

In the 'canonical' literature, other attempts to qualify the combinations of values and general cultural traits compatible with the existence of the ID have been made. In particular, a climate of trust, solidarity and cooperation as a governance mechanism in interfirm relations, have been emphasized by Italian and international scholars.

A more dynamic view of IDs may derive from relying on the socio-economic attempts (Granovetter, 1985, 1992) to recast the ID as an organizational form strongly *embedded* in a network of peculiar social relationships localized in a bounded territory. In this approach, 'culture is not a once-for-all influence but an ongoing process' (Granovetter, 1985, p. 484), and therefore is a context-driven feature. Most of the canonical literature focussed on the basic attitudes of the local population. Those who applied the socio-economic approach to IDs have particularly emphasized the strength of 'weak ties' in the local context and the degree of embeddedness of its SMEs in the local culture (Grahber, 1993).

1.5.3.   The Role of Cooperation in Industrial Districts

The specific intermingling of cooperation and competition identifies a peculiar form of governance between two extremes: on the one hand the market and, on the other hand, the community which, taken together, Dei Ottati names 'Communitarian Market'. The same author introduces the concept of trust as a secondary regulating mechanism emerging, implicitly, as a result of cooperation.

Dei Ottati maintains that the necessary condition for districts to succeed is a particular use of cooperation: 'in order that a model of cooperation and competition may function, it is necessary that firms belong to a social context where a particular custom of cooperation extended to economic relationships has built up over time' (Dei Ottati, 1987, p. 121).

It is exactly this local custom of cooperation that sustains the success of IDs. This emerges by analysing the function of cooperation that may be derived from the canonical literature:

1. the sustaining of ID dynamics;
2. encouragement of flexibility, with respect to firms and labour;
3. innovation spurring;
4. effective coordination of strictly complementary activities;
5. contribution to production and transaction costs' reduction.

Cooperation reduces the risks associated with the starting of a new activity or investing in new products or processes. In fact, in the district 'community' those whose results are unsuccessful are weakly sanctioned and tend to be helped by the local population. Unlike other places, the stigma associated with those who fail in an economic venture is lower and people are not afraid to start again. As a result, mobility is encouraged and high density of entrepreneurs as well as a high rate of start and closure of firms should be expected in IDs.

Dei Ottati asserts that, normally, the workforce in IDs is distinguishable for its qualities (skillness, specialization, versatility, initiative, ability to react to new situations), each of which are very apt in helping to cope with new external demand characteristics such as variety in tastes and volumes. However, unlike other authors she adds that workers qualities are not sufficient to explain production flexibility. On the contrary, local actors must rely on trust in community help, 'they are sure to find a place in the local community'. In Dei Ottati's paper (1987), trust refers to the expectation of a subcontracting firm that has lost orders for its specific products to receive an order from a different commissioning firm, or of a worker who has been made redundant by a failing firm either to find another job or to find an economic subsidy from the family or family firm or other local institutions. This is what may be called 'inclusiveness' of the local community.

Proximity of firms and population ensures a continuous flow of technical and commercial information as well as the diffusion and local rootedness of competencies and skills. Dei Ottati recognizes that strict complementary links among specialized firms permit cooperation and communication among firms, but she also asserts that cooperation aptitudes allow the diffusion of innovative processes: 'it is the cooperative element, peculiar to the inter-subjective relationships taking place in the district, which makes possible innovation as a diffused process' (1987, p. 134). Along this line of interpretation, Sabel and Zeitlin (1982) define innovation as a 'collective' process.

According to Piore (1990), technological dynamism is an essential criterion for the identification of an ID. Technological dynamism of the districts and the combination within them of the apparently contradictory traits of competition and cooperation are the two factors at the top of the list of the salient features of the ID.

Coordination functions are also performed in a efficiently and effectively way in IDs. The exchange of goods between firms in a subcontracting line is speeded up by informal relationships of trust, and hence subcontractors save money avoiding the signing of detailed contracts. Savings extend to other transaction costs, such as those involved in searching external suppliers or acquiring information on traders. Hiring costs are also compressed because of neighbouring relationships or cooperation with other entrepreneurs, or merely thanks to the spillover information on reliability and skills of workers.

The role of cooperation, or the particularly supportive role of social environment, in IDs has been underlined by many authors. Lorenz (1993), who implicitly identifies the ID as a communitarian model, argues that differences in the degree of flexibility and technological dynamism among IDs (or in the same district over time) can be accounted for by differing levels of trust among actors. Scott and Storper (1989) identify 'trust relations', 'system-wide co-ordinating institutions', a consolidated 'industrial atmosphere', and 'social consensus' as key features in the continuing success of IDs. In the Gremi approach (Aydalot, 1986), the 'milieu' is defined as a 'territorial set, integrated in network fashion, of material and non-material resources, dominated by a historically constituted culture, a vector of knowledge and know-how and based on a cooperation/competition-type relational system of local actors' (Lecoq, 1989, p. 44).

Furthermore, Becattini has recently claimed that the existence of an ID requires local actors following certain norms of fairness, such as moral constraints to the practice of 'selling high and buying cheap' (Becattini, 1997).

1.5.4. Cooperation as a Rule of Governance of Industrial Districts

The 'communitarian market' of Dei Ottati pinpoints one of the most distinctive features of what we have named the 'canonical' approach. Cooperation and an extended division of labour distinguish canonical IDs from mere agglomerations of firms. In this world, cooperation among local actors allows the internalization of a district's external economies, supporting Sraffa's claim that external economies are *external* to firms and *internal* to the (localized) industry. These economies are therefore merely potential or latent and may be acquired by local actors only thanks to cooperative attitudes.

Therefore, we may conclude that at least three conditions must operate to have a successful ('canonical') ID: external economies of scale (and economies of agglomeration), extended division of labour and cooperation.

To explain how cooperation works, Dei Ottati (1987) borrows the concepts of opportunism and asymmetry from transactional analysis. She asserts that the custom of cooperation should prevent local actors from behaving opportunistically, as they should have interiorized an implicit rule of behaviour antagonistic to opportunism. According to Williamson (1975, 1985, 1992), opportunism may easily arise when transactions are characterized by 'asset specificity', 'uncertainty' or 'low frequency'. If one looks at the economic features of canonical IDs, one has to conclude that some of these conditions are very rare, as the ID is, by definition, characterized by a large number of operators (subcontractors, commissioning firms, designers and traders) and by a decomposable cycle of production. As a consequence, interdependent linkages are more typical than one-sided relationships, while specific assets are distributed among many subcontractors. In addition, a second-hand market for used machinery, a dynamic labour and financial market exist that lowers exit costs. The practice of commissioning firms to finance the seed capitals of their subcontractors is well documented in some well-known IDs. With cooperation as a governing rule in IDs, there is no space for opportunism to operate, since there are no 'structural' conditions for opportunism to arise. Heretically, we may say that the market is perfectly 'contestable' (Section 1.4).

Whether we admit that asymmetries exist in IDs, in conditions of uncertainty and ambiguity abuse of one part by the other may appear. This may be facilitated by the absence of formal contracts and by idiosyncratic supplier or employment relationships. It is here that cooperation may contain the disruptive effects of opportunism. In fact, the threat of social sanctions in the face of opportunistic behaviours is effective for those operators who live long term in the area. Hence, reciprocity is guaranteed by social mechanisms, rather than by contractual arrangements because of proximity of population.

Similarly, the problem of opportunism also dissolves in Piore's view. Recalling the approach of Hanna Arendt to human action and recognizing that the economic structure of IDs is embedded in the social structure, the paradox of competition and cooperation simply disappears.

> [If the] ID is seen as essentially a forum for action, it becomes clear that what is involved is not competition and cooperation at all. We have mistaken competition for the individual's attempt through action to differentiate him or herself. What appear to be his/her collaborators in the market model are really interlocutors in the discourse through which the differentiation of the individual occurs and the audience for the story of a life which actions create. (1990, p. 67) [7]

That problem of opportunism, in fact, derives from the model in which activity is a means towards the end of individual income. Moreover, if production is conceived of as a realm of action, as Arendt suggests, the other members of the community cannot ever be dispensed with, without making one's acts meaningless. The critical concept in Arendt's view of action – and by extension the understanding of IDs – is the notion of 'a community of equals'. Only within such a democratic community can one differentiate self. If the other members of the community are not alike, they cannot appreciate each other's differences. It is therefore clear that the ID emerges as a new model of social and economic organization, able to displace the old paradigm of mass production (see Section 1.5.5).

The role of cooperation as a governance mechanism in IDs has been emphasized more forcedly by many non-Italian authors than by Becattini. The emphasis on trust has favoured the interpretation of IDs as an organizational mode or an institution in itself in antithesis to the market (Thompson, Levacic and Mitchell, 1991), which, if invaded by pure market rules, is doomed to perish (Section 1.11).

Apart from the theoretical analysis of cooperation, other contributions offer empirical evidence of different forms of cooperation or emphasize the role of cooperation in the success of IDs. A wide catalogue of cooperative behaviours in IDs is offered in the literature. The main form this takes is interaction between commissioning and subcontracting firms, but other manifestations include sharing of technical information or equipment; lending of money or instrumental goods; subcontracting out to less successful competitors; and refraining from poaching workers and from underpricing (Becattini, 1989, 1990; Dei, 1999). Ranging over the case-study literature, evidence also emerges of cooperation leading to joint programmes for the provision of collective goods; notably training and research and development, but also medical care and unemployment insurance. Collective goods are generally provided under the auspices of some local institution: a business association, trade union, or possibly the local or regional government (Brusco, 1986; Sabel and Zeitlin, 1982, pp. 146–49; Lorenz, 1992).

Other researchers have emphasized attitudes besides cooperation that are conducive to innovation and technological dynamism (Section 1.7).

1.5.5. The Success of the Idea of Industrial Districts in the International Debate

The appeal of the idea of IDs has been appreciated by those authors who have used them as an empirical reference for the concept of 'flexible specialization'. This notion has been extensively discussed in the book *The Second Industrial Divide* by Piore and Sabel (1984), but it was already present in their previous work with Brusco and Zeitlin. Their starting point was the economic crisis of the capitalist system and of its paradigmatic big corporation, which began in the 1970s and 1980s in most industrialized countries. Flexible production systems are interpreted as a new socio-economic paradigm, replacing the system of rigid mass production and standardized goods.

In flexible specialization systems such as IDs located in the so-called 'Third Italy'[8] (Bagnasco, 1977) a large number of small enterprises engage in small batch production, adopting flexible production procedures that require close collaboration between the factory and the client. The flexible use of microprocessor-based technologies is combined with craft skills; collective business services are provided; and strong informal or institutionalized structures ensure the provision of minimum pay scales and acceptable working conditions to regulate interfirm cooperation and competition.

IDs have served as examples for several other definitions and conceptualizations within reflections on the evolution of modern capitalism: Storper, Harrison and Scott introduced the concept of 'regional production systems' (Harrison and Storper, 1991; Scott and Storper, 1989) as embracing IDs. Following this wave of ideas, many empirical studies have also been carried out, identifying successful agglomerations of small specialized firms in France (Benko, Dunford and Heurley, 1997), Denmark (Kristensen, 1992) and Germany (Grotz and Braun, 1997; Herrigel, 1996) among others countries.

In Best (1990), 'Third Italy' and its IDs are cited as a leading example of the success of the 'new competition' model. In particular, Italy is identified by the author as a paradigmatic case of how the 'new competition' may reconcile the interests of workers and employers. Italian firms 'pursue a strategy of continuous innovation, deploy flexible production methods and integrate planning and doing in work' (pp. 203–4). These firms, according to Best, cooperate with similar firms by exchanging technology, market information and training, and they employ multiskilled, high-paid, unionized labour. Best also mentions the institutional capacity of IDs to continuously learn, adjust and improve their economic performance (1990, p. 235).

The diffusion of professional know-how allows skilled workers to leave the factory and become small entrepreneurs, guaranteeing a high degree of social mobility within the areas characterized by flexible specialization (Sabel and Zeitlin, 1982).

High social mobility in IDs has also been emphasized in the works of Brusco (1982, 1990) and Becattini (1990). The large extent of job opportunities in the district as a condition and, at the same time, as a result of, the high work mobility creates a 'continuum of work positions' (home-based work, part time, waged work, self-employment, entrepreneurship). This means that the district manages to allocate each individual to his/her optimal place, at least to a certain extent. In addition, Becattini remarks on the fact that specialization of the worker – which is sometimes firm-specific and sometimes district-specific – is lost only to a very limited extent when the worker moves from one firm to another. His specialization remains part of that 'public good' which Marshall labels 'industrial atmosphere'.

As a result of social mobility, high activity rates coupled with low rates of unemployment and a strong tendency to independent work may be observed in IDs. The allocative effects of IDs were already visible when we discussed the implications of a vertical model of labour division.

In the works of Becattini, Brusco, Sabel and Zeitlin it is also implied and often stated that wages and labour conditions are superior to those registered in other non-ID areas. The documented presence of strong trade unions in some IDs ensures very rewarding levels of wages and quality of work (Bagnasco and Trigilia, 1984), but generally the level of wages is supposed to be higher on average in IDs because of the superior degree of qualification of workers. Becattini insists that wages and fees paid to subcontractors are 'fair' and more stable, rather than merely higher or lower than average levels (see also Section 1.4). However, the evidence in this respect is highly controversial (Amin, 1988; Solinas, 1982).

The works of Piore and Sabel, as well as those of Scott and Storper and Best, have been very influential in the international academic context. The association between IDs, cooperation and flexible systems of production has become automatic. The perception of IDs as innovative and cooperative systems has been reinforced by the conceptualization provided by the Gremi approach, which encompasses such extended areas as Third Italy, the Jurassic Arc and Baden Wurtemberg. The influence has also been strong in organization sciences, where IDs have been discussed in the context of socially embedded networks (Section 1.11).

1.6. THE ROLE OF INSTITUTIONS IN INDUSTRIAL DISTRICTS

The role of cooperation in IDs would not fully be understood if social and economic institutions were not mentioned. In the canonical literature, social and economic institutions are essential ingredients of an ID's success. In Becattini's view, social institutions (market, firms, extended families, technical schools, churches, political parties, trade unions, employers' associations, and so on) arise spontaneously and reflect, legitimate and reproduce dominant values (Becattini, 1989). Scholars in economics and sociology have emphasized the economic rationale of extended families, which act as internal labour markets (Trigilia, 1990) and benefit from unified budgeting (Paci, 1982; Solinas, 1982).

Economic institutions are different from the market or the firm, and although they are an expression of local attitudes towards, for example, associationism, they are specifically designed to complement the activity of economic operators. The relevant institutions in IDs are often depicted as 'intermediate' (Arrighetti and Seravalli, 1999) and include local employers' associations, trade unions, local councils, education structures, consortia and stable rules, which locally supply public goods for specific economic categories in order to relieve them of some costs.

In Trigilia's view (1986, 1990), local social and economic institutions and, above all, local political subcultures support the local community. Their interaction with economic life describes a *local* regulatory model, as opposed to a *national* one more closely linked to large firms' environments. Local councils, trade unions, and business associations furnish and 'compensate' the local population with, respectively, social services, higher wages or job security, and business services, and thus economize on production costs.

According to Piore (1990, 1992), institutions are essential for the survival of the ID model as he understands it:

> Italian IDs are not markets: the intensity of communication that occurs within them and the social structures in which they are embedded make it very unlikely that they could ever be compatible with a competitive price system. Moreover, there is a real question about the externality of the economies associated with these kinds of network organizations. The research on both the network corporation and the Italian IDs suggest that they survive and prosper only if the economies that are external to particular productive units are internalized as parameters in the decisions of some higher-level organization unit – for example, the corporate headquarters in large organizations and municipal government, trade unions, and

business associations in the geographic region. (1992, p. 43)

Brusco (1990), from a different point of view, distinguishes between what he calls ID *Mark One* from ID *Mark Two*. ID Mark One arose in the mid-1970s in a context of growing domestic and international demand for consumer goods, and it developed spontaneously without local government intervention. By contrast, this last factor became of major importance in districts Mark Two, which derived from the evolution of the former. The underlying contention is that new markets and new technologies have developed since the beginning of the 1980s, posing a problem for both large and small firms.

> The district is characterized by a sort of strong, heavy inertia. It goes on learning the technology in a deep, personal and creative way, but it is very difficult to move this huge mass of people . . . Therefore, industrial districts must now face the problem of how to take on the new technologies which are necessary to revive a process of creative growth. It is here that the need for government intervention appears. (1990, p. 17)

The distinction made by Brusco also suggests that various institutions in a district play different roles in distinct periods of time (see Chapter 5). The important role of institutions is similarly emphasized in other contributions, which, however, point out the role of institutions in technological transmission and diffusion (Saxesian, 1994; Maillat, 1995; Corò and Rullani, 1998).

None of the studies surveyed thus far take institutions to be an unnecessary component of canonical IDs. Rather, they are conceived as an important part of the 'package' of private and public arrangements allegedly responsible for the vibrant economic growth of the regions in which IDs arise.

This literature focuses on at least three different functions of institutions, which parallel those performed by cooperation:

- supporting SMEs in order to offset their diseconomies;
- strengthening local competencies and attitudes;
- triggering innovation.

The first two functions enhance the efficiency of IDs, while the third is intended to foster districts' change in particular. In order to envisage a possible industrial policy, Chapter 5 focuses on the role of social and economic institutions and on the transformations that occurred in a sample of IDs in the 1990s.

1.7. INDUSTRIAL DISTRICTS AS INNOVATORY SYSTEMS

1.7.1. Technological Externalities

According to the 'canonical' literature, innovative processes and change in IDs, as well as static performance, may be explained in terms of local values and attitudes. Along a pure Marshallian line of interpreting, however, the concept of external economies may be used fully to explain innovations in IDs. The competitive pressure on firms, and the local diffusion of commercial and technical information ('the mysteries of the industry . . . are in the air'), force them to continuously innovate and ameliorate their performance, thereby increasing their capacity to survive. Whether the allocative static efficiency of agglomeration (reduction of production and transaction costs) has been sufficiently discussed in the literature, the role of proximity in nurturing processes of growth, knowledge creation and diffusion has been stressed by a recent and already mature stream of literature. For this reason, the idea of external economies is used as a crucial explanatory variable in the context of regional and country growth theories (Glaeser et al., 1992; Henderson, 1996; Henderson, Kuncoro and Turner, 1995). Since spillovers of knowledge are localized, as Marshall noticed, firms and/or households tend to cluster together and therefore the growth of that industry or city is faster (see Chapter 4).

Along the Marshallian line, other geography authors have emphasized the innovative capacity of IDs. Maillat and Lecoq (1992) define the general category of Italian IDs as an example of 'endogenous innovative milieu or technological district'. The concept of milieu, in further contributions of the Gremi research project, has been applied to cases of technological dynamics in certain regions or even smaller territories, covering a number of territorial phenomena other than the ID.

Similarly, Camagni (1991) stressed the role played by districts in the reduction of uncertainty in innovation processes due to imperfect information, as well as difficulties in precisely defining the effects of innovative decisions and problems in controlling the reactions and behaviour of economic actors. Because of proximity, local actors are able to gather and screen information through informal interchanges and a process of 'collective learning' through the mobility of a skilled labour force, customer–supplier interchanges and imitation processes takes place.

1.7.2. Modern Theory of Innovation and Industrial Districts

In modern innovation theory, the crucial role played in innovative processes by territorial agglomeration is clearly stressed: regional production systems, IDs and technological IDs are becoming increasingly important (Lundvall, 1992).

In the theory of technological competence (Cantwell, 1989, 1992, 1994), technology is defined as partially tacit, specific to the context in which it has been created or adapted, and tied to the skills and routines of those who have developed and operate it. The significance of the 'regional dimension' of an innovative system has emerged as the logical consequence of the interactive model, which put the emphasis on relations with information sources external to the firm. Such relations – between firms and science infrastructure, between producers and users at interfirm level, and between firms and the institutional environment – are strongly influenced by spatial proximity mechanisms that favour processes of polarization and cumulativeness (Lundvall, 1988). Moreover, the employment of informal channels for knowledge diffusion provides another argument for the tendency of innovation to be geographically confined (Hägerstrand, 1967; Lundvall, 1992).

The theoretical basis for the argument that agglomeration may be accompanied and indeed fosters innovation has found some confirmations in the discovery of agglomeration processes within very innovative industries: Silicon Valley and Route 128 in the USA, the M4 in the UK, and the Scientific City of the Southern Paris region in France, among others (Saxenian, 1994; Scott and Storper, 1989; Storper, 1992) are the places where the context-specific and local nature of technology are combined with more codified elements. The sources of codified knowledge in these cases are universities or scientific parks, thus pointing to a crucial source that is not historically present in Italian IDs, where the means of competencies formation and transmission depend on more traditional institutions such as schools and family.

Economies of agglomeration may also largely explain international flows of direct investments, greedy to tap specialized centres of production in order to benefit from cost advantages due to the high specialization of local manpower or expertise of suppliers and subcontractors, or in order to enter into the process of learning. As a consequence of virtuous mechanisms of cumulative causation, international poles of excellence in the production of final products or components or in R&D activities may, *inter alia*, attract footloose foreign direct investment (Amin and Thrift, 1992; Cantwell, 1989, 1992; Dunning, 1988, 1992 and 1993).

1.7.3. The Process of Learning

The issue of learning has received a large attention from scholars in economics interested in IDs. Following the seminal contribution of Polanyi (1962), a distinction is made between codified and tacit knowledge, the former being abstract, communicable and conveyed by symbols and language; the latter being uncommunicable and embedded in practice, people and organizations and being somewhat idiosyncratic, specific to particular problem-solving activities. Some authors have emphasized the typical pattern of learning in IDs, while more recently others, relying on the scheme provided by Nonaka (1994), have pointed at the interaction between tacit and codified knowledge that occurs in IDs.

Since the beginning of research on IDs, it has been emphasized how local knowledge in IDs is normally tacit or uncodified, and incremental, tending not to be formalized (for example, Bellandi, 1989). Learning processes therefore suit those of 'learning-by-doing' and 'learning-by-using'. The largely *incremental* rather than *radical* nature of innovations is due to the specific features of IDs. Firstly, as cooperation occurs mainly along vertical lines, between commissioning and subcontracting firms for example, this limits the scope for horizontal technological cooperation, which is more associated with radical innovations. Secondly, there is normally a fierce horizontal competition in strongly competitive markets between firms producing the same products or carrying out the same production functions. Finally, independent firms very often lack both human and financial resources to build up and support the necessary level of research and development activity (Asheim, 1994). The largely incremental nature of dominant technologies in IDs, as our research confirms, raises the question of whether IDs are structurally incompatible with radical innovation or not. Specifically, does the introduction of radical innovations cause IDs to be transformed into a different form of organization? The empirical part of this book offers some answers to this question.

Other authors, Becattini himself, underline how IDs are a formidable engine for the creation and reproduction of knowledge as conceptualized by Nonaka (Becattini and Rullani, 1993; Belussi and Pilotti, 2000; Corò and Rullani, 1998; Pilotti, 1997). According to Nonaka, knowledge is created by the interaction between explicit and tacit knowledge. The conversion of tacit knowledge into explicit knowledge is a circular process that can be conceptualized in four different stages: (1) *socialization*: collective sharing of tacit knowledge; (2) *externalization*: conversion from tacit to explicit or codified knowledge; (3) *combination*: reuse of various types and sources of tacit and codified knowledge and (4) *internalization*: conversion from explicit to tacit knowledge.

The above mentioned authors show that the spiralling process of knowledge creation and reproduction takes place in IDs thanks to the existence of cultural, social and physical proximity, which favours common cognitive processes.

This approach grasps the self-organized nature of IDs, which are able to select external knowledge and adapt it to their own specific needs and codes (see Section 1.9). Moreover, the approach may offer a prescriptive scheme with which to analyse the competitiveness or innovation of IDs, this being the result of the ability to internalize external codified knowledge and externalize internal tacit knowledge. The extent to which all IDs are able to convert tacit into codified knowledge according to the spiralling process envisaged by Nonaka, and how to operationalize tacit knowledge, are open questions in the empirical literature, where there have been some first applications (see Section 1.11).

1.8. COMPETENCE THEORY OF THE FIRM AND INDUSTRIAL DISTRICTS

Most of the empirical research, as well as our results themselves, show that the technological content of the productive cycle in IDs is, on average, low to intermediate. The paradigms governing the industries where IDs are specialized are almost exhausted. Rather than insisting on IDs as an innovatory system, some authors therefore believe it more realistic and appropriate to depict them as repositories of competencies, thus departing from the incremental nature of IDs' typical technological progress.

Lawson (1998), Morgan (1997) and Maskell and Malmberg (Maskell, 1999; Maskell and Malmberg, 1999) find many points of convergence between the resource-based view of the firm (Wernerfeld, 1984) or, in the most recent literature, the competence theory of the firm (Langlois, 1988; Langlois and Robertson, 1995; Prahalad and Hamel, 1990) and the explanation of the sustained competitive advantage of regions. It is therefore suggested that this theory should be extended to regions and IDs. Several features of IDs may justify extension of such a broad current of theory. The ID, conceived as the mere agglomeration of SMEs and persons, is the result of an historical interaction between people and firms. Agglomeration always implies a rootedness of competencies and know-how. Wherever a geographically bounded productive system exists, a process of 'collective learning' takes place. This process can be defined as the creation, dissemination and further development of a stock of common knowledge among the actors within it. As a result of local interactions, a bundle of relationships, practices, routines, knowledge, rules of conduct, and technical know-how develops and evolves, thereby creating the basis for the area's competence creation. Competencies or capabilities lie at the heart of the structure of regions and IDs, accounting for their typical specialization and thus for their sustained competitive advantage or disadvantage.

Lawson (1998) goes a step further in the application of competence theory to territories by recasting some of the analytical categories developed by Rumelt in the context of the theory of the firm in regional terms. He lists these as follows:

> First, (regional/corporate) span: competencies not only span products but firms themselves at any point in time. Second, temporal dominance: competence may not only be more stable and evolve more slowly than products, but may be more stable and evolve more slowly than firms themselves. Thus firms, like products, may be only the temporary expression of a region's competences . . . Both firms and regions consist of bundles of competences; which set is more enduring, explanatorily dominant etc. at any moment in time is an open question. Third, learning by doing: competences are not only gained or enhanced by work but by trade and other interfirm interaction . . . Fourth, competitive locus: the relative performance of regions as well as the relative performance of firms is merely the superficial expression of a deeper competition over competences. (Lawson, 1998, p. 160)

The competence perspective crucially depends on the nature of learning assumed to be dominant in territories, regions or IDs. Different types of learning may be distinguished and each may have a differing impact on the structure of interfirm linkages and on the sustainability or endurance of IDs.

The competence perspective is able to account for the dynamic process of change. Since learning is a continuous sustained process, the relationships that sustain and facilitate different types of learning must be thought of as changeable. Moreover, assuming that the specialization observed in one period of time is only one specific manifestation of a deeper and more robust heritage of competencies, we may expect the diversification of other (likely) contiguous industries to be a new form of embodiment of latent competencies. If, however, the formation and consolidation of skill traditions in an area are believed to result from a long-term historical process, then a region bereft of the skills necessary at a particular evolutionary moment is bound to decline. This approach does not thoroughly develop the theme of learning processes (as does the cognitive approach), nor does it examine the role or entry of new actors (as does the population ecology, for example), except in so far as it interprets the birth of new specializations as the expression or emergence of latent capabilities on the basis of an *ex post* reconstruction. It is here that the competence-based approach reveals a weakness, since it has not yet provided a method with which to measure the degree of ownership and the real span of competence, or to find the competitive locus of a district. This may carry the consequence that any evolution by an area toward a different specialization may be traced back to the original specialization by way of an *ex post* exercise unless an operationalizing criterion is found and applied.

1.9. INDUSTRIAL DISTRICTS AS 'SELF-ORGANIZING' SYSTEMS

1.9.1. A Biological Metaphor for Industrial Districts

The search for the essence or invariant nature of IDs, now that the pure proximity of firms and people is not considered sufficient to explain their structure and evolution, has stimulated attempts in this direction by organization scholars. IDs have been interpreted as 'autopoietic' (Dematteis, 1994; Corò and Rullani, 1998) or 'self-organized' systems (Biggiero, 1999), that is, a product of highly specific interactions among their components and of autonomy with regard to their environment. The concept or paradigm of autopoiesis was first introduced in the scientific community by an article published by Varela, Maturana and Uribe (1974), to be refined and developed in other contributions (Varela, 1981). The adaptation of a biological theory or paradigm to an economic phenomenon would be welcomed by the discoverer of IDs, Marshall, the author who wrote that 'The Mecca of the economist lies in economic biology rather than in economic dynamics' (Marshall, 1950, p. xii). Attempts to use biological concepts in the social sciences are now relatively common; but it is biological theory that has discovered an organizational and therefore social component in the 'autopoietic' or 'self-organized' biological processes of adaptation and evolution. The already mentioned 'new geographical economics' also assumes that the processes of geographical agglomeration are self-organized in nature (Krugman, 1996).

The legitimacy of extending the autopoietic approach to social science lies in the recognition that both biological and social systems interact with the external environment, preserving their invariant traits or 'identity' without changing or being dominated. This feature of biological and social systems is also referred to as organizational closure. This closure is 'operational' in that the internal organization of a system changes or adapts, not according to external dictates (input control) but according to its own internal rules (Varela, 1981). These rules select external signals and react to them by preserving their compatibility with the internal structure.

Apart from operational closure, autopoietic systems have other attributes. A strict assessment of their significance for IDs and social systems in general would exclude their belonging to the autopoietic paradigm. More convincing is the extension of second-order cybernetics proposed by Biggiero (1999). At the core of this approach lie concepts like self-organization, which is based on feedback properties, and system identity. If autopoiesis is inapplicable to social systems and IDs, second-order cybernetics may instead yield understanding of social systems, if concepts like self-organization, self-reference and autonomy are interpreted as a question of degree and not as on–off conditions (Biggiero and Sammarra, 2001).

1.9.2.   The 'Identity' of an Industrial District

Following this second line of interpretation, cybernetic concepts may be applied, and the structural origin of district identity (or interorganizational networks) may reside in the recursiveness of interactions. In addition, some authors distinguish between the characteristics (and nature) of identity, on the one hand, and the forces (causes) of identity creation on the other (Biggiero, 1998). As for individual identity, organizational identity can be described and classified in many ways, but this is an issue different from that of understanding *identity creation, maintenance* or *reinforcement*.

The latter involve individuals, firms and institutions and may emerge either in unintentional and thus 'spontaneous' orders (or states of the system) or as a result of the action of 'systemic integrators' or catalysts. By means of interactions with the community, the individual helps reproduce the conditions for the survival of the collectivity (or the system) to which s/he belongs. This view requires that the critical resources for the reproduction of the system (for example, knowledge) are not completely internalized by single firms but are rather put into circulation through spontaneous mechanisms of interaction or by the action of some catalysts. The endurance of the ID is thus ensured by what Varela calls the '*blind watchmaker*', and not by a superior rationality.

Hence, adaptation by these systems is not deterministic in its structure; rather, it leaves a multiplicity of organizational responses and evolutionary paths open. In this respect, some sort of evolutionary relativism is evoked, and a *cognitive domain* comprising all the possible organizational responses of the system results.

Having explained how district identity emerges does not exhaust understanding of IDs as distinct objects of analysis. The density of relationships, and therefore their continuous interaction, must be driven by some kind of *similarity* and *interdependence* among the constituent parts of the network. In the case of a district, similarity derives from a dominant (industrial) specialization, and therefore from diffused competencies accompanied by a shared learning process and generally typical entrepreneurial origins or professional backgrounds. Shared competencies facilitate processes of labour division able to create interdependencies among firms, individuals and active institutions. Proximity, and therefore continuous interaction among people, also fosters imitative and homogeneous behaviour.

It is evident that social cohesion in IDs emerges as a result not of specific attitudes but of continuous interactions. What was implicitly attributed to historical processes operating outside the realm of economics (Dei Ottati, 1987) under the cybernetic approach is more clearly related to recursive interactions.

The interpretation of an ID as a self-organized system has many virtues in explaining the inertia of IDs, as emerges from many of the cases analysed. Common cognitive maps, owing to the causes explained above, may impair the perception and understanding of environmental (technological or market) changes. Interrelatedness and imitative behaviours also have the effect of propagating disturbances. The approach is able to explain why innovations are incremental rather than radical while a process of learning by doing prevails, or why firms may diversify into other niche markets without changing their organizational structure. In fact, to the extent that radical innovations require new theories and routines, no continuity with the existing knowledge or specialization in an ID may be expected.

Under the view of IDs as open (to some degree) self-organizing systems, change may originate from external sources, but the IDs may not evolve into different forms. Rather than offering complex operational concepts (for example, a measure of recursiveness is cumbersome to build, involving a count of the number of interactions), the cybernetic approach raises a fundamental question concerning whether change may originate from outside the ID or from its internal structure. The emphasis on the mechanisms of identification allows one to gauge whether mimetic or differentiation processes emerge, the former implying continuity and the latter change. The empirical section of this book presents an analysis of IDs as areas characterized by a certain degree of interaction within a bounded territory by examining the variety of structures (that underlie identities and cognitive maps) that may coexist within the same ID and that may engender change rather than decline in IDs.

1.10. AN ECOLOGICAL APPROACH TO INDUSTRIAL DISTRICTS

Another organizational approach germane to cybernetics that contributes to the understanding of the problem of change in IDs adopts an ecological perspective (Hannan and Freeman, 1989). An ID may be interpreted as an intermediate form of organization consisting of competing but interdependent communities of 'populations' of firms. A population is 'a set of organizations characterized by a particular organizational form and dependent on a common set of material and social resources' (Carroll, 1997, p. 120).

Population ecology stems from the idea that the processes of organizational change within firms and industries are not so endemic as the traditional theory pretends, and that there are strong factors of inertia. This theory explains organizational forms (structures, strategies, and so on) as the result of selection mechanisms by focusing on the distribution of resources and the terms on which they are available.

According to this approach, populations are related by three types of relation: symbiotic, competition, and predator–prey. The number of members/individuals of a population – consisting in the number of members having, for example, the same productive specialization – and their density both give rise to different degrees of organizational variety.

Population ecology is fruitful in explanation of why some IDs are unable to evolve towards different organizational forms by adopting new practices and structures or by reverting to new paradigms, once the external environment changes. One reason for the inertia of IDs is that, for example, if certain individually rational behaviours are adopted by all firms, they become irrational and destructive for the survival of all species. However, as regards the imitative mechanisms that operate among the various firms' populations in a district, the ecological approach fails to draw all the implications of learning processes, which, like species replacement mechanisms, may generate organizational changes. It may therefore be fruitfully merged with the cognitive approach, which instead concerns itself with the processes of knowledge creation and diffusion.[9]

Staber (1997, 1998) uses concepts and propositions from organizational ecology theory to highlight the entrepreneurship features of the ID model. He views business start-ups (and dissolutions) as a source of change at the level of organizational populations. Change is supposed to occur more through business start-ups, which introduce new organizational forms and routines and destroy outdated forms, than through the radical transformation of existing firms.

Lazzeretti and Storai (1999) apply ecological concepts in explanation of the evolution of the Prato district in the post-war period (1946–93), examining the number of populations – defined according to firms' specialization – and their density. The populations (specializations) considered concern activities classified under industry codes. The micro-data consist of the birth and death rates of firms.

The ecological perspective partly overlaps with cybernetics theory. Since this theory presumes that change is introduced by new actors with new identities, it assumes that new populations induce a change in the system. The 'natural' outcome of selection pressures is that less effective organizations are eventually driven out of the population. Inertial forces within organizations are seen as limiting the capacity to change with sufficient rapidity to keep pace with environmental changes. Thus, most change occurs at the population level, as organizations of outdated form are replaced by organizations that introduce new forms.

Viewed from the ecological perspective, an ID is a competitive response by a business population, or group of populations, to the problems of adapting to changes in the environment.

1.11. INDUSTRIAL DISTRICTS AND/OR NETWORKS

1.11.1. Networks (and Industrial Districts) between Market and Hierarchy

The literature on interfirm and intrafirm networks often overlaps with that on IDs because both phenomena – assuming they are not coincident – may be, and indeed are, studied from different disciplinary perspectives, thereby yielding abundant insights and fostering dialogue among various fields of the social sciences.

Here we shall focus on those studies in which network concepts are applied to IDs and vice versa, by default concentrating mostly on organizational and territorial studies. The latter have used the concept of networks in an instrumental way simply in order to describe the openness of territorial systems and their linkages with other places of resources or market seeking. The Gremi approach assumes the network as its principal organizational metaphor since the milieu is itself a network of actors in a region. Implicit in most of the studies is a normative value of the network form as able to sustain competitiveness in the face of globalization processes (Axelsson and Easton, 1992). Most of these studies interpret interfirm networks as constituting a broader category, which includes IDs and other organizational forms.

The inclusion of IDs among network forms in organizational studies derives from two implicit assumptions. On the basis of the well-known examples of IDs as Prato or Carpi, many authors have assumed that IDs are characterized by a network, that is, a close-knit (both horizontal and vertical) division of work. Accordingly, they have analysed the governance rules of IDs from a perspective that contrasts IDs, as well as networks, with markets and hierarchies. This portrayal of both networks and IDs as alternatives to integrated firms governed by hierarchy, on the one hand, and the market as mediated by price coordination through firms' competition, on the other, is based on two different interpretations. Firstly, there are those who define an interfirm network as an 'intermediate' or 'hybrid' form of the organization of economic activities with respect to markets and firms (hierarchies) (Jarrillo,

1988; Thorelli, 1986; Williamson, 1991). Secondly, there are those who dispute this view and maintain that a network is a 'third type' or a 'pure' organizational form, with characteristics and properties qualitatively different from those of both markets and firms (Casson, 1995; Di Bernardo and Rullani, 1988; Johanisson, 1987; Powell, 1990).

Hybrids are social subsystems formed by the interplay of trust and power, while networks are assumed to be pure organizational forms governed by non-market mechanisms such as trust, language or informal codes of communication. Hutter and Teubner (1993) make the interesting point that hybrids are not just an alternative to the market or hierarchy – as argued by transaction theory – but are 'parasitic' in the positive sense that they can draw on both the qualities of organization and the qualities of individuals.

The discovery of the network as a third or pure form of organization between market and hierarchy has apparently gained much more consensus than the alternative view of networks as intermediate forms. The already mentioned depiction of IDs as a 'communitarian market' (Dei Ottati, 1987), and the concept of milieu are attempts to mediate between market mechanisms of coordination and trust.

Once having put trust at the very foundation of networks, some authors have applied the network concept to very dissimilar phenomena or contexts (franchising, joint ventures, subcontracting, putting-out, A-forms, N-forms, U-forms, JV, interlocking directorates, IDs and so on), often in mutual contradiction, generating a substantial semantic confusion and ambiguity (Nohria and Eccles, 1992) similar to that which occurred in relation to IDs. What is unsatisfactory from a theoretical point of view is that, once again, 'functional equivalents' are not isolated. Organizational features may vary according to the history of interfirm or intrafirm relationships, or to their context, but the functions performed may be the same. We are therefore left doubting whether these descriptive forms are really alternatives based on antagonistic principles of organization or whether they are descriptive taxonomies associated with distinct efficiency or equity results.

By way of a first conclusion, it seems that in order to define the typical governance mechanisms of a network it would be wiser to look at their structural features. In itself, a network is only a set of interconnected elements, which means that *complementary* linkages exist among these elements while *similarity* relationships identify only pure sets. All organizations are networks differentiated according to their degree of internal interconnectedness. Merely considering them as organizational forms, IDs may therefore be depicted as networks. Others emphasize the variety of organizations interconnected (or institutional and economic inter-organizational networks) within an ID, and therefore their nature as 'hypernetworks' (Biggiero, 1999; Pilotti, 1997).

Network analysis provides a wide array of concepts and tools to study networks (number of links among the 'nodes', relational or spatial density, distance, and centrality) (Wasserman and Faust, 1994). This approach has several merits in that it provides workable concepts with which to differentiate among different forms. The compatibility of this approach with a non-deterministic and evolution-based view of networks depends crucially on whether it is possible to devise workable concepts for the information exchanged and the content of relations, as well as for their geometric properties. Linkages may concern flows of goods, but they may also involve information. Observation of a network in different periods of time may yield a sequential picture of its evolutionary pattern. The problem with this approach is the large amount of information needed: in fact, only few applications to larger systems of firms are to be found in the literature: more common are studies on smaller groups of firms. More workable is to look at the degree of interdependence, which may easily be determined in order to derive the governing (coordination) mechanisms.

Thompson (1967) identifies a parallelism between types of interdependence ('pooled', 'sequential' and 'organic') and types of coordination (codes and standards, planning and mutual adaptation). In this regard, Grandori (1997) proposes a typology[10] of IDs with respect to the typical coordination mechanisms enacted in responses to types of interdependence given the external context of converging preferences and low information complexity that characterizes social networks and IDs in general.[11]

Table 1.1 Types of interdependence and forms of social networks: an application to industrial districts' governance

Pooled interdependence: 'Marshallian' IDs	Intensive interdependence: Differentiated and integrated IDs
Sequential interdependence: 'Constellations'	Reciprocal interdependence: Informal ID subcontracting

Source: Grandori (1997, p. 912).

1.11.2. The Structural Distinctive Features of a Network

Other authors have focused on the distinctive features of networks as applicable to IDs, rather than on their governing mechanisms, such as 'autonomy' and 'entrepreneurship' (Di Bernardo and Rullani, 1988), coordination and ownership integration (Grandori, 1997) and learning capabilities (Langlois and Robertson, 1995).

Di Bernardo and Rullani (1988) conceive of a network as a specific form of work organization that marks a passage from Fordist to post-Fordist society. Autonomy and entrepreneurship are the two attributes identified by the authors that may easily be applied to distinguish among different models of labour division and therefore among different paradigms of society. Autonomy is defined in terms of property rights and decision-making independence, while entrepreneurship refers to self-reference and control over core competencies.

Langlois and Robertson suggest looking at the type of firms' knowledge (tacit versus codified knowledge). Firms or individuals that base their competitive advantage or competence on tacit knowledge or capabilities have non-dependent relationships. Entirely coincident in substantive terms, although differently phrased, are the two distinctive features of networks emphasized by Belussi and Arcangeli (1998): the degree of flexibility (or the physical shape of the interconnected nodes of the network) and the learning capabilities of all agents (rather than merely the 'nodes') involved in each relational network. The combination of these two features gives rise to different types of networks: steady-state networks, retractile and reversible networks and evolutionary networks; a set of notions which the authors apply to a group of Italian IDs. The first type is characterized by a low degree of operational flexibility and by static incremental learning. Firms' activities are organized within a given framework, the specialization of firms is relatively low, and there is little accumulation of knowledge. The second type of network exhibits, by contrast, the attributes of flexibility ('retractility' or 'reversibility'). Firms' linkages are mobile; tasks and functions are subject to decentralization or recentralization according to the needs of the 'principal' firm, changes in demand, and/or technological developments. Firms belonging to the network develop an adaptive learning capability focused on incremental innovations, which may be localized only in some of the network nodes. The most complex type of network is the evolutionary one, which possesses attributes of high flexibility (reversibility and retractility) and is characterized by various forms of creative learning and capacity for growth. According to Belussi and Arcangeli, since the performance of firms in 'Third Italy' IDs is based upon tacit, idiosyncratic knowledge, the steady state and retractile forms of network are most common within Italian IDs, while the evolutionary networks are relatively insignificant and occur in very few cases – for example the Montebelluna area – although the authors predict that Italian IDs will evolve into this form. Other authors have placed great emphasis on the 'innovative network', exemplified by Silicon Valley and Route 128.

Once the nature of the relationships and the distinctive features of the nodes have been defined, the governance rules of networks, trust or power, can be determined. Similarly, Belussi and Arcangeli (1998) and Belussi and

Pilotti (2000) point to learning capabilities of actors as predictors of the nature of the relationships and therefore of the nature of networks.

Competence theory of the firm may also be rephrased in terms of network characteristics. According to a competence view of the firm, ownership is based upon competence. A wide distribution of ownership therefore implies a wide distribution of the competence that underpins it.

The ecological perspective also offers a dynamic approach to networks, which are interpreted as an organizational form linking firms to their environment. The source of change in networks is not in the adaptation of existing firms, nor in changing the strength of ties, in the administrative form of relations, or in the content of connections, but rather in the entry of new firms that weed out less efficient members of the network. According to Staber, 'Routines based on investments in the networks and external dependencies constrain organizational change and lock firms into their network positions. Strong network embeddedness is therefore a liability, limiting firm's adaptability in volatile environments'[12] (1998, p. 705).

On closer inspection, the structural features of networks have much in common whit what we discussed in the section on the determinants of labour division. Entrepreneurship relates to the integration of execution and conception within the same node, and this explains why networks are taken to be paradigmatic examples of post-Fordist models of work organization. These two categories can also be used to describe a 'vertical' division of labour, whereby each firm specializes in a particular task and produces goods, products or services by relying on its own design or competencies alone. These categories therefore permit the recasting of interfirm relationships in a more genuine organizational language. The attribute of autonomy, for example, enables assessment of whether or not Marshallian IDs correspond to a network. Notwithstanding the multiplicity of linkages among the nodes, what Marshall described was a system – that is a set of interconnected nodes – but not a network, because all the firms were under the same proprietary roof and lacked decision-making autonomy.

The literature on networks thus far surveyed points out that a network, as a third form of organization, is characterized by a specific form or type of relationships among 'nodes'. This a question concerning not so much the density of relationships as their nature.

A feature latent in each framework concerns the location of conception and design competencies. The 'extended division of work' described by Brusco, or the flexible specialization of IDs, and network definitions that stress autonomy, entrepreneurship, learning or competence: these are all features indicative of the integration of execution and conception as a distinctive trait of IDs, and can be used as a predictor of their success. What is not clear in all the approaches to IDs as networks is whether the distinctive features, summarized here as the reintegration of conception and execution, must be possessed by the ID as a whole or by a certain proportion of firms (or nodes), and if the latter, then how large this proportion has to be. Is this only a question of degree and not of essence? Do the most closely integrated nodes also need dependent nodes in order to work?

The research questions we are left with concern whether IDs are networks, and, if they are, which typology applies to Italian IDs? Given their nature as networks, are they efficient organizational forms? And finally, what are the rules of governance of networks?

1.12.　CONCLUSION: A PRELIMINARY EVALUATION OF THEORIES

The interest of various scholars from different disciplinary traditions confirms that IDs may be seen as a multi-disciplinary meeting point (microeconomics, development economics, institutional economics, industrial organization, geography, sociology, socioeconomics, and so on), or as a 'master key' for reviewing hotly debated questions of basic economic theory (patterns of labour divisions, 'embeddedness' of economic relations, regional growth, role of trust in economics, and so on).

The reader of the foregoing brief survey of the literature on IDs may have gained the impression of an abundant and often redundant 'supply' of theories on IDs that converge in identifying the question of change as crucial under a theoretical and empirical point of view. Whether or not the reader has a declared preference for one approach rather than others, s/he should have objective criteria of evaluation.

The theory of technological competence, the competence perspective, population ecology, the cognitive interpretation of IDs and the self-organizing approach are the most promising research programmes towards explaining the evolution of IDs; while all the other approaches, such as the transaction-based theory or the 'communitarian' idea of the ID, are mainly static in nature, these are able to take full account of the evolution of IDs.

There are, however, weaknesses in *all* the approaches surveyed. Some of these concern their theoretical foundations, which may conflict with the 'objective' or factual nature of the phenomenon under investigation (or with the beliefs of the critic), while others relate to a poor heuristic value of the approach itself. The Gremi approach, for example, fails to specify precisely the economic logic of a milieu.[13] Overall, a limited extension of applied studies has to be recognized for the more innovative approaches. Whether these deficiencies will be made up for in time (some approaches are in their infancy), or whether they point to an idiosyncrasy of the theory to be operationalized, makes a major difference, and we have the suspicion that the latter is the more likely case. Concepts like span of competencies, degree of interaction and trust are very difficult to express in observable indicators. Operationalization – as a preliminary step before empirical testing – is even more important for those concepts that hinge on questions of degree rather than essence, like the cybernetic approach for example. They are all plausible, but do not lend themselves to testing the explanatory value of the determinants of ID performance.

Advantages and limits of operationalization are discussed in detail in Section 2.3. Suffice here to remark that above all, operationalization may show that the same indicator, or a combination of these may 'serve' or be compatible with different theories. This illustrates that with IDs, as with other social systems, conflicting theories may converge, although using a different 'language'. Only where a bi-univocal correspondence between indicators and theory does not exist is it possible to point to the real differentiation of theories and to their real heuristic value.

We believe that the crucial item on the ID research agenda, and therefore the golden rule when assessing theories, is the ability of a theoretical framework to provide testable hypotheses for a general assessment of IDs and to answer the research questions set in the introduction. Are IDs a successful and sustainable socio-economic phenomenon, or are they not? Is agglomeration by itself sufficient to account fully for the efficiency and growth of IDs? Is cooperation a pervasive rule of ID governance? Do IDs change yet preserve their identity, or do they evolve towards different forms? How, or who, are the actors introducing change in IDs? Whether change occurs, will IDs be able to conjugate competition and social competitiveness in the face of globalization?

Not all these questions are answered in this book, partly because IDs are still in a phase of transition that makes easy identification of directions difficult. A variety of structures and strategies results from our study that precludes the identification of a simple pattern of evolution, a one way for IDs, especially if only spontaneous mechanisms of adjustment are taken into account.

NOTES

1. An insight into this idea may be found in Bianchi (1989), although the author did not offer an explicit treatment of IDs as contestable markets.
2. 'It is possible to divide the process of production into several stages, each of which can be performed with the maximum of economy in a small establishment (and thus yielding a district consisting of) a large number of such small establishments specialized for the performance of a particular stage of the process of production' (Marshall, 1920, p. 221).
3. Again, 'in all but the earliest stages of economic development as localized industry gains a

great advantage from the fact that it offers a constant market for skill . . . The owner of an isolated factory, even if he has access to a plentiful supply of general labour, is often put to great shifts for want of some special skilled labour; and a skilled workman, when thrown out of employment in it, has no easy refuge' (Marshall, 1950, p. 271).

4.   Again, 'the economic use of expensive machinery can sometimes be attained in a very high degree in a district in which there is a large aggregate production of the same kind, even though no individual capital employed in the trade be very large. For subsidiary industries devoting themselves each to one small branch of the process of production, and working it for a great many of their neighbours, are able to keep in constant use machinery of the most highly specialized character, and to make it pay its expenses, though its original cost may have been high, and its rate of depreciation very rapid' (ibid., p. 271).

5.   'And presently subsidiary trades grow up in the neighbourhood, supplying it with implements and materials, organizing its traffic, and in many ways conducing to the economy of its material' (ibid., p. 271).

6.   The book contains another relevant contribution, Amin and Robins (1990), which is however very critical with respect to Piore and Sabel's approach especially.

7.   The opposite model is that 'in which production is a means, and the ends which it serves are the product which can be sold in the market or income. They imply a district the members of which are ultimately motivated by profit. Each individual is a potential competitor because his or her sales threaten the profit which any other can obtain. Co-operation can only be understood by the ultimate need of the individual for the help of the other members and of the district as a whole, if profit is to be learned at all' (1990, p. 67).

8.   The notion of 'Third Italy' describes the specialization of some regions of Italy, mainly northern and central-eastern Italy, based on small firms.

9.   Among the mechanisms which select human social constructs, one should consider the selective diffusion of successful organizational variations through imitation of the forms adopted by firms, and the selective retention of successful variations through observations of the results achieved by firms over time.

10.   A theoretical or *ex ante* classification is a typology (see p. 102).

11.   The author carefully warns that the typology by no means exhausts the variety of possible effective applications of interfirm informal cooperation, even in the realm of ID governance; also that interfirm relations in IDs are not always characterized by perceived convergence of interests and informal cooperation.

12.   Similarly, in the collection of contributions on the embeddedness of industrial networks edited by Grabher (1993), is accurately discussed how 'strong ties' cause mechanisms of inertia as well.

13. Storper (1993) sharply remarks: 'The Gremi group . . . has never been able to identify the economic logic by which the milieu fosters innovation. There is a circularity: innovation occurs because of a milieu, and a milieu is what exists in regions where there is innovation' (p. 13).

2. Operationalizing Industrial Districts

'Concepts without percepts are empty'
I. Kant
'Percepts without concepts are blind'
S. Greer

2.1. INTRODUCTION AND OUTLINE

This chapter focuses on some critical methodological issues on the ID research agenda. Criteria of identification and operationalization are treated as pertaining to two conceptually distinct operations. As regards identification, it examines the criteria used for the working definition of IDs assumed in this book, while operationalization is assumed to be a broader concept aimed at finding indicators for the variety of concepts offered in the literature. The question of identification combines two issues: identification of the areas complying with the definition assumed – those which actually consist of an operationalization of the definition – and identification of the physical boundaries of IDs.

The methodological phases of the research design used in this book may be summarized as follows:

- territorial identification of the units of analysis;
- selection of the sample;
- operationalization of the concept of ID;
- collection of data and surveys at a local level;
- interviews and mail questionnaires to selected 'qualified' observers;
- calculation of indicators;
- multivariate and econometric analysis.

Territorial identification is the first step towards obtaining a meaningful taxonomy of IDs and the empirical testing of hypotheses. Boundaries are a constitutive element of IDs, because only in a geographically bounded territory is it possible to observe the development of a shared culture or identity as a product of a common history. In economic geography the issue of spatial scale is central, since it seems likely that different forms of externality operate at different geographical scales (Martin, 1999). Boundaries are also relevant when IDs are considered as networks, since the degree of interdependence and similarity or the effectiveness of coordination mechanisms may diminish when there are too many actors or when they are heterogeneous.

Any disregard of ID boundaries – and the selection of too large a geographical unit; for example, an entire 'province'[1] – may detract from research on IDs. The sample was accordingly selected by adopting two objective criteria – territory and industry – which took account of relevant exogenous dimensions that may affect the structure and performance of IDs. Territory defines the cultural and social context that accomodates the formation and evolution of an ID, while industry sets the technical constraints and demand conditions that account for its specific model of labour division and competitiveness. These features constitute the exogenous conditions under which any taxonomy of IDs holds and appears to be less or more stable.

Section 2.2 reviews the main attempts in the literature to identify, on a quantitative basis, the existence of IDs, according to explicit or implicit definitions. The advantages and shortcomings of a quantitative approach to IDs are discussed in Section 2.3. As already pointed out in Chapter 1, a quantitative approach has found few followers; it is submitted, however, that it may instead have many advantages since it allows comparison among different IDs and relating concepts in a logical framework, and the establishment of cause/effect relationships. Obviously, the methods used to quantify concepts, and the notional number of indicators that can be built for each concept, are numerous. Illustrated here is an attempt to translate the distinctive features of IDs – as related to 'population of firms' and 'community of people' as stressed by the literature – and their performance into quantitative indicators. Owing to constraints related to the availability of data, research resources and the intrinsic limits of any translation, what follows is only an attempt – among others that may ensue – to specify the ID concept. After the limitations and advantages of operationalization have been contrasted in Section 2.4, the micro-foundations for the operationalization of IDs are provided in Section 2.5.1, while the data sources and indicators used to approximate the ID notion are described in Sections 2.5.2 to 2.5.4. Finally Section 2.6 discusses the indicators and the techniques best suited to testing IDs' performance.

2.2. THE IDENTIFICATION OF INDUSTRIAL DISTRICTS: QUANTITATIVE STUDIES

A preliminary question on the research agenda is the territorial identification of IDs. The territorial boundaries of IDs are often disregarded in the literature and most studies examine data at the provincial or even regional level, rather than at the local one, although this is the level best suited to observation of proximity effects.[2] The debate during the 1970s on the 'multiregionality of development' in Italy already showed that economic and social development differs from place to place, even within a single small province (which is therefore only an administrative division). The statistics available at a local level enable one to avoid generic territorial references and to proceed from mere intuition of an ID to its analytical localization in Italy by means of a meaningful unit of enquiry.

The difficulty of this task – as will become apparent later – does not entirely thwart the search for a satisfactory, if not optimal, criterion with which to distinguish IDs from other geographical areas comprising small firms. A case-study approach is frequently applied to areas selected on the basis of a 'common knowledge' or merely intuition as to their correspondence with the ID model. Other studies rely more closely on the work of the few scholars who have tried to identify ID areas. Among these, Sforzi (1987, 1990) and – to some extent – Garofoli (1983, 1991a and 1991b) have made the first rigorous attempts to find criteria through which to identify IDs. Their methodology, although it could be amended, is an important benchmark for our research, as will become clearer in the pages that follow. The various attempts to identify IDs in Italy are now surveyed, and these then follows discussion of their differences or similarities with respect to the approach used here.

2.2.1. Sforzi: the Identification of 61 Marshallian Industrial Districts

Sforzi's analysis was an attempt either to identify or to operationalize the definition of the Marshallian ID propounded by Becattini, using quantitative variables. Sforzi applied a multi-step algorithm using economic as well as social variables drawn from 1981 census data.

Sforzi took as his unit of observation the 995 Local Labour Market Areas (LLMAs) identified by ISTAT-Irpet (1989) on the basis of the 1981 Census of Population and Industries. The notion of LLMAs is more familiar to British geographers as 'Travel-to-Work-Areas' (Coombes, Green and Openshaw, 1986; Spence et al., 1982), and it denotes an area that includes a group of municipalities distinguished by a certain concentration of jobs, where the majority of the resident population is in employment and employees can change their jobs without changing their place of residence. The local labour market is spatially delimited, and relatively self-contained in the sense that job supply and demand tend to be in equilibrium with respect to the area over which they extend, because the majority of the resident population works within that area and employers recruit workers from the constituent localities.

In the light of these considerations, the concept of LLMA seemingly encapsulates the features of a locally bounded community, given that it identifies a restricted area in which interactions between firms and population are very dense.

The next stage in Sforzi's approach consisted in subjecting all 995 LLMAs to a multivariate analysis based on 61 socio-economic census variables and resulted in the clustering of 15 groups according to their socio-economic characteristics. According to Sforzi, one of these clusters, comprising 161 local systems, displayed the typical socio-economic features of the 'light industrialization' model; a model that exhibited a typical socio-economic pattern identified by the following discriminatory variables: the presence of entrepreneurs and workers in small manufacturing firms, working wives, young workers, large households with elderly people, and amenities (theatres, cinemas, sports centres, and so on).

As a final step, the economic structure of local labour markets complying with the pattern of light industrialization was analysed according to the specialization rate; that is, the prevalence of one industry or a cluster of subsections closely related in terms of the number of employees in total manufacturing employment.

The outcome of the analysis was identification of 61 areas, defined as Marshallian IDs, mainly located in north-eastern and central Italy.

Sforzi's selection strikes one as disappointingly restrictive, because it does not contain several well-known industrial areas referred to in the literature as IDs (for example, Biella and Schio), nor does it include more recent ones (for example, Putignano). The reasons for this lie in the method used. Sforzi was not concerned simply with the identification of IDs; his aim rather was to operationalize the 'canonical' ID: indeed, a direct line of descent from Becattini's work is immediately apparent. Because his method subjected a predetermined set of LLMAs to a double set of conditions on social and productive structures, the result was a small final subset that included neither areas of very recent industrialization (those not yet organized around a leading sector), nor older industrial areas (those already mature and with a different social structure).

Secondly, areas in which different industries coexisted, often intertwined but generally distinct, were deliberately excluded from the analysis. The reason for this was Sforzi's belief – stemming from Becattini's approach –

that a single industry plays a very important role in identity building or in the external 'image' of an ID. Moreover, because of the social constraint imposed by the author (the predominance of self-employed people), the areas in which larger firms were present, and hence those in which the dominant social class consisted not of self-employed people but workers, could nonetheless exhibit an extended division of labour which the indicator selected failed to grasp. This is the case, for example, of the ID types yielded by the multivariate analysis in Chapter 3.

2.2.2. Garofoli's 'Local Systems'

Garofoli (1991a and 1991b) attempted to build a typology of what he called 'models of local development' in Italy, only one of which was the ID. His aim also was to identify distinct territorial entities in order to apply different and specific territorial and economic policy measures. The territorial boundaries of the areas selected by Garofoli were derived only by referring to the degree of specialization of proximate municipalities. More precisely, those adjoining municipalities that displayed a high rate of specialization in the same industry were aggregated with the 'local system'.

However, in the absence of precise algorithms to calculate the relevant degree of specialization, one gains the impression that in some cases boundaries may be determined on the basis of *ex ante* knowledge, or according to administrative partitions.

Garofoli's analysis combined qualitative criteria with indicators conventionally employed in economic geography. Quantitative variables were calculated on the basis of census data, while qualitative ones were 'inferred' from existing surveys or values assigned subjectively (Garofoli, 1991a). Cross-referencing these variables yielded three different types of local economies based on SMEs:

1. Areas of productive specialization: a 'horizontal' division of labour among firms generally prevails in these types of area, which are usually young ones performing specialized tasks (often more labour-intensive ones) for commissioning firms located in other regions.
2. Local production systems: these are areas with a denser web of vertical and horizontal relationships among firms specialized in the same industry.
3. System areas: these coincide with 'clusters' of SMEs specialized in different tasks and in various complementary sectors.

Garofoli's main contribution was his use of an extended set of variables besides those to be drawn from census statistics, and in the broad perspective of his analysis, which was not limited to IDs alone but embraced 'local economies' as well (Garofoli, 1983, 1991a). This comprehensive approach emphasized change. Although neither a necessary transition from one type to another nor a predefined sequence will be followed, the different types may depict different phases of a development process impinging upon manufacturing SMEs.

2.2.3.   ISTAT Method

A recent contribution to identification of IDs has been made by the Italian central statistical office (ISTAT). ISTAT's procedure is based on a multistage method, which is similar to the approach used by Sforzi, who was involved in its design (ISTAT, 1997). The 784 LLMAs identified on the basis of 1991 census data were taken as the starting point, and 279 of them were defined as manufacturing LLMAs – the others being urban, rural or tourist areas – in that they had a proportion of employment in manufacturing industries above the national average. Among this group, 199 LLMAs were identified as IDs, because they exhibited a higher-than-average territorial concentration of SMEs in at least one of the manufacturing subsector in which the LLMA was specialized.[3] ISTAT's procedure is much simpler and more flexible than all those discussed thus far, although the concentration threshold may be overly rigid compared to the average for Italian manufacturing; the idea of an ID presupposed by this method, which defines it only in terms of industrial specialization and concentration, not in social terms, is consistent with our definition of IDs, and it is therefore the one that was chosen for the research set out in this book.

The IDs thus far defined are particularly widespread in the north-west and north-east of Italy (mainly in Lombardy, Veneto and Emilia Romagna), and in the central regions (Tuscany, Marche, Umbria), where they account for over 74 per cent of total establishments and for 79 per cent of employment. A few are to be found in the south of Italy, the so-called *Mezzogiorno*, and along the Adriatic coast (Abruzzo and Apulia), but there are none in insular Italy (Table 2.1).

ISTAT's IDs comprise 'fashion-wear' or design industries such as tanning, textiles, clothing, furniture and ceramics, but also mechanical engineering (Table 2.2). IDs represent, according to the 1996 census, 52 per cent of total employment and 70 per cent of manufacturing employment (around 2.2 million employees).

2.3.   IN SEARCH OF APPROPRIATE CRITERIA TO IDENTIFY INDUSTRIAL DISTRICTS

2.3.1.   Merits and Demerits of the Notion of LLMA

One of the most notable aspects of Sforzi's work is its intuition of the LLMA as a good geographical approximation for ID self-containment. The use of LLMAs also supports the idea that IDs are circumscribed areas in which interactions take place among people and between the local population and economic businesses, thereby generating that recursiveness of interactions which lies at the core of the cybernetic and network approaches. Provided that an LLMA's boundaries and constitutive municipalities are stable over time, major processes of common cultural and historical development may take place.

In order to identify the boundaries of IDs, an alternative to the LLMA might be the aggregation of only contiguous municipalities specialized in the same industry, which was Garofoli's approach. This procedure, however, may fail to grasp the functional specialization of municipalities located in the same area. Even if there is no firm engaged in the 'lead' industry in a municipality, the local population may provide a reservoir of manpower for the latter. In other words, the focus is solely on the degree of specialization; the important trait of functional specialization within the area may be lost.

Notwithstanding its validity, the concept of LLMA poses notable practical and theoretical problems. One concerns the 'mobility' of an LLMA's territorial boundaries; for example, between 1981 and 1991, most – though not all – LLMAs changed their composition in terms of enclosed municipalities. Because these local markets in Italy were identified between the 1981 and 1991 censuses, it may happen that, in the last census year, an LLMA includes a number of municipalities different from those identified in 1981. There are also some rare cases in which the 'core' municipality giving its name to the LLMA in 1981, then became part of another LLMA in 1991, thereby losing its centrality.

Proponents of the LLMA concept emphasize that these are not closed systems. On the contrary, they are open systems that exchange people, information and goods across their boundaries. As a consequence of these exchanges, they may enlarge or restrict their boundaries.

The problem of mobility is difficult to ignore, since for analytical purposes the object of enquiry must be stable. However, in this case the analysis assumes a retrospective or prospective rather than an evolutionary nature.[4]

Another difficulty similar to the previous one arises when two contiguous LLMAs are specialized in the same industry. Should these be considered two different LLMAs, and therefore two different IDs, or would it be more

Table 2.1a Italian districts by specialization of industrial sector and geographical location (by region), 1991

	Textiles and clothing	Tanning	Footwear	Furniture and fixtures	Mechanics and metals	Rubber and plastics	Paper and printing	Food	Musical instruments, toys and jewellery	Total
Piedmont	5			3	5		1	2		16
Lombardy	19			3	13	4		3		42
Trentino-A.Adige	1			1	2					
Veneto	15	1	2	10	5				1	34
Friuli-V. Giulia				2	1					3
Liguria								1		1
Emilia Romagna	4		1	5	6		1	7		24
Tuscany	6	1	3	4	1		2	1	1	19
Umbria	2			2			1			5
Marche	11		14	6				1	2	34
Lazio				1			1			2
(Abruzzo-Molise)	3		2	1						6
Campania	1	1	1	1						4
Puglia	2		1							3
Calabria								2		2

Source: ISTAT (1996).

Table 2.1b Italian districts by specialization of industrial sector and geographical location (by territorial partition), 1991

	Textiles and clothing	Tanning	Footwear	Furniture and fixtures	Mechanics and metals	Rubber and plastics	Paper and printing	Food	Musical instruments, toys and jewellery	Total
North-West	24			6	18	4	1	6	1	59
North-East	20	1	3	18	14		1	7	1	65
Centre	19	1	17	13	1		4	2	3	60
South Islands	6	1	4	2				2		15
ITALY	*69*	*3*	*24*	*39*	*33*	*4*	*6*	*17*	*4*	*199*

Source: ISTAT (1996).

Table 2.2 Manufacturing establishments and employment in Italian industrial districts, 1996

	Establishments		Employment	
	No	per cent	No	per cent
North-western Italy	90 496	36.7	914 875	41.2
North-eastern Italy	91 721	37.2	841 735	37.9
Central Italy	56 452	22.9	397 564	17.9
Southern Italy	8 032	3.3	67 059	3.0
Insular Italy	0	0.0	0	0.0
Total	*246 701*	*100.0*	*2 221 233*	*100.0*

Source: Author's calculation on ISTAT (2000).

correct to aggregate them as if they constituted only one? (And what should be done if there is more than one LLMA specialized in the same industry?) If we decide to aggregate them, when should we halt the process? Becattini (1990) suggests a size limit of 200 000 inhabitants should be imposed on an ID, while Brusco (1990) proposes a limit of 20 000 workers. One criterion with which to solve these contingencies might be to take all the LLMAs specialized in the same industry and aggregate them into what may be called a 'functional area', generally smaller than a province (ISTAT–Irpet, 1989; ISTAT–Irpet, 1997). This device, however, is better suited to grasping interdependencies among individual LLMAs, rather than their self-containment, and it may in fact be appropriate for some cases in the sample (see Section 6.3.2).

Again, as regards the notion of the LLMA, one may question whether the commuting period (between 7:30 and 9:30 a.m.) taken into account when identifying an LLMA is appropriate if employment relationships with more flexible working hours predominate in an area. That particular period is in fact typical of dependent employment. However, to the extent that IDs are mainly composed of industrial employees, the criterion is appropriate.

Besides the problems concerned with the LLMA as a unit of observation, measurement of the degree of specialization within an ID also raises difficulties. The case of *hidden* or *invisible* IDs may be a serious impediment against the use of statistical data for parameterization, especially when the classification of industry data is too aggregated to grasp some specific specialization. These cases, however, appear to be confined to highly specific productions like biomedical instruments, bicycles, kitchenwares, taps and fittings, and toys, which although relevant to a regional or local economy, play only a minor role in the national economy.

The case of IDs where specialization in one end-consumer good, such as shoes, has fostered the development of machine tools is different, these being easily extractable from the statistics. Indeed, an industry should be defined in terms of a *filière* comprising the upstream and downstream phases of production classified under different industry digit numbers.

Compared to the advantages of the notion of the LLMA, its disadvantages appear less serious than those of other criteria. Furthermore, the notion is compatible with most of the conceptualizations of the ID reviewed in this book.

We may consequently take the LLMA to be our unit of observation, while remaining mindful of its limitations. In particular, this study takes the 1991 LLMAs as its unit of observation (ISTAT, 1997), so that their evolution is observed back to 1961/1951 in a retrospective analysis, and forward to 1996. In addition, we consider single LLMAs, even where more than one LLMA is specialized in the same industry (as in the Marche region), resorting if necessary to the concept of 'functional area' for a further refinement.

Under this approach, the population from which the units of observation are selected must be sufficiently inclusive to comply with our 'agnostic' definition of ID; and the population that best fits this criterion is the one used by the above-mentioned ISTAT survey (1997) (Tables 2.1a and 2.1b).

2.3.2. Selecting the Sample

As useful and general criteria with which to discriminate between LLMAs of SMEs, we chose two critical factors: industry and space, thereby obtaining a sample of industrial systems located in different regions of Italy and specialized in different industries. The rationale for this choice was that the industrial sector sets the technical constraints (and hence the range of variability) of different forms of interfirm relationships, while the local space is the geographical *locus* in which particular relationships and systems of values develop, influencing the linkages among firms, people and institutions.

Various criteria can be used to differentiate and classify industries. If the criterion of technological innovativeness (Pavitt, 1984) is employed, two main categories of industries can be distinguished within the specialization industries of the IDs listed in Table 2.1: 'traditional' industries, which cover the majority of areas, and a smaller number of 'specialized supply' industries, like metalworking and engineering industries. Different technological opportunities, cost features, competencies and learning patterns are associated with these two industries. Consequently, both of them are included in the sample in order to give it an adequate degree of variety.

With regard to geography, Italy was divided into three macro-areas according to the canonical distinction: North, Centre-north, and Centre-south. It was decided to set the sample size at 39 units of observation (20 per cent of the total numbers of ISTAT IDs). In fact, the number of IDs considered for the multivariate and regression analyses was only 37, after the Matera and Casarano areas had been excluded on the grounds that they can be recognized as IDs only if a lower threshold is used for ISTAT's discriminatory variables.[5] This number seemed appropriate both to allow a sufficient degree of freedom in applying statistical methods and to gain more qualitative information not available from the Census data.

The sample is inevitably unbalanced with respect to the number of IDs in each geographical partition since the centre-south regions generally show a lower density of IDs and do not include certain specializations, like mechanical engineering. The sample is not probabilistic: it has a high degree of representativeness (Table 2.3) and includes an adequate combination of variety and homogeneity. The employment in the specialization industries of the IDs selected represent about 20 per cent of the corresponding industries in all 199 Italian IDs. When all the industries in the sample areas are considered in relation to total manufacturing in Italian industry, the representativeness rises to 25 per cent.

Table 2.3 Representativeness of the sample (specialization industries alone), 1996

	Establishments No	Employees No	Establishments %	Employees %
Textiles	10 410	62 321	33.0	22.1
Clothing	3 177	18 489	11.6	8.1
Knitwear	2 431	13 239	19.6	13.9
Footwear	3 597	34 507	29.2	30.0
Furniture	1 234	11 016	6.1	8.2
Agricultural machines	116	1 604	5.0	6.4
Tannery	1 788	19 567	83.9	77.4
Ceramics	1 306	29 145	13.7	25.1
Sample total	24 636	179 055	23.4	19.3
Total Italian IDs	105 362	925 762	100.0	100.0

Source: Author's calculations.

The final sample is set out in Table 2.4 and Figure 2.1.

2.4.   ADVANTAGES AND LIMITS OF OPERATIONALIZATION

2.4.1.   The Need to Operationalize and Measure the Concept of the Industrial District

The key advantage of a quantitative approach used here is that it provides a robust methodological framework while being flexible enough to admit replication and amendment. As already mentioned in Chapter 1, the features describing 'canonical' IDs are several but often lack quantitative precision. In most of the contributions surveyed, it is also clear and reiteratively stated that a superior performance is associated with the ('canonical') ID. Hence, even if

Table 2.4 The final sample

	Fashion-led industries							Innovative industries	
	Upstream industry: tannery	Downstream industry: furniture	Downstream industry: leather footwear	Downstream industry: sport and leather footwear	Upstream industry: textiles	Downstream industry: knitwear	Downstream industry: clothing	Non-specialized industry: ceramics	Specialized industry: mechanical engineering
North	Arzignano (Veneto) **C**	Desio (Lombardy) **C** Bassano del Grappa (Veneto) Oderzo (Veneto)	Vigevano (Lombardy) San G. Ilarione (Veneto)	Montebelluna (Veneto)	Biella-Cossato (Piedmont) Schio (Veneto)	Ostiglia (Lombardy)	Palazzolo sull'Oglio (Lombardy)	Marostica (Veneto) Sant'Ambrogio in Valpolicella (Veneto)	Suzzara (Lombardy) **C** Vigevano (Lombardy)
Centre-north	Santa Croce dell'Arno (Tuscany) **C**	Pesaro (Marche) **C** Poggibonsi (Tuscany) **C**	Fermo (Marche) **C** S.Elpidio (Marche) **C**	Civitanova (Marche) **C** Montecatini T. (Tuscany)	Prato (Tuscany) **C**	Carpi (Emilia Romagna) **C**	S. Benedetto Tronto (Marche) Senigallia (Marche)	Sassuolo (Emilia Romagna) Castellarano (Emilia Romagna) **C**	Guastalla (Emilia Romagna **C**) Cento (Emilia Romagna) **C**
Centre-south	Solofra (Campania)	Matera (Basilicata)	Guardiagrele (Abruzzo) Casarano (Puglia)	Barletta (Puglia)	Ascoli Piceno-Val Vibrata (Abruzzo)	Giulianova (Abruzzo)	S Marco Cavoti (Campania) Putignano (Puglia)	Civitacastellana (Lazio)	not existing

Note: The letter **C** denotes Sforzi's IDs.

57

Figure 2.1 Map of Italy

it has not been explicitly proposed as a normative model – for example, Becattini proposes his idea of ID only as a 'framework for analysis', rather than a model or a theory – it appears to be so. However, in the canonical literature a formal treatment of the relationship between the distinctive characteristics of the model and the performance is not offered, neither is there a structured, logic placement of concepts. In particular, it is not clear whether all the listed characteristics of IDs are necessary or just sufficient conditions for their success. The listed distinctive features appear to be all similarly essential for yielding increasing returns, competitiveness or innovation. A likely distinction between 'necessary' and 'secondary' or sufficient conditions is not present. The drawback of most of the canonical literature in providing a workable notion of IDs and a theory based on a logical construct of concepts raises the suspicion that it is valid on a 'narrative' level only.

In addition, there appears to be confusion between 'structural' or explanatory factors, on the one hand, and 'behavioural' or performance conditions of IDs on the other. This is particularly evident when Becattini claims that IDs are characterized by a continuous tension leading to change, which guarantees their survival. It is difficult to accept this claim on objective grounds, as we expect the structural characters of the ID to ensure the conditions of survival and not the reverse. If the ID is a normative model, a problem appears when a superior performance is shown by those empirical IDs not sharing all the requisites of the 'canonical' ID model.

We are quite convinced that operationalization may help provide a theoretical grounding for the concept of IDs in all its variants. Comparisons on the basis of controllable criteria may permit the emergence of 'functional equivalents' (Pyke and Sengernberger, 1990); that is, enable us to identify the mechanisms that ensure certain results without becoming embedded in given static historical and contingent forms.

Operationalization may also enable us to distinguish between those conditions that are responsible for the specific effects of the ID (such as competitiveness and certain positive welfare effects), or that ensure their stability, survival or innovation. In addition, an attempt to measure and operationalize the list of criteria helps us recognize that some requisites are implied in others and thus their listing may be considered valid on a 'narrative' rather than explanatory level.

For understanding IDs' structure and evolution, an operationalization, namely a measurement of concepts, is necessary. Once data are available, a comparison of different IDs and an assessment of the explanatory factors of their performance will be feasible. An analytical framework must also identify the explanatory factors of the particular performance of IDs, making clear whether they can be reduced to economies of agglomeration, or whether they are related to other factors.

We are also interested in distinguishing different forms of IDs as different forms in an evolutionary pattern. According to external technological and demand conditions or endogenous factors in the specialization industry, districts may mutate from one type to another.

Given the general and specific aims of our research, we need, as a first step to examine, the operationalization of the distinctive features of IDs as underlined by the literature so far reviewed. As illustrated in the previous sections, we are not primarily concerned with the mere geographical identification of IDs. Identification is but an intermediate step, since we are more interested in verifying the normative value of the models of IDs and assessing to what extent the model of the 'canonical' ID is empirically significant and associated to a superior performance.

2.4.2.   Limits of Operationalization

Operationalizing basically concerns the process of linking abstract concepts to empirical indicators. Such a process, which may be interpreted as a translation, involves misunderstandings or the use of inappropriate indicators (the 'words'), which, for example, may have a semantic content not necessarily intended by the author to be translated. The task is fairly complex as abstract concepts do not have a one-to-one correspondence with empirical indicators. It may be objected that the conceptualization of IDs could never be exhausted and reduced to empirical variables, but that they retain an unattainable intuitive value. Some authors have even criticized attempts to identify IDs geographically, since they are conceived as models valid only on a conceptual level (Franchi and Rieser, 1991).

By emphasizing the need for operationalization, it is not implied that concepts have definitive denotations (essence) and that they may therefore represent completely dichotomous meanings. Furthermore, even if variables are well specified and clearly depicted, whether quantitative or qualitative, a certain amount of subjectivism is always implied in their interpretation or in the identification of threshold or discriminant values. We simply assert that operationalization is the only instrument by which a researcher may make 'replicable' and falsifiable, in the Popperian sense, propositions, and therefore theories, built on these assertions. Therefore, since concepts can be operationalized and measured in an almost infinite variety of ways, our design is only one attempt, among many, which may be controlled, amended, criticized, superseded or dismissed by other researchers. In selecting the indicators, we have been guided by some constraints, due to the non-availability of data at the level of breakdown desired. However, most of the indicators have been used quite comfortably in these different disciplines.

The construction of indicators may be effected either using available raw statistics or data deriving from ad hoc surveys extended to a larger sample of areas in order to overcome the constraints and rigidities of available sources. Whether the latter solution is ideal, it is also quite obvious that it would require an enormous financial effort, affordable only through a joint research project combining financial and human resources, which has not been our case.

2.5. THE RESEARCH DESIGN

This section attempts to translate some of the ID conceptualizations discussed in Chapter 1 into testable hypotheses. Testable relations between phenomena are then derived from propositions and, as a third step, indicators and parameters are associated with these phenomena. A consistent set of related propositions, or a model, based on a well-developed micro-founded model of IDs, is not constructed here but some 'building blocks' are given.

2.5.1. Micro-Foundations of Industrial Districts

A point of departure is the alleged superiority or, more specifically, the greater efficiency, of the canonical ID. It may therefore be expected that the performance of an ID will be positive in at least some respects. The first problem arising from this statement is the level at which performance should be measured: at that of the firm or of the system level. The second concerns the economic or social nature of this performance, which first requires definition of the nature of an ID; namely, as a mere agglomeration of firms or rather as a socio-economic system.

The location of a firm in an ID may give rise to better performance in the form, say, of high profitability or stable market leadership, if it internalizes local externalities by hiring high-skilled workers, buying cheaper intermediate products or specialized services, economizing on transaction costs or introducing the new techniques, organizational procedures or technologies available in the local environment. Better labour productivity may also derive from exchanges of information and worker mobility (from one firm to another). Non-pecuniary economies account for the diffusion of entrepreneurship, or for its higher productivity or innovativeness, which is another production factor often neglected in the literature. The relationship among input factors, externalities and firms' profitability in an ID may be formalized by a firms' cost function, where the cost of individual inputs depends on a measure of agglomeration. Soubeyran and Thisse (1998), one of the few works in the literature on IDs with an analytical model, draws on a previous formalization by Arrow and Stockey to describe the cost function of a firm located in a district as a decreasing function of the industry output accumulated in that district. The implication is that the profits of ID firms increase with the local stock of competencies and knowledge. This model only considers labour productivity, although it could be complicated by adding further variables and factors emphasized in the literature. The supply of entrepreneurship may be viewed as dependent on the same factors that affect labour productivity; that is, the local tradition; so that history is inserted into a production model. A formalization of this kind is compatible both with a competence theory of the ID and with technological externalities.

Various indicators may be used to measure the diffusion of competencies besides the cumulation of production. Both entrepreneurial density (that is, the number of firms in relation to inhabitants) and the number of employees in relation to inhabitants in the specialization industry may be suitable. For the reasons given in Section 1.7, however, we maintain that the skills and knowledge peculiar to an ID are also embodied in firms, and not solely in individuals. Neglecting the organizational and technological competencies developed within a firm may incur the risk of overlooking a more typical feature of IDs as they have been structured in the last decades, where the role of larger and more complex firms has expanded, while workers' skills may be more compatible with an artisan type of ID. In keeping with a 'competence-based' approach to IDs' and the cognitive perspective, we also claim that 'learning by doing' and a spiralling process of knowledge creation may be related not only to cumulated production but also to the proximity of firms and population, or better to the density of firms and employees. This may result from an area's long tradition in its specialization industry.

Having outlined a possible formalization of the linkage between firm's profitability and location in a district, we may now turn to the question of whether the allegedly higher profitability of firms is related to an ID's overall performance. We may assert that the condition for the existence of a normative ID is that a firm's profitability must translate into better ID performance. The more firms are profitable, the higher the district's overall performance, as pointed out by various streams in the literature mentioned in Chapter 1. The self-contained nature of IDs emphasized by numerous studies also typifies their mechanisms of capital accumulation. The profits earned by local firms are either reinvested in the firm, or deposited in local banks, or spent on goods and services acquired locally. The same applies to wages. A virtuous circle of saving–investment–consumption operates at a strictly local level. A district's labour market, moreover, has to be characterized by full employment, high wages related to high productivity and mobility. The mechanism of re-investment offers a first insight for a micro-foundation of IDs which explains macroeconomic or collective performance in terms of local income, production, sales and global productivity. Krugman has also stressed that a concentration of firms in a location ensures both a lower probability of unemployment and a lower probability of labour shortage (1991b).

A collectively better performance by an ID also relates to urbanization economies, namely infrastructures (public roads, industrial and social facilities, and amenities). Institutions are also considered to be 'an essential ingredient' in an ID's success. A model of an ID's performance should therefore include all these factors.

Apart from the benefits accruing to the firms or people located in a district, one may also suggest that a country as a whole may benefit from the location of a large number of IDs on its territory, given the network externalities that may exist among different IDs. If intermediate or final ID products are effectively more competitive, national buyers may profit from their purchase. This, in fact, is what has happened in the user sectors of machinery produced in several Italian IDs (see Section 3.3.5). But, recalling Marshall's view on the matter (see p. 7), IDs also offer economies of purchasing or transaction, which may be to the benefit of firms in other industries or to the benefit of final consumption. Any synopsis of the propositions put forward in the literature would be incomplete if cooperation were neglected. How, thought, should one formalize cooperation? The only possible approach is to refer to its explanatory causes. If these are believed to be the local population's values, the researcher must parameterize them; or rather, expect that in an econometric function this unmeasured component will be entirely captured by the u residual. If instead one views cooperation as a product of recursive interactions, the age of the industry or the temporal process of cumulative production may be taken to be predictors of cooperation. The pattern of labour division is a further variable that needs to be inserted in a model. In the network perspective, efficiency increases with the thickening of linkages and exchanges among nodes.

The indicators used in the empirical research (Chaper 3) are discussed in the following sections. The Appendix illustrates the algorithms of each variable and data sources.

2.5.2. Selecting the Data Source

To ensure objectivity and comparability, it is crucial to choose a reliable and homogeneous data source for all the units of observation. Census data (Census of Population and Census of Industry) fit the requisites of reliability, homogeneity in space and time and breakdown at municipal level. The ten-yearly censuses conducted by ISTAT are systematic and reliable sources of data. They cover the entire national territory and are available from 1951 at ten-year intervals until 1991. An intermediate industrial census, the results of which are now available, was carried out in 1996.

Census data, however, have their shortcomings. A first limitation is their stock nature, which prevents study of the evolution of a phenomenon over time, permitting merely its description in a given period of time. Official statistics do not include economic trend data at the local or even regional level, and generally speaking they do not cover long periods. For example, statistics on value added or production at a two-digit code (for example, textile industry) dating to the 1950s are not available. A too-aggregated level of classification also concerns the birth and death rates of firms. The data available have been calculated at the province level and refer to the period 1980 onwards. This, for example, hampers application of an ecological perspective intended to assess the birth, consolidation or decline of organizational populations. Listing the data necessary to test all the theories discussed in the previous chapters would, however, be too cumbersome to undertake here.

Secondly, the degree of industry classification in census data is not homogeneous across the years surveyed.[6] While it is possible to obtain data on different specializations within an industry (at a three digit code: for example, knitwear industry in the textile industry) from the last industry census, this is not possible for previous years. Finally, since census data do not cover all the features we are interested in, it is necessary to resort to alternative ones, or to build indicators as proxies for the data available, in order to measure all the features of the ID models.

Qualitative information has been derived from secondary sources (recent and less recent surveys) and from interviews with 'qualified observers' or opinion leaders (for example, trade unionists and entrepreneurs, local administrators, managers of export consortia, and so on) resident in the areas studied (between one and five interviews were conducted in each area). In addition, a semi-structured questionnaire on the characteristics of the labour market designed to collect data on unionization was administered to the local branches of the main trade unions.

2.5.3.   The Indicators for Industry Structure

For the purpose of proxying the economic features of IDs, we calculated the indicators conventionally used in economic geography as well as in other theoretical frameworks, such as the rates of localization, specialization and concentration (variables are cited by means of the italicized labels given to them in the Appendix). These indicators can be defined by various algorithms, and the choice depends, as usual, on the purpose of the analysis.

Finding appropriate measures for agglomeration and labour division is not an easy undertaking. Some recent empirical studies on the relationship between Marshallian external economies and growth have used an index of specialization to measure the former (Glaeser et al., 1992). Since the econometric estimation results were not significant at this point, we prefer here to begin with a larger set of indicators, some of which may be subsequently discarded according to their statistical value. Given the constraints of the available data, the following indicators are discussed (all indicators have been calculated on data at a municipal level):

1. the firms' or entrepreneurial density index: the ratio between local productive units in the leading industry and the resident population (*finh*);
2. the employee density index: the ratio between the number of employees in the leading industry and the resident population (*einh*);
3. the absolute number of establishments[7] and employees (*firm, empl*);
4. the degree of specialization (by number of firms[8] or employees) in the leading industry (*spcf, spce*);
5. the degree of specialization (by number of establishments and employees) in ancillary manufacturing industries (*secf, sece*) as defined in note nine; [9]
6. the degree of specialization (by number of firms and employees) in ancillary machinery industries (*mechf, meche*);
7. the degree of diversification in manufacturing industries (first ten industries) calculated as a Herfindhal index (*HH*);
8. the percentages of micro-firms with fewer than ten employees (*C1*), small firms with between 10 and 50 employees (*C2*), medium-sized firms with more than 50 employees (*C3*).
9. the average size of firms (*size*);
10. the proportion of artisan firms among all firms in the leading industry (*arti*);
11. the distribution of the population in industry by employment status. The categories are self-employed workers (*isem*), entrepreneurs (professionals, owners of companies, members of cooperatives) (*enti*), dependent workers (*work*), clerical workers (*icle*), ancillary workers (*ancy*), managers (*mana*); [10]
12. the degree of concentration of production (the percentage of local production controlled by the first five firms: *C5*).

A spatial concentration of firms in a bounded territory and in a given industry is a prerequisite for external economies. Required to grasp this feature is a proxy of the density of firms in a local context, rather than indexes of localization or specialization, which are instead better suited to measuring the territorial distribution of one industry in a given territory, for example a region or a province. In fact, the rate of specialization has been used by ISTAT to select IDs. The concept of an agglomeration of firms or people seems to come closer to the idea of a large number of small firms, rather than to the densest concentration in a given region. In fact, in an area poor in firms, an index of specialization may yield high values relative to the presence of other industries in the area, but the number of firms may in any case be too small to generate significant external economies. For this reason, two indicators of density are calculated as the ratios between inhabitants and, respectively, firms (*finh*) and employees (*einh*). Another fundamental reason for calculating the indicator *finh* resides in the view of the firm as a stock of knowledge or a repository of competencies, as in the approaches surveyed in Chapter 1.

In order to measure the concentration of one industry in an area, the absolute values of firms and employees in that industry were also included. *Firm* and *empl* are further indicators of agglomeration, given that it is to be expected that a greater industry size in a given location will permit the pursuit of greater specialization.

Another hypothesis prompting the choice of indicators for the number of firms and employees (*firm* and *empl*) is that the larger the industry, the more the local industry is fragmented; and the higher the specialization rate, the more extended the labour division. It might also be noted that *firm* and *empl* measure the density of a 'population' belonging to an industry, on the basis of an organization ecology approach and the number of nodes in a network analysis.

The rate of specialization calculated both for the leading industry and for the other main industries of the *filière* encapsulates the dominant presence of one or a few complementary industries in an ID. By convention, ancillary industries were defined *ex ante* as related to the leading industry's technological constraints.[11] Owing to the classification of data available, it was not possible to assess the complementarity between industries pertaining to different processes or products but classified under the same code. The complementary industry specialized in the production of instrumental mechanical goods were defined as distinct from the other ancillary industries.

The indicator of firms' average size (*size*) and the indicators of size distribution (*C2*, *C2* and *C3*) capture a distinctive feature of IDs and their market structure: their high degree of competition and labour division. In fact, the larger the number of firms and the smaller their size, or the larger the percentage of small firms in the total, the more extended the division of labour will be. Similarly, the larger the number of independent firms, the higher the proportion of (a) entrepreneurs and (b) self-employed people. A large proportion of small firms and independent workers (in an industry) also indicates low barriers to entry, and therefore a large competitive market in the industry. The correlation matrix provides significant correlation values between the presence of entrepreneurs and the size typology of firms.

However, caution is required when analysing data on distribution of firms by size, because a similar one may conceal different interfirm relationships. Consequently, these data were complemented by the indicator *auto* and other information (see also Section 3.3).

The market structure also affects the rate of growth of an industry. The indicators related to growth are discussed in Chapter 5. Authors who stress the value of non-pecuniary economies maintain that spreading the same employment over several firms increases the diffusion and dissemination of knowledge, which promotes growth. This result is also compatible with the view that small firms grow faster, although this does not perfectly fit the Marshallian model or other evidence.

The proportion of artisan firms in the leading industry gives further information on the nature of the production process, since one may expect to find that the larger this proportion, the less mechanized the latter will be. When commenting on this variable, however, it is essential to bear in mind that, owing to fiscal and labour regulation in Italy, many small firms prefer to preserve their artisan status even though they are not particularly small in size and the process is not particularly traditional. Under Italian legislation, a firm may be recognized as artisan if it employs the labour of its owner and fewer than 25 employees (more in certain sectors).

The social weight of entrepreneurs (*ient*) and self-employed people (*isem*) is a variable of crucial importance: in Piore's view of the ID as a 'community of equals' especially, since the role, income, status and competencies of employers, *vis-à-vis* workers do not differ significantly. The more an industry is characterized by self-employed and ancillary workers, and by a high proportion of small firms, the closer it approaches an artisan, pairwise and family-based model of labour division. The precondition for an extended class of small entrepreneurs is, in fact, high work mobility. This in turn explains, according to several contributions (Becattini, 1990; Brusco, 1982, 1990; Sabel and Zeitlin, 1982), how internal mobility in districts creates job opportunities, high activity rates, very low rates of unemployment, and a strong propensity for independent work.

The choice of indicators capturing the distribution of population by employment status is borne out by other socio-economic studies in Italy, which have used the structure of the population by employment status as a proxy for the social structure of local areas or countries (Bagnasco, 1988; Sylos Labini, 1974).

Variable *C5* was introduced to test whether processes of supply/enterprise concentration were occurring in IDs. The consolidate turnover of companies or networks of firms (see Section 3.3.7) – whether present – rather than the individual company turnover, was taken as the unit with which to calculate this indicator. Unlike the other indicators selected, the degree of concentration of production was extracted from secondary sources (see Appendix) or estimated similarly with the variable on turnover (*saled*).

Neither of these indicators is able to distinguish between firms with reciprocal, one-way or any other exchanges of information and goods, although this may be possible inductively after comparison with qualitative information. For example, the size parameter for firms is unable to discriminate between a subcontractor and a final firm coordinating a flow of goods and information. Similarly, relatively larger firms may be either more integrated or less efficient firms, without clues as to their level of technological innovation or leadership position. A localized industry consisting of very small firms may be compatible either with an extended division of labour based on a large proportion of firms, each specialized in a different task (vertical division of labour), or with the totality of firms specialized in the same task (horizontal division) working for non-local commissioning firms. In the latter case, the area is simply one of work having been 'decentralized' from external areas, while in the former it comes close to the idea of a canonical ID. Complementary information analysed within the framework of the other indicators of human capital allowed construction of a parametric variable able to discriminate between different types of labour division. First, a distinction between independent and subcontracting (or supplier) firms was drawn by considering the former to be those that sell more than 60 per cent of their turnover to final markets (directly or indirectly), and the latter to be those for which more than 60 per cent of their turnover was accounted for by one or a few commissioning firms. Subcontractors and suppliers could be further distinguished according to the extent to which their (semifinished) products are produced by relying on their own design or otherwise, and according to whether or not their commissioning firms are located in the district area. These distinctions have been only partly parametrized, although details on each area are given in Section 3.3. The parametric variable (*auto*) assumes the following values: nought, when more than 60 per cent of local (district) turnover was accounted for by subcontracting firms dependent for more than 60 per cent on commissioning firms (generally not located in the area); 1, when it was covered by mostly independent firms (more than 60 per cent); 0.5, when the contribution to local turnover by independent firms was between 40 and 60 per cent; and 0.7, when the contribution to local turnover by independent firms was more than 60 per cent, but subcontracting firms sold more than 60 per cent of their turnover to commissioning firms not located in the area. The construction of this variable required a large amount of data which was available in most cases thanks to secondary sources (see Appendix) or interviews.

An obvious risk of inaccuracy was present, however, especially if one considers that the proportion of turnover accounted for by commissioning firms or market orders may be unstable for each single firm. Borderline cases are also common (for areas whose local turnover is close to being equally divided between subcontractors and independent firms). Correlation analysis suggests that this variable is strongly correlated with the degree of concentration ($C5$), so that areas with a value of *auto* equal to 1 have a low degrre of concentration and those with *auto* equal to 0.7, have a very high value of concentration. It is also negatively related to the illiteracy rate (–0.6) and the unemployment rate (– 0.5), and positively to the unionization rate (0.5) and the proportion of clerical workers (0.5). This is perfectly understandable, since dependent firms are unable to generate high value added and do not activate a local circuit of accumulation and investment, so the development of the industry is unable to ensure jobs for all the population. This is also impaired by the low quality of human capital outside firms (illiteracy). The disequilibrium in the local labour market is also mirrored by the weakness of trade unions.

With respect to innovative capacity, which plays such an important role in IDs according to some of the studies surveyed, indicators of innovative activity at municipal level may prove very difficult to find. Census data only enable calculation (for 1991 and 1996 years, only) of an index of specialization in R&D activities (*RDsp*); that is, the number of employees in local units specialized in R&D activities over total employment. This indicator, however, is a very imperfect indicator of the innovative propensity of an area dominated by SMEs, since these activities are not necessarily performed in specialized units or by specialized workers. Similarly, R&D expenditure indicators are entirely inappropriate in areas where small firms tend not to formalize or create dedicated departments for their innovative activities. Moreover, data published by ISTAT (2000) report the number of employees in R&D activities of private firms only, excluding institutions. A low propensity to patent is also to be expected, since innovative processes in areas like IDs concern incremental advances that are unlikely to be patented (Archibugi, 1992; Cantwell, 1989). Taking account these drawbacks, we also examined such indirect indicators as export performance.

Most studies agree that the diseconomies of the often very small firms constituting an ID are offset by the supply in the local area of a wide array of business or financial services delivered by private or publicly funded organizations, or by local trade associations. The supply of business services was measured by calculating the relative indicator of specialization (number of firms specialized in business services over total firms: *isef*). Similarly, the density of financial and banking services was measured by a rate of specialization in the relative sector by number of firms (*bankf*) and by number of employees (*banke*).

The presence of social and cultural services (or 'amenities'); namely gyms, cinemas, theatres, libraries, and so on has been measured by the variable *sosf*, which is, not surprisingly, significantly related to income, since the expenditure in amenities requires income availability. The provision of infrastructure, too, is an external facilitating condition in the environment surrounding small firms in IDs. The index of infrastructure endowment (*infr*) may be interpreted as an outcome of an interventionist or active industrial policy at the local level. The population's sense of belonging should create the political instruments that equip the local area with the necessary infrastructure. As a localization factor that enhances the competitiveness of firms, the index *infr* is therefore a proxy measure for an industry's economies of urbanization.

2.5.4.   The Indicators for the 'Community of People'

2.5.4.1.   Measurement of a shared culture and a stable community
One of the most frequently cited features of IDs is what has been called their 'homogeneous system of values and views' (for example, in Becattini, 1990, p. 39).

Coherently with the choice of LLMAs as the unit of enquiry, we may expect the population of each to display a high degree of interaction and interdependence, and therefore a common cultural background and shared attitudes. The reproduction of a shared culture is facilitated by the tendency of people to stay in the same area. Constant interactions among people foster the sharing of common values, behaviours and codes of conduct. However, interdependence among the residents of a particular LLMA may derive from merely contingent economic factors (for example, the localization of a new factory, which may attract an inflow of immigrants), and not from a shared historical heritage. Therefore, in some cases the population of an LLMA cannot be expected to be culturally homogeneous.

It has already been shown in previous sections that LLMA boundaries are unstable, and it has also been admitted that functional specialization may take place within them, with each municipality performing a specific function springing from different cultural attitudes and history. Notwithstanding these likely internal cultural differences, we may assume that the degree of cultural variance within LLMAs is lower than it is between them.[12]

Used as a more direct and appropriate proxy for cultural homogeneity was the presence of a dominant political subculture, which is evidenced when a political party achieves a relative majority of votes in national elections. The variable *poli* measures the percentage of votes obtained by the largest party or coalition in the elections of 1992, this being the election year closest to the Census data considered.

2.5.4.2.   The indicators for human and social capital

The distribution of the population by educational qualifications is a good proxy for human capital at a local level. Accordingly, the following indicators were calculated: the proportion of the population with a higher qualification (*high*) (degree + upper-secondary diploma); the proportion of the population with compulsory schooling (*comp*); and the proportion of illiterates (*illi*). A measure of vocational training would be more suitable for investigation of the human capital available to industrial activities, but this information is not forthcoming at the municipal level. In order to prevent these ratios from reflecting the qualifications of the older generation (for example, illiteracy is generally more typical of elderly people), the 1991 census provides data on qualifications by age group (*qual34*, *qual44*, *qual19*) and the drop-out rate in the 19-to-24 age group (*drop*). The average level of qualifications among workers (for example, the proportion of managers in 1991) is another typical indicator of human capital. The distribution of the population in industrial sectors by employment status may provide insights in this regard.

The aforementioned indicators do not exhaust the cultural dimension of a local area; the cultural attitudes of its residents are determined by their families, education and professional backgrounds; and a shared political allegiance may comprise different cultural attitudes towards work or the community. In the recent past, however, a communist political allegiance has been taken to imply specific attitudes to work (against the capitalist owner), common goods and females (Capecchi, 1990), while a Christian Democrat allegiance has been related to solidaristic attitudes (Bagnasco and Trigilia, 1984). In the 1990s, these ideological distinctions have significantly blurred, making the notion of political subculture identified by Trigilia (1990) less cogent. Because of these limitations, evidence from secondary sources can make an important contribution to deriving a more accurate picture of the areas examined.

Institutions are also another typical feature of 'canonical' IDs in other studies. Verification was made of the frequency of 'extended families' (*famy*), technical colleges, employers' associations and trade unions, and local banks (*bank*). Extended families, including parents and grandparents, aunts and nieces/nephews, have always played an important role in the emergence of small entrepreneurship. Sforzi (1987) has proxied them with the relative weight of 'large household with elderly members', finding that they are a distinctive feature of his 'Marshallian' districts (and of light industrialization as well). The rate of membership in employers' associations has been found to be related to the rate of unionization (*unio*) by studies carried out at regional level; hence only the latter is used here.

A questionnaire sent to the leading workers' organizations at the local level was used to assess the rate of unionization, either in order to gain a measure of associationism and cohesion among workers or to ascertain the existence of one of the preconditions for a consensual pattern of industrial relations. In order to assess the level of prices paid to subcontractors, also verified was the existence of agreements between final producers and stage producers.

The presence of local banks was surveyed directly and accounts may be found in Chapter 5; the multivariate exercise only considered specialization rates in banking and financial services (*bankf* and *banke*) indicators, as obtained from census data.

As mentioned earlier, one effect of action by institutions and interest organizations is a fair distribution of rent or wealth among the local stakeholders in an ID. Statistics on per-capita income – which are the only ones available – are not appropriate, but a measure of inequality at a local level is impossible to construct.

2.5.4.3.   The indicators of inclusiveness and the labour market
IDs are also characterized by a 'continuum of work positions' (home-based work, part time, waged work, self-employment, entrepreneurship), which signals the ability of a district to include all the components of local society. The inclusiveness of IDs was tested by calculating the activity rate, the rate of housekeeping as an indicator of female non-participation in economic activity, and the proportion of young people involved in industry activities (variables *hous*, *apyo*). It was not possible to devise indicators of work mobility within areas.

The variable relative to the presence of immigrants (*immi91* and *immi99*, calculated respectively for 1991 and 1999) is another indicator of the degree of inclusiveness of the local labour market and, by extension, of local society. High immigration rates are generally indicative of the vitality or attractiveness of an area and its labour market, though with some controversial aspects, as discussed in Chapter 5.

The frequency of associations other than those representing distinct stakeholders may be taken as a proxy for solidarity, trust in other people, a sense of belonging and 'civicness' (see Chapter 1). A census conducted on all local as well as national associations (amateur soccer clubs, choral societies, hiking clubs, bird-watching groups, literary circles, hunters' associations, Lions clubs, and the like) in Italy (Mortara, 1985), enables specification of this variable for each area in 1981. Unfortunately, a similar survey was not carried out in the 1990s.[13]

2.5.4.4. The allocation of the concept of trust

As discussed in Chapter 1, trust is taken here to be an outcome of, rather than a prerequisite for, IDs. Its frequency relates to structural rather than subjective characteristics. Consequently, the analysis is of a structural type and is intended to explain the emergence of trust as a consequence of objective circumstances, rather than the emergence of subjective attitudes as a lack of opportunism.[14]

Chapter 3 offers evidence from secondary sources or interviews on the following features:

1. control mechanisms between manufacturers and suppliers;
2. the ease with which agreements between firms engaged in the same task are reached.

In a narrow sense, trust is used in economic or business activities and may be defined as: 'confidence in or reliance on the ability and intention of a buyer to pay at a future time for goods supplied without present payment' (Good, 1988).[15]

2.6. THE ECONOMIC RATIONALE OF INDUSTRIAL DISTRICTS. TESTS AND INDICATORS

2.6.1. Measurement of Industrial District Performance in the Literature

Few attempts have been made to offer sound and accurate measurement of the economic rationale of IDs on a comparative basis (Fabiani and Pellegrini, 1998; Pietrobelli, 2000; Signorini, 1994). An initial attempt to measure the performance of firms in IDs, the so-called ID's effect', is reported in Signorini (1994). This study is based on the balance sheets of firms engaged in woollen cloth production and located in the province of Florence (which includes the district of Prato), and it compares their financial and economic ratios against the average of woollen cloth manufacturers located outside the province. In a more recent work, the profitability and productivity ratios of firms belonging to the areas defined as IDs by ISTAT (1997) and Sforzi (1990) are analysed in comparison with a control sample of firms with the same characteristics in terms of size and specialization (Fabiani and Pellegrini, 1998). The analysis confirms the existence of positive externalities for firms located in an ID, like higher profitability measured by ROE (Return

On Equity), ROI (Return On Investments) and gross operating margin over sales, and superior technical efficiency, as measured by a parametric function. Profitability is higher even when different industries and average size of firms are taken into account. Conversely, area-specific factors, like proximity to outlet markets, are not significant. Fabiani and Pellegrini conclude that the ID is an efficient organization mode, and that external advantages are higher for firms belonging to a specialized industry than for those belonging to different industries in the same ID. Another outcome of agglomeration discovered by these authors is a lower per capita cost of labour.

This study conceives of IDs as an alternative model of local development with respect to areas characterized by large firms, but there is no structural analysis of areas selected in terms of interfirm linkages, the presence of networks, and so on. This prompts the question as to whether such results are due to agglomeration factors only, or whether they are determined by additional conditions like pervasive cooperation, a virtuous mechanism of learning or a flat division of labour.

Secondly, Fabiani and Pellegrini's study deals only with economic performance, neglecting its effects on societal well-being. A further doubt concerns the representative nature of a sample derived from a balance sheet database that includes figures only on limited companies. In fact the most common legal form of enterprise in IDs, as well as among SMEs, is a non-limited company.

One may therefore argue that there is such wide variety within IDs that it may be erroneous to treat them as homogeneous. Rather than testing the superiority of clustering with respect to other ideal types a further direction for research would involve examination of the multifaceted world of IDs.

Above all, this new avenue of research would dispel the intangibility of the Marshallian 'industrial atmosphere' and demonstrate that an analytical framework of hypothesis testing can be applied to IDs.

2.6.2.   A Composite Indicator of Performance

According to Becattini, superior performance is associated with the 'canonical' ID; these are providers of good jobs and are affected by long-term stability and dynamism. A normative although implicit view of the ID as a paradigm of flexible specialized systems is also apparent in Piore and Sabel (1984), Best (1990), Scott (1988a, 1988b) and Saxenian (1994).

In order to test the economic rationale of IDs, a number of indexes of performance were calculated, each mirroring a particular aspect of ID structure.

Performance is a multifaceted concept that can be measured at the firm or system level. Whilst firm performance has its standardized indicators, it is more difficult to select the indicators for the performance of a system of firms, as in the present case. However, it was decided not to look at data at the firm level, for two reasons.

First, because the nature of the concept of ID, as explained in Chapter 1 and Section 2.4.1, requires analysis of collective, that is social and economic, performance. Second, because the data on non-limited companies, like those that would constitute a representative sample of each of our areas, are not available. It was thus decided to restrict the definition of performance to the indicators for average labour productivity – for the overall productive system – competitiveness, and social welfare. Competitiveness may result from superior intrinsic qualities of the product, while social welfare derives from the internalization by local society of the rent extracted from productive activity. The former concept is generally linked to export performance, but this feature is particularly pertinent in the case of IDs, given that these are cited as responsible for Italy's leading position on foreign markets.

Consequently, the following features, given *i* as the specialization industry, were examined (all the data refer to 1991, unless otherwise stated):

1. Percentage variation in exports 1986–91: *exp1* (normalized by the corresponding variation in the same industry at the national level) and the 1991–96 variation: *exp6* (normalized by the corresponding variation in the same industry at the national level).[16]
2. Per capita turnover. The average value of turnover for each district (and industry) was divided by the corresponding average indicator at national level, in order to take account of the different structural features of each industry. Data on sales were collected from a variety of sources for each ID (see Appendix). Where published data were not available, as in most of the smallest IDs, data were collected by asking local trade associations or local institutions, or by conducting estimates on the basis of the available information.[17] All the data refer to 1996.
3. Percentage variation in the number of employees and establishments in the leading industry *i* between the census years 1951, 1961, 1971, 1981, 1991 and 1996 (*vale*, *vafi*).[18]
4. Labour-market dynamic. This feature is measured positively by the rate of economic activity of local population (*inac* inverted), female labour-market participation (measured negatively by the rate of housekeeping: *hous*) and young worker participation (*apyo*), and measured negatively by the rate of unemployment *(unem)*.
5. Private well-being and household wealth: per-capita income (*inco*)[19] and housing facilities: average number of square metres per dwelling occupant (*m2av*), average square metres per inhabitant (*m2in*) and

average number of rooms per occupant (*room*).

Performance can also be analysed in terms of innovative capacity. However, as said, it was not possible to find appropriate measures of innovation, because this process is mainly informal in nature, while data on patenting are aggregated at the provincial/regional level.

The indexes listed above are liable to be ambiguous, as they have a semantic content larger than the objects which they are intended to denote. This suggests that they should be used with caution, and their results critically appraised, rather than relying on the evidence of one or two in isolation.

ISTAT issue statistics on the time series of imports/exports since 1985 are classified according to a by goods' classification (which roughly corresponds to a three-digit-level industry classification). Unfortunately, the data are at a provincial level. The indicator of export variation is not properly a measure of an area's or industry's competitiveness since even if an area's exports increase more than the national average in the same industry, the country's exports may diminish to the advantage of other competitors. A growth in value of exports may be due to an increase in quantity or prices. One indicator of the relative price of exports is the ratio between their average price and the average price of imports. This index, however, is very difficult to construct for some classes at the provincial level, owing to the inaccuracy of the figures on imports.

Where most of the provincial employment of one industry is localized in the ID observed, the data may be taken to be a good approximation of the area's exports. In the sample, apart from the cases of Ostiglia, Bassano, Palazzolo and San G. Ilarione, localization rates are generally very high.

Another possible objection against the use of export data as an indicator of competitiveness is that in areas more closely focused on their internal rather than international market, export variations may concern only a very small proportion of local firms, though the national market may be too restricted for firms to be competitive.

The variation of total exports by the specialization industry is an appropriate indicator of the competitiveness of its product, since, to some extent, it is less closely related to the export capacity of the local system. We may also expect there to be external economies in export activity, in that the exporting of one product, say a machine, may induce the exporting of another complementary product. Proximity of manufacturers of complementary products may induce a buyer to economize on transaction costs by allocating a differentiated order to several contiguous specialized firms in a district. Also in the case of exports not intermediated by a buyer, the initial exporter may put forward the names of neighbouring firms, often its suppliers, when asked for complementary products that it is unwilling to produce. Local proximity favours economies of scope and scale for exporters, buyers or traders. A buyer or an exporter economizes on transaction costs when it can put together a varied/composite supply merely by contacting and comparing producers located in the same area.

The indicators measuring variation in the number of employees and firms (*vale* and *vafi*) are discussed in Chapter 4.

As far as income and sales are concerned, few objections can be raised on theoretical grounds, given that these are typical economic performance indicators. The passage from firm and ID competitiveness to private income as captured by average productivity is fairly linear. Objections can be raised as to their reliability or the manner in which they have been calculated. The indicator of income is in fact an average value, which may conceal major inequalities in the distribution of wealth among the local population, while the drawbacks of the procedure to calculate data on sales were already underlined.

As to inclusiveness or labour-market dynamic (*unem, inac, hous, apyo*), we have been already discussed how a high rate of participation by the local population in economic activity characterizes a 'canonical' ID. These indicators appear as indicators of both structure and performance.[20]

2.6.3. Hypotheses

This section summarizes from various frameworks a sequence of causal relationships linking explanatory or independent variables with dependent ones. Taken together, the various approaches conclude that a localized industry fosters:

- economies of specialization for all the inputs employed in the production processes of firms;
- economies of specialization at the firm level;
- economies of learning;
- economies of urbanization;
- economies of transaction.

These advantages derive from specialization, agglomeration or the recursiveness of interactions, and the reiteration of transactions. More controversial is the role of the social and economic institutions that provide a wide array of inputs (land, training, labour, business services, and so on) at a lower cost. On the basis of the causal relationships described in previous pages, we may therefore expect the performance of IDs to be higher than in non-ID areas, and the IDs closest to the ideal ID to exhibit the best performance in terms of:

- average labour productivity;
- profitability of firms;
- per-capita income;
- rate of (incremental) innovation;
- wealth per household;
- level of employment;
- export performance;
- rates of firms and employment growth.

Table 2.5 Explanatory factors of the 'ID's effect': a summary scheme

	Explanatory factors
Efficiency	
Higher labour productivity	Specialization, widespread labour skills, strong trade unions
Lower cost of intermediate inputs	Specialization, contestability of markets, widespread entrepreneurial competencies
Lower cost of capital	Proximity, risk hedging, local banks
Lower dynamic transaction costs	Proximity, face-to-face relationships
Effectiveness	
Time to market	Flexibility
Innovativeness	Large number of strategies of experimentation and innovation; user-producer pattern of innovation, interaction between tacit and codified knowledge
Product differentiation	Large number of operators and co-ordinators
Quality/reputation	Historical tradition in manufacturing, cumulating of expertise
Social welfare	
Low rates of unemployment	Extended labour division, trade unions, efficient search and job match possibilities
Less dramatic reduction of employment or demand	Extended labour division
High infrastructural endowment	Sense of belonging, political subcultures
High amenities	Sense of belonging, community identity

Source: Author's calculations.

Table 2.5 offers a stylization of the various linkages between the distinctive features and performance of IDs that may be derived from the literature.

2.6.4. Research Tools between Economics and Sociology

In order to verify the causal relationships between the explanatory variables and the indicators of performance, a two-step and flexible methodology was used.

For hypothesis or causal relationships testing, at least three instruments are available: multivariate analysis, correlation analysis and econometrics. From a purely economic point of view, the core of the idea of an ID is the Marshallian concept of external economies. An economist would expect performance to be fully explained by external economies, with good regression results, provided that the terms of the equation are adequately specified.

Econometric methods seek to uncover causal relationships among variables. Recent developments in econometrics have challenged the capacity of the classical linear model to have real explanatory value, but it is still a useful point of departure.

Under Becattini's conceptualization, but in other approaches as well, it is quite clear that performance results from a complex interaction among different factors. Hence, proxying these explanatory causes with only one variable may be misleading or disappointing. Multivariate techniques may consequently be more appropriate. However, these are conceived mainly as descriptive tools by economists, more suited to the social or natural sciences which prefer 'harder' and more robust tools of analysis, such as econometrics, deemed to have explanatory value.[21]

However, multivariate analysis may even have predictive value provided certain conditions are satisfied. Concerning cluster analysis in particular, for a taxonomy (which is an *ex post* classification as compared to a typology, which is an *ex ante* classification) to have scientific value (and not to be a metaphor or an idea), it must have two features. First, the resulting 'types' or 'clusters' must have predictive and explanatory capacity. The cluster must forecast or explain differences in the behaviour of the systems belonging to the various clusters. In other words, what is important from a scientific point of view is to be able to say that if an object belongs to a cluster then other common features not already included in the clustering must derive from it. The second requirement of a good cluster analysis is that it must specify the conditions (efficiency, equilibrium, and so on) under which the classification has value (Grandori, 1990). In our case, cluster analysis may have another aim: that of verifying whether the conceptual category of the canonical ID, which is indeed a theoretical typology, corresponds to an empirical unit or group, and then whether this cluster is associated with a similar and superior performance.[22] For this reason, the cluster and factor analysis will consider only 'independent' variables. In fact, in our sample, external conditions are taken into account as far as the different geographical location of areas, their different cultures and histories are concerned. What is considered exogenous to IDs is demand. Different periods of time for the various industries included in the sample yield different demand scenarios. Clusters may therefore include IDs specialized in industries subject to different external circumstances.

Both multivariate analysis and econometrics are used here, in the belief that they are more complementary than mutually exclusive. Factor analysis can be used to reduce the number of explanatory variables, which is to be recommended if the aim is to test a socio-economic notion like the ID, where a close correlation among variables is very likely. Factor analysis yields 'independent' factors, which are linear combinations of orthogonal variables. The factors obtained may subsequently be regressed on the performance indicators.

NOTES

1. Italy is administratively divided into 20 regions. Each region is formed by provinces (*provincia*), corresponding to the three-digit level of NUT classification, which are then divided into municipalities (*comuni*).
2. In Becattini's terms (1990), a district is an intermediate area between the Italian Comune and the Provincia, of a small size (not exceeding 100 000 inhabitants) and normally comprising between 2 to 40 municipalities.
3. As previously stated, small firms are defined as those with fewer than 50 employees, medium sized firms as those with fewer than 250 employees and large firms as those with more than 250 employees.
4. Identification of LLMAs in 1961 and 1971 is not available.
5. We considered them in order to fill the box of the southern regions in the table of selection (Table 2.3) and to provide the reader with interesting information in the descriptive sections of this book (see, in particular, Chapter 3, Section 3.4). Multivariate analysis considered the two areas as 'illustrative', and they are consequently not included in the regression analysis.
6. Comparison of industry census data at two-digit levels of classification has only recently become possible: in November 1998, when ISTAT published a new data-set of industrial activities in Italian municipalities between 1951 and 1991, using a common classification (ISTAT, 1998).
7. An establishment or local unit coincides with a single-unit firm. Many establishments may belong to one company, which is the legal entity comprising various establishments owned by the same person or group of persons.
8. The term 'firm' always stands for establishment (or local unity).
9. For each of the five industries considered in the sample, ancillary manufacturing industries (excluding mechanical engineering) have been defined as described in the table below.

Classification of upstream and downstream ancillary industries

Specialization or leading industry	Upstream ancillary industry	Downstream ancillary industry
Textiles	–	Clothing and upholstery
Clothing	Textiles	–
Tanning	Chemical products (chrome)	Footwear and leather clothing, upholstery
Footwear	Tanning and plastics	–
Agricultural machines & tractors	Metals and motors	Other machinery
Ceramics	Other non-ferrous products	Paper

10. Entrepreneurs: individuals who run their own businesses using not their own or their family's manual work but that of employees only.

Self-employed: individuals who own their own businesses but, unlike entrepreneurs, undertake the manual and administrative work themselves.

Professionals: individuals who practise a profession (accountants, engineers, lawyers, and so on).

Ancillary workers: individuals who collaborate with a member of the family who owns his/her own business, without a regular contract of work.

Managers: individuals with supervisory positions.

Clerks: white-collar workers. Individuals who carry out administrative tasks or technical supervisory functions.

Workers: foremen, skilled workers, unskilled workers, auxiliaries, apprentices, home-workers, and members of Corps.

11. Industry data at the municipal level between 1951 and 1961 are provided by ISTAT at a two-digit level classification. This means that mechanical industry comprises the manufacturing of all machinery, not only that used by the specialization industry. Even considering that in 1991 and 1996 a four-digit industry classification became available, it is very likely that the case of a strong mechanical industry and a scant presence of 'specialized' manufacturers is not possible, given the high degree of interrelatedness among different industries and therefore the ease with which the knowledge accumulated in the production of one piece of machinery can be transferred to the manufacturing of a different one, provided there is demand for it.

12. The permanency of a local population over time affects its cultural attitudes. On the basis of census data, the degree of permanency can be measured by means of two indicators: rate of emigration (ratio between present and resident population), and the percentage of people owning rather than renting a private dwelling. These indicators are included in the author's database, but are not discussed here.

13. For the purpose of comparisons with the last two observation periods of our research, the same rate of associationism was assumed in 1991.

14. Measuring trust is a very difficult undertaking, although some interesting attempts have been made (Glaeser et al., 2000). Various indicators can be built, but they require in-the-field research. Let us suppose that we want to survey a sample of entrepreneurs. In this case, we may ask whether subcontracting to sub-suppliers takes place with no quality control of products and processes, or whether their reliability is tested in various ways. Other methods are to ask other sub-suppliers about the fairness of prices charged, or to visit the subcontractors' workshops and check on procedures and quality. Similar questions may be asked of appropriate samples of owners and workers or moneylenders in order to ascertain trust relationships among them.

15. In order to measure this conception of business distrust, a ratio between protested bills and inhabitants could be calculated, as done in a previous work by the author (Paniccia, 1999). This indicator, however, captures only a very restrictive notion of trust, and is also an indicator of performance. It measures the extent to which expectations of future payments are fulfilled, and therefore captures the state of health of contractual relations among the local population.

16. The classification used for the export data is illustrated in the table below.

Classification of export data

Industry	Groups of goods code	Industry	Groups of goods code
Tanning	95–96	Furniture	144, 146
Leather garments	97	Wood products	
		Non-ferrous minerals	
Textile raw materials	99–106	and ceramics	199–204
Textile fabrics	106–112	Sanitary wares	202
Woollen	113–117,		
garments	122–125	Ceramic tiles	203
		Mechanical	
Knitwear	118–121	engineering	169–70
		Agriculture machines	
Clothing 1	130–133	and tractors	172, 190
Clothing 2	134–135	Plastics	216
Footwear (leather, non-			
leather)	136–137		

17. Estimates were conducted taking into account the available number of firms, their size and their distinction between subcontractors and commissioning firms. These information were also used for the construction of the indicator *auto*. Data provided in a variety of sources (see Appendix) were also considered.

18. Calculation of variation in the number of firms and employees at two-digit level and a municipal level since 1951 was made possible by a new data-set issued by ISTAT (1998), in which the figures for the various Census years are comparable.

19. Source of data: for year 1987: Banco di Santo Spirito, 1987; for year 1996: estimations on data provided by Istituto Tagliacarne, 2000.

20. Author's data-set includes other indicators depicting other relevant aspects of LLMAs, which, however, are not included here because they do not derive from the frameworks discussed earlier.

21. One may also object that multivariate techniques can be manipulated; but it is very hard to argue that manipulation is a peculiar or exclusive feature of multivariate analysis and not of econometrics as well.

22. Although the terms 'taxonomy' and 'typology' are distinguished in this study, they are used very generally.

PART TWO

Empirical Results

3. Organizational Variety and Performance of Industrial Districts

3.1. INTRODUCTION AND OUTLINE

This chapter examines the organization of industry and society in IDs in order to identify the sources of possible variety, and the determinants of their competitiveness or decline. It therefore endeavours to supersede generic or simplistic notion of IDs and to lay their structure bare. This analysis will permit identification of possible sources of change and discontinuity and enables us to address the specific research question of whether or not a successful ID requires the existence of all the canonical conditions. To this end, a multivariate technique is used to determine whether different typologies of IDs can be identified. This will also enable us to test the empirical significance of canonical IDs in Italy.

The following section reports the results of multivariate analysis as applied to 'structural' social and economic indicators (Sections 3.2.1 to 3.2.3). Four typologies of IDs emerge either in 1981 or 1991, confirming that agglomeration *per se* is not able to produce all the externalities deemed to characterize Italian IDs. The agglomeration that is subsumed in the definition of an ID is combined with different patterns of labour division and a different width of externalities. Comparison between the typologies obtained in the two periods of observation offers evidence that the areas in the sample are undergoing a process of evolution. The canonical IDs, moreover, reduce significantly in number between the two observed decades.

Section 3.2.4 goes beyond the mere description of data or typologies and relates structural indicators to performance indicators through a regression analysis, in order to determine which typology and which 'factors' are most closely related to superior economic and social performance. The factors obtained from the multivariate analysis are regressed on the performance indicators selected in order to test their significance in 1991, and the overall average performance of the resulting typologies is examined, while Sections 3.2.5 and 3.2.6 focus more on the export (internationalization) and dynamic performance.

Section 3.3 examines interfirm linkages within each typology to produce a stylization of IDs' typical network structures. The section provides a brief description of the business or market structure in the specialization industry for each of the areas included in the sample, with a list of useful references where available. The evolution of the mechanisms of coordination in the last two decades is examined in Section 3.4, with a focus on the new organizational forms of 'groups' or 'networks' of firms. The market structure of IDs is also examined in terms of their contestability conditions. Analysis of coordination mechanisms permits reassessment of the role of cooperation and the drivers of change in IDs (Section 3.5).

3.2.   THE DISTINCTIVE 'FACTORS' OF THE ECONOMIC AND SOCIAL STRUCTURE OF INDUSTRIAL DISTRICTS

The first methodological question addressed in the multivariate analysis was whether social variables should be separated from industrial ones in order to distinguish more homogeneous and more consistent typologies of IDs. On the one hand, considering that economic phenomena cannot be understood outside the social context in which they are embedded, superimposing a social structure on a business structure may fall into the 'oversocialization' trap that Granovetter warned against; and it would clash with the agnostic approach adopted here. This problem, in fact, was eased by the results of correlation analysis, which pointed to very high correlation values between some of the social variables and the business variables. After having dropped the highly correlated variables that might have caused statistical redundancy, we considered as explanatory only some of the social variables included in our data-set, such as those related to the social structure and the degree of inclusiveness of the labour market. Therefore the resulting typologies are also socially characterized but their social features are not taken as discriminatory.

3.2.1.   Characteristics of Factor Analysis

This section presents the results of a multivariate analysis carried out on the variables operationalizing the distinctive features of IDs' social and industrial structure. In this exercise, we included only 'independent' (that is, 'structural') variables in order to obtain the explanatory factors of performance, the indicators of which were considered to be dependent variables. For the same reasons, the rates of variation of the variables were not considered among the independent variables. Moreover, we dropped closely correlated variables and those indicators the sum of which amounted to 100 (for example, all the composition indexes), retaining only those with the highest statistical explanatory value, the purpose being to avoid statistical redundancy.

A total number of 31 independent variables were considered by the multivariate analysis, and eight of these were deemed to be active in both 1981 and 1991 (see Table 3.2 for the list). 1991 results alone are presented here, while those for 1981 are mentioned only when they are significantly different and therefore indicate that evolution has taken place.[1]

Depending on the degree of correlation between factors and observations, we obtained different typologies or clusters (here 'cluster' obviously differs in meaning from the term used in network analysis or by Porter (1990)). A distinction is usually drawn in cluster analysis between 'typology' and 'taxonomy' (Grandori, 1990). The former is an *ex ante* classification with predictive value and the ability to explain variables not contained in the *ex ante* classification – irrespective of whether it results from an empirical analysis – while a taxonomy is an empirical classification.

In order to ensure the comparability of the analyses carried out in the two years, the loading factors obtained in the 1991 analysis were included in the 1981 analysis as illustrative variables. Comparison between the results of factor and cluster analysis in the two periods revealed the main changes that had occurred in the meantime.[2] The procedure comprised the principal component method for factor analysis and then a hierarchical method of clustering.

The most critical step in factor analysis is the choice of m, the number of factors. Several criteria have been proposed for choosing m, but they are generally equivalent. Caillez and Pages (1976) list the following:

- criterion 1: choose m equal to the number of factors necessary for the variance accounted for to achieve a predetermined percentage, say 70 per cent, of the total variance;
- criterion 2: choose m equal to the number of eigenvalues greater than the average eigenvalue.
- criterion 3: use the 'scree' test based on a plot of the eigenvalues of the matrix. If the graph drops sharply, followed by a straight line with much less slope, choose m equal to the number of eigenvalues before the straight line begins;
- criterion 4 chooses only the most relevant factors: that is, those which differ by more than 10 per cent.

Many empirical studies use shorter thresholds when the first criterion is selected and economic applications of multivariate analysis generally refer to less tight criteria. For this reason, we chose m equal to the first three factors that account for more than 61 per cent of the total sample's variance (Table 3.1).

3.2.2. The Distinctive Factors of Industrial Districts in 1991

Table 3.1 Histogram of the first eight eigenvalues, 1991

Eigen-values	Per cent of variance	Cumu-lative per cent	
1.9	23.9	23.8	**
1.6	22.7	46.5	***
1.2	14.7	61.2	***************************
0.8	12.4	73.7	**********************
0.7	9.9	83.6	*******************
0.5	8.1	91.6	***************
0.4	4.9	94.4	***********
0.2	3.5	100.0	********

Source: Author's calculations.

According to the loading values and their signs (variables on the negative quadrant are placed in parentheses), the first factor, the one with the highest explanatory value, clearly denotes an industry based on firms employing a relatively lower (higher) proportion of clerical workers, generally of a smaller (larger) size and of an artisan nature, generally non-unionized, mainly dependent on external clients (mainly independent); while the specialization industry appears not to be integrated (integrated) with mechanical engineering activities. The low (high) proportion of young workers and immigrants (among the illustrative variables) and the high (low) rate of housekeeping) together with high rates of unemployment and illiteracy describe the features of a non-inclusive (inclusive) and marginal economy mainly based on traditional services rather than industry (Table 3.2). This factor may be termed the *marginality factor*, when the positive segment (quadrant) of the axis is considered and the *firms' tertiarization, concentration* and *integration factor* when the variables negatively correlated are considered (henceforth, the first name of the factors' label is related to the variables on the positive quadrant, and the second to the negative variables).

The second factor, which explains 23 per cent of the total variance, summarizes on the negative quadrant the features of an economy based on family-owned, artisan and often independent enterprises run by self-employed workers, employing 20–50 units on average, and being typical of a society where the relative weight of extended families is still substantial. It also combines most of the (both active or illustrative) indicators that describe the features of an extended labour division, based on a densely concentrated and sizeable leading industry, where the degree of market concentration is low and the leading industry is highly specialized. On the same negative quadrant, the rate of unionization also appear as highly correlated (Table 3.2). Since all the indicators of agglomeration and specialization, and of an extended labour division based on self-employed and ancillary workers are closely (with a negative sign) correlated with this axis, we call it the *non-canonical/canonical* factor.

Factor 3, which explains a lower amount of variance, is a specification of factor 1 that, on the negative quadrant, stresses diversification (specialization) and low employment of young workers, but a low rate of housekeeping. Looking at the illustrative variables, it appears that the specialization industry is not homogeneously extended or geographically concentrated, while the rates of specialization in the service sector and the proportion of highly educated people (on the positive quadrant) are highly correlated. All together these variables point to still immature processes of industrial agglomeration and specialization. It is therefore apparent that a fragmented business structure may arise even when the size of the industry is not large (Table 3.2). This factor may be termed the *diversification/specialization* factor.

3.2.3.   Results of Cluster Analysis in 1991

In order to obtain a cluster partition, a hierarchical procedure was followed. Hierarchical clustering techniques are very common in multivariate analysis, and compared to optimization techniques they involve less arbitrary steps. When this technique is used, the data are not partitioned into classes in one single step. Rather, they are first separated into a few broad classes, each of which is further divided into smaller classes. Then, each of these smaller classes is further partitioned, and so on, until terminal classes are generated and these can be no further subdivisions. Using an agglomeration method, a distance matrix between the entities is accordingly selected.[3] The method developed by Ward clusters the units of observations in a manner that yields the minimum increase in the error sum of squares (ESS) (Everitt, 1981). The clusters obtained in 1991 by applying this procedure were as follows:

Cluster 1: Solofra, Vigevano, Marostica, Carpi, Civitanova, Pesaro, Guastalla, Desio, Poggibonsi, S.B.Tronto, Fermo, Montecatini Terme, Sant'Ambrogio in Valpolicella.
Cluster 2: Santa Croce dell'Arno, Porto Sant'Elpidio, Prato.
Cluster 3: Arzignano, Bassano, Montebelluna, Sassuolo, Civitacastellana, Cossato, Suzzara, Cento, Schio, Oderzo, Palazzolo sull'Oglio, Castellarano.
Cluster 4: Giulianova, Ostiglia, Ascoli Piceno (Val Vibrata), Barletta, S.G.

Cavoti, Senigallia, Putignano, S.G.Ilarione, Guardiagrele.

The forth cluster groups together areas belonging to the same geographical partition, while areas in northern and central Italy areas are split in all four clusters.

Table 3.2 Coordinate values of explanatory factors, 1991

Variables	Factor 1	Factor 2	Factor 3
Active variables			
Arti	0.49	− 0.17	0.35
HH	0.22	− 0.52	− 0.62
Medium	− 0.61	0.44	− 0.08
Clei	− 0.74	− 0.21	0.36
Isem	0.09	− 0.84	− 0.02
Hous	0.30	0.40	− 0.40
Apyo	− 0.39	0.29	− 0.51
Auto	− 0.67	− 0.57	− 0.18
Illustrative variables			
Einh	0.36	0.31	0.45
Empl	− 0.21	− 0.57	− 0.03
Serve	0.32	0.02	0.31
Micro	0.32	− 0.69	0.07
Small	0.63	− 0.03	0.06
C5	− 0.61	0.23	− 0.03
Enti	0.37	− 0.47	− 0.16
Iwor	0.32	0.79	− 0.15
Meche	− 0.35	− 0.20	0.31
Immi91	− 0.40	0.18	− 0.15
Famy	0.35	− 0.38	− 0.01
Isef	− 0.30	− 0.23	− 0.04
Bankf	− 0.32	− 0.32	− 0.12
Unio	− 0.23	− 0.42	0.06
High	− 0.14	− 0.20	0.44
Unem	0.48	0.10	− 0.13
Asso	− 0.22	− 0.17	0.01
Illi	0.69	0.15	0.02
Drop	0.06	0.27	− 0.02

Source: Author's calculations.

3.2.3.1. Cluster 1: Craft-based or urbanized/tertiarized industrial districts

The first cluster is positively correlated with the *non-canonical/canonical* factor and with the *diversification/specialization* factor (the values of correlation are respectively – 2.3 and 3.0). It is therefore explained by an extended division of labour based on family-owned and family-run firms that have few employees and are reliant on family members or relatives. The structure of the industry is highly fragmented, in that it consists of independently owned firms scattered among small units. The distinctive features of this cluster are the relatively large proportion of entrepreneurs and self-employed workers, a low rate of schooling drop-out, extended families, high rates of associationism and unionization, and political subcultures. These areas, however, are not homogeneous as concerns, for example, shared political subcultures, their unionization rates, infrastructures and specialization in mechanical engineering industry (Table 3.4a). When the *auto* indicator is analysed, together with indicators relative to the quality of human capital and unionization rates, internal differences emerge in the areas with strong agglomeration economies.

Table 3.3 Correlation values between clusters and factors, 1991

	Factor 1: marginality/firms' tertiarization and concentration	Factor 2: non-canonical /canonical	Factor 3: diversification/ specialization
Cluster 1	0.2	2.3	3.0
Cluster 2	1.0	– 3.6	– 3.5
Cluster 3	3.8	3.2	0.5
Cluster 4	– 4.7	1.5	– 1.1

Source: Author's calculations.

This typology comprises IDs like Civitanova, Pesaro, Poggibonsi and San Benedetto del Tronto, in which a productive structure based on an extended labour division in a leading industry is embedded in a typically urban context: which demonstrates that an ID may be compatible with a non-manufacturing environment. The large weight of the variables *micro*, *high*, *arti*, and *serve* (see Appendix) suggests that these IDs should be called 'craft-based' or 'urbanized/tertiarized' IDs.

3.2.3.3. Cluster 2: Canonical (or quasi-canonical) industrial districts

The second cluster, which consists of a small number of IDs, exhibits the largest number of 'canonical' features. Therefore they coincide on average

Table 3.4a Distinctive features of craft-based industrial districts, 1991

	immi	high	illi	drop	qual34	hous	apyo	enti	clei	isem	ianc	umio	poli	asso	serve	sosf	bankf	RDsp
Solofra	2.2	14.0	22.8	21	27.2	46.6	18.8	8.1	18.1	17.7	1.5	40.0	38.2	0.4	35.2	603.6	0.8	0.0
Vigevano	4.8	20.0	10.6	14.8	38.1	20.0	14.7	6.4	20.2	15.6	2.5	50.0	24.0	1.9	42.6	631.5	1.1	0.1
Carpi	10.8	21.2	12.7	36.0	35.0	14.0	18.0	5.9	14.9	20.2	2.1	60.0	37.7	3.2	35.5	347.3	1.2	0.3
Marostica	5.2	15.9	10.0	10.1	19.1	30.4	25.1	4.8	9.1	16.2	2.2	20.0	40.0	2.2	35.7	693.3	0.8	0.0
Bassano	9.3	20.4	9.9	12.0	26.4	30.6	22.7	6.6	13.4	12.6	1.7	20.0	39.4	3.2	40.5	200.0	1.6	0.0
Civitanova	9.4	21.3	15.8	38.6	41.6	31.8	14.9	7.1	11.4	15.6	1.8	30.0	38.8	1.9	44.8	603.6	0.2	0.0
Pesaro	7.6	27.1	12.4	9.3	44.9	32.2	14.0	7.8	17.9	16.4	1.9	50.0	38.0	2.5	61.6	455.6	1.0	0.3
Guastalla	5.0	29.2	13.1	13.9	36.1	24.0	18.1	5.2	16.6	16.2	1.7	60.0	48.0	1.0	34.5	399.9	0.4	0.1
Desio	7.1	21.0	9.4	19.9	35.5	35.0	13.6	4.7	20.3	14.4	1.3	35.0	25.0	0.5	38.0	470.6	1.7	0.1
Poggibonsi	5.9	18.4	16.6	37.6	40.4	27.0	12.1	6.7	15.5	15.1	0.9	60.0	43.0	2.1	42.0	482.7	1.1	0.2
Montecatini T.	5.0	16.8	13.1	30.2	31.7	24.2	12.7	6.5	10.1	18.4	2.9	50.0	41.0	2.7	56.2	200.5	0.4	1.1
Fermo	5.6	24.3	16.9	11.7	43.2	29.9	13.0	7.7	12.2	18.7	3.0	30.0	33.0	4.2	52.2	517.7	0.6	0.2
Valpolicella	22.6	19.2	18.7	11.4	34.8	42.1	17.2	7.3	14.2	15.9	1.4	30.0	30.0	2.1	52.4	598.5	0.7	0.0
S.B. Tronto	10.6	22.9	17.2	11.7	43.2	34.7	14.4	1.5	36.8	16.7	3.5	40.0	32.0	1.6	56.7	254.2	0.4	0.8
Average	**7.9**	**20.8**	**14.2**	**20.2**	**34.9**	**30.2**	**16.4**	**6.2**	**16.5**	**16.4**	**2.0**	**41.1**	**36.3**	**2.1**	**44.8**	**461.4**	**0.9**	**0.2**
Std Dev	4.7	4.0	3.8	10.8	7.2	8.1	3.7	1.6	6.6	1.8	0.7	13.7	6.5	1.0	8.9	156.3	0.4	0.3
Italy average	10.1	22.4	14.3	15.4	38.8	31.7	10.7	5.6	17.5	13.9	1.4	18.0	38.0	13.2	58.6	90.0	3.2	0.1

Table 3.4a Con't.

	finh	einhi	auto	arti	firm	empl	meche	size	HH	C1	C2	C3	isef	C5
Solofra	107.4	7.4	1.0	58.7	253.0	3648.0	2.3	14.4	2225.1	23.9	50.2	25.9	6.9	20.0
Vigevano	208.5	22.0	1.0	75.8	539.0	4962.0	19.8	9.2	38.4	28.0	53.2	18.8	7.7	25.0
Carpi	60.9	5.6	1.0	74.0	1300.0	7878.0	0.5	6.1	270.6	45.2	40.3	14.5	13.0	10.0
Marostica	123.9	9.1	1.0	91.5	263.0	1753.0	0.1	6.7	25.8	30.8	59.2	10.0	9.8	30.0
Bassano	95.4	9.2	0.5	75.5	583.0	6046.0	0.0	10.4	260.3	21.7	38.5	39.8	6.9	15.0
Civitanova	242.7	25.7	1.0	87.2	441.0	2794.0	0.1	6.3	12.4	30.1	40.8	29.2	29.0	20.0
Pesaro	142.5	13.0	1.0	58.4	764.0	7390.0	8.7	9.7	83.5	27.3	45.5	27.2	15.3	30.0
Guastalla	237.0	14.0	0.5	75.8	243.0	3683.0	0.6	15.2	41.3	33.6	52.4	13.9	9.3	45.0
Desio	106.7	17.3	1.0	83.4	4446.0	23322.0	0.9	5.2	22.4	43.9	36.1	20.0	12.6	15.0
Poggibonsi	237.8	22.8	1.0	55.1	274.0	2226.0	14.7	8.1	23.0	31.8	57.1	11.1	13.8	30.0
Montecatini T.	168.9	19.1	1.0	76.6	636.0	4240.0	0.7	6.7	22.2	38.0	48.7	13.3	13.7	20.0
Fermo	77.8	10.3	1.0	78.9	838.0	6206.0	0.6	7.4	393.2	33.8	50.2	16.1	8.5	20.0
Valpolicella	239.4	19.6	1.0	56.3	270.0	2843.0	3.8	10.5	32.3	17.3	43.8	39.0	7.9	20.0
S.B. Tronto	360.3	25.7	0.5	62.0	249.0	3086.0	0.4	12.4	12.9	12.0	54.7	33.4	9.7	15.0
Average	**172.1**	**15.8**	**0.9**	**72.1**	**792.8**	**5719.8**	**3.8**	**9.2**	**247.4**	**29.8**	**47.9**	**22.3**	**11.7**	**22.5**
Std Dev	*84.8*	*6.6*	*0.2*	*11.5*	*1054.8*	*5213.6*	*6.2*	*3.0*	*560.8*	*9.0*	*7.0*	*9.8*	*5.5*	*8.6*
Italy average	*61.6*	*22.4*		*66.1*			*9.2*	*8.8*		*57.9*	*21.9*	*20.2*	*11.0*	

Source: Author's calculations.

93

Table 3.4b Distinctive features of quasi-canonical industrial districts, 1991

	Immi	High	illi	drop	qual34	hous	appo	enti	clei	isem	ianc	unio	poli	asso	serve	sosf	bankf	RDsp
Santa Croce	7.0	15.9	15.1	29.2	32.2	28.3	18.2	6.9	10.4	16.3	2.0	60.0	35.6	2.2	37.2	361.9	2.1	0.1
Sant'Elpidio	7.0	15.2	17.1	18.2	29.8	24.8	20.1	7.8	6.6	18.4	4.1	30.0	33.0	1.4	27.1	645.6	1.0	0.1
Prato	8.2	17.9	13.0	32.1	32.1	32.6	16.4	9.1	15.9	32.4	4.4	60.0	41.8	3.0	41.9	513.3	1.2	0.7
Average	**7.4**	**16.3**	**15.1**	**26.5**	**31.4**	**28.6**	**18.2**	**7.9**	**11.0**	**22.4**	**3.5**	**50.0**	**36.8**	**2.2**	**35.4**	**506.9**	**1.4**	**0.3**
Std Dev	*0.6*	*1.1*	*1.7*	*6.0*	*1.1*	*3.2*	*1.5*	*0.9*	*3.8*	*7.1*	*1.1*	*14.1*	*3.7*	*0.6*	*6.2*	*115.9*	*0.5*	*0.3*
Italy average	*10.1*	*22.4*	*14.3*	*15.4*	*38.8*	*31.7*	*10.7*	*5.6*	*17.5*	*13.9*	*1.4*	*18.0*	*38.0*	*13.2*	*58.6*	*90.0*	*3.2*	*0.1*

Table 3.4b Con't.

	finh	einhi	auto	arti	firm	empl	meche	size	HH	C1	C2	C3	isef	C5
Santa Croce	86.6	4.9	1.0	59.3	1020.0	8757.0	2.8	8.6	3822.4	30.8	60.0	9.2	17.5	7.0
Sant'Elpidio	25.9	3.9	1.0	83.9	1398.0	9322.0	0.6	6.7	12084.5	42.8	49.1	8.0	12.0	10.0
Prato	28.9	5.5	1.0	75.3	8032.0	38380.0	2.3	4.8	869.0	45.6	42.9	11.6	15.2	7.0
Average	**47.1**	**4.8**	**1.0**	**72.8**	**3483.3**	**18819.7**	**1.9**	**6.7**	**5592.0**	**39.7**	**50.7**	**9.6**	**14.9**	**8.0**
Std Dev	*27.9*	*0.7*	*0.0*	*10.2*	*3220.1*	*13833.2*	*0.9*	*1.6*	*4746.6*	*6.4*	*7.1*	*1.5*	*2.3*	*1.4*
Italy average	*10.1*	*22.4*		*66.1*			*10.7*	*8.8*	*13.9*	*57.9*	*21.9*		*20.2*	*11.0*

Source: Author's calculations.

with the canonical IDs. The group is in fact correlated with the second and third factors with respective values of –3.6 and –3.5. Indeed, this cluster groups together the best-known and most frequently studied IDs, with Prato often taken as a paradigmatic example – although even a glance at its descriptive statistics shows that it is hardly imitable. The degree of fragmentation of production in these IDs is even more extreme than in the previous case (the quota of employment in local units with fewer than 50 employees is over 80 per cent). Self-employment is one of the main distinctive social features of these IDs, as in the case of Sforzi's Marshallian IDs (1990). The most distinctive features include a high specialization, a high proportion of self-employed people and ancillary workers, a wide extension of the leading industry, and entrepreneurial density.

The social cohesion of these areas may be deduced from their relatively pronounced political subcultures, and from a high level of social associationism and trade-unionization (with the exception of Porto Sant'Elpidio), although unionization is also a distinctive feature of typology 3. A weakness of this cluster of areas is their relatively high rate of schooling drop-out, which reveals a distinct attitude towards education among the local population (Table 3.4b). Education is perceived as a means to achieve social and economic emancipation; but this concerns only compulsory schooling, while higher education is not regarded as providing easier entry to the local labour market (see Chapter 5). Another distinctive feature of this typology is the high proportion of financial and business services, including R&D private centres, which confirms that while firms are lean and focused on manufacturing, they are able to rely on an abundant supply of services provided by public and private organizations in their neighbourhood. This is the case of Santa Croce and Prato in particular (Table 3.4a). For craft IDs, the evidence is instead inconclusive in this regard, since these are generally tertiarized areas where firms specialized in business services tend to locate.

3.2.3.3.   Cluster 3: Concentrated and organizationally upgraded industrial districts

This cluster is characterized by a high proportion of clerical workers matched by a relatively low proportion of ancillary workers. Firms within these IDs tend to be larger, and most of them have more than 50 employees (Table 3.4c). The predominant specialization is integrated with a strongly-developed mechanical industry, which makes the tools and machines used in the production process of the leading industry. Society and industry comprise high proportions of immigrants and young workers, while housekeepers are only a minority in the female population. Considering that the most significant variables for this cluster are *medium*, *C5*, *apyo*, *auto*, *immi* and *clei* (see Appendix), we may call these IDs 'concentrated', 'inclusive',

3.4c Distinctive features of concentrated industrial districts, 1991

	immi	high	illi	drop	qual34	hous	apyo	enti	clei	isem	ianc	unio	poli	asso	serve	sosf	Bankf	RDsp
Arzignano	21.3	14.4	9.6	14.7	24.3	38.2	27.2	5.3	21.5	8.6	0.8	20.0	33.9	1.0	30.3	745.4	1.6	0.0
Sassuolo	10.5	20.0	13.2	33.9	33.6	23.9	19.3	6.0	29.8	18.8	1.3	40.0	41.0	0.9	33.1	698.4	1.5	0.3
Civitacastellana	11.1	16.6	17.1	29.3	32.2	46.1	13.0	4.3	10.1	13.1	1.1	55.0	38.0	1.2	49.4	900.0	0.6	0.2
Cossato	7.3	15.4	9.4	12.5	38.1	12.4	21.1	4.6	21.2	13.2	1.1	30.0	22.8	1.7	37.0	550.0	1.2	0.2
Montebelluna	10.3	16.9	10.7	29.0	28.6	32.5	23.6	5.9	12.3	12.3	1.4	30.0	33.2	1.4	34.2	598.0	0.8	1.1
Suzzara	6.2	19.1	12.4	38.0	36.7	36.7	17.4	4.2	15.2	15.4	2.4	40.0	46.0	1.2	33.0	400.0	1.0	0.1
Cento	5.6	21.4	12.3	28.8	40.9	19.5	15.3	4.3	19.4	14.5	1.9	50.0	48.0	1.2	41.3	400.0	1.7	0.0
Oderzo	8.3	17.8	13.7	32.0	31.7	37.8	22.5	6.5	10.1	12.7	1.1	30.0	28.0	1.7	42.3	587.5	0.7	0.7
Schio	12.7	20.6	8.4	8.9	32.9	27.3	22.3	5.0	16.4	9.6	0.9	45.0	34.0	3.8	34.5	273.6	0.8	0.0
Palazzolo	11.6	13.9	8.9	15.1	25.6	35.0	30.2	5.5	11.8	11.5	1.6	35.0	32.0	0.4	38.9	272.0	1.0	0.1
Castellarano	9.6	15.9	17.7	28.8	40.9	24.2	21.9	4.7	14.6	14.0	0.9	60.0	38.0	9.7	20.0	266.3	0.8	0.1
Average	**10.4**	**17.5**	**12.1**	**20.8**	**33.7**	**30.3**	**21.2**	**5.1**	**16.6**	**13.1**	**1.3**	**39.5**	**35.9**	**2.2**	**35.8**	**517.4**	**1.1**	**0.3**
Std Dev	*4.1*	*2.4*	*3.0*	*9.1*	*5.1*	*9.4*	*4.7*	*0.7*	*5.7*	*2.6*	*0.5*	*11.6*	*7.1*	*2.5*	*7.2*	*203.1*	*0.4*	*0.3*
Italy average	*10.1*	*22.4*	*14.3*	*15.4*	*38.8*	*31.7*	*10.7*	*5.6*	*17.5*	*13.9*	*1.4*	*18.0*	*38.0*	*13.2*	*58.6*	*90.0*	*3.2*	*0.1*

3.4c Con't.

	finh	einhi	auto	arti	firm	empl	meche	size	HH	C1	C2	C3	isef	C5
Arzignano	108.8	10.0	1.0	57.6	510.0	7400.0	2.3	14.5	25.9	16.7	52.3	31.0	10.9	30.0
Sassuolo	341.9	7.0	1.0	31.8	323.0	15333.0	4.9	47.5	104.2	2.1	16.5	81.4	14.0	30.0
Civitacastellana	345.4	10.5	1.0	34.2	105.0	3410.0	0.5	32.5	825.5	3.4	21.5	75.2	9.0	40.0
Cossato	92.4	4.3	1.0	55.2	636.0	12578.0	4.0	19.8	42.1	10.7	29.8	59.5	15.0	7.0
Montebelluna	164.1	11.6	1.0	74.3	612.0	8013.0	2.7	13.1	32.3	17.3	43.8	39.0	12.9	50.0
Suzzara	372.7	10.5	1.0	70.8	191.0	5259.0	6.4	27.5	10.5	9.7	14.7	75.6	10.0	35.0
Cento	219.7	12.7	1.0	73.0	383.0	5772.0	5.8	15.1	10.4	13.4	22.1	64.5	9.1	30.0
Oderzo	359.6	13.7	1.0	47.2	183.0	2218.0	0.6	12.1	18.1	14.1	55.1	30.8	14.4	15.0
Schio	585.6	11.8	1.0	68.9	114.0	3428.0	4.9	30.1	47.5	7.1	27.8	65.1	12.9	30.0
Palazzolo	252.4	10.1	1.0	77.1	291.0	2621.0	3.3	9.0	112.8	19.3	56.2	24.5	13.1	15.0
Castellarano	356.3	9.2	1.0	15.6	74.0	2739.0	1.1	37.0	8.4	1.1	29.5	69.3	6.6	45.0
Average	*290.8*	*10.1*	*1.0*	*55.1*	*311.1*	*6251.9*	*3.3*	*23.5*	*112.5*	*10.4*	*33.6*	*56.0*	*11.6*	*29.7*
Std Dev	*136.0*	*2.6*	*0.0*	*19.6*	*193.0*	*4111.7*	*2.1*	*11.7*	*239.2*	*6.1*	*14.8*	*19.7*	*2.6*	*12.5*
Italy average	*61.6*	*22.4*		*66.1*			*9.2*	*8.8*		*57.9*	*21.9*	*20.2*	*11.0*	

Source: Author's calculations.

97

'organizationally upgraded' and 'integrated' (with the mechanical engineering industry).

The proportion of clerical workers is greater than that of self-employed. As discussed later, a less 'extended' division of labour has formed in this group. Clerical workers include those occupying positions of responsibility in product development, sales or quality assurance departments. These workers are required to satisfy the increasing demand for innovation, and also to meet the requirements of internationalization and quality control. This indicator therefore points to the inclusion of new professional figures in the production cycle. The integration of the leading industry with its ancillary industries corresponds to clusters of activity *à la* Porter (1990). Garofoli would describe these districts as 'system areas' (1991), while they resemble (for example, the Montebelluna area) the areas identified as evolutionary networks by Belussi and Arcangeli (1998) (see Section 1.11.2).

3.2.3.3. Cluster 4: Peripheral/embryonic or Schumpeterian industrial districts

The third typology is significantly explained by all the three factors. This suggests a relatively higher internal heterogeneity that is in fact mirrored in a higher degree of inner inertia and by the standard values for the single indicators (Table 3.4d). The correlation values are −2.0, −3.4 and −2.6 respectively for the first three factors. This typology includes not only all the southern IDs, with the significant exception of Solofra, but also areas located in the so-called 'Third Italy' regions (those with the highest density of districts), notably Lombardy and Veneto. The districts of San G. Ilarione and Ostiglia may in fact be viewed as offshoots of larger and stronger IDs in contiguous LLMAs.[4] The Southern areas do not all display the same pattern of labour division. Ascoli Piceno and Giulianova are slightly more upgraded than San Giorgio dei Cavoti or Guardiagrele, while Matera and Casarano, on the other hand, display a model of labour division based on small firms and more vertically integrated industries coexisting side by side (Table 3.4d).

This cluster includes IDs where the industrial vocation is still weak, given the small extent of the specialization and the manufacturing industry, and this impacts on the local labour market, which is characterized by high levels of unemployment. A metalworking or mechanical engineering tradition, and, more generally, the development of pecuniary external economies, are absent from southern areas. With regard to social features, the most significant and distinctive variables in cluster 4 are rate of unemployment, rate of inactivity and rate of illiteracy. As shown below, a negative social performance, a low level of infrastructure, and social services (*sosf*) qualify these areas.

3.4d Distinctive features of marginal industrial districts, 1991

	immi	high	illi	drop	qual34	hous	Apyo	enti	clei	isem	ianc	unio	poli	asso	serve	sosf	RDsp
Giulianova	6.2	20.8	19.0	37.8	40.6	32.1	16.9	6.2	8.4	12.1	1.5	20.0	36.0	1.0	44.2	700.0	0.2
Ostiglia	7.4	19.4	22.8	39.5	38.9	32.7	15.8	4.5	13.3	15.3	2.5	30.0	33.5	1.3	53.7	400.0	0.0
Val Vibrata	4.7	24.8	16.2	12.6	44.4	34.0	14.8	5.5	13.8	10.5	0.8	20.0	34.0	2.9	48.7	575.2	1.0
Barletta	3.9	14.8	22.8	31.6	26.9	57.3	15.6	6.6	8.0	13.8	1.5	20.0	22.2	0.5	43.8	766.9	0.2
S.M. Cavoti	2.6	13.3	28.3	23.2	35.1	15.1	9.4	4.5	9.1	15.7	1.5	20.0	43.0	0.9	45.8	1349.0	0.1
Senigallia	6.0	24.6	13.3	36.6	51.3	30.3	11.2	6.1	10.9	17.0	1.3	35.0	31.0	3.7	49.7	438.2	0.1
Putignano	2.5	10.3	25.9	22.8	30.3	30.9	14.7	6.6	8.6	13.2	0.9	35.0	37.0	2.2	51.2	810.5	0.0
S.G. Ilarione	9.6	8.6	14.1	18.7	14.7	16.8	28.5	3.7	5.5	10.2	1.7	30.0	30.0	0.0	45.2	398.1	0.0
Guardiagrele	6.2	17.6	25.2	22.0	35.1	47.0	14.2	8.2	10.4	9.9	1.1	30.0	40.0	1.5	28.5	289.4	0.0
Average	**5.5**	**17.1**	**20.8**	**27.7**	**37.4**	**32.9**	**15.7**	**5.8**	**9.8**	**13.1**	**1.4**	**26.7**	**34.1**	**1.6**	**45.7**	**636.4**	**0.2**
Std Dev	*2.2*	*5.5*	*5.1*	*8.1*	*6.0*	*12.4*	*5.1*	*1.3*	*2.5*	*2.4*	*0.5*	*6.2*	*5.7*	*1.1*	*6.8*	*304.6*	*0.3*
Italy average	*10.1*	*22.4*	*14.3*	*15.4*	*38.8*	*31.7*	*10.7*	*5.6*	*17.5*	*13.9*	*1.4*	*18.0*	*38.0*	*13.2*	*58.6*	*90.0*	*0.1*

3.4d Cont'd.

	finh	einhi	auto	arti	firm	empl	meche	size	HH	C1	C2	C3	isef	C5	bankf
Giulianova	376.5	18.3	0.0	47.5	203.0	3614.0	0.0	17.8	34.2	6.4	56.0	37.6	10.0	40.0	0.9
Ostiglia	360.5	26.6	0.0	89.2	102.0	626.0	0.6	6.1	29.2	51.8	48.2	0.0	10.0	35.0	1.0
Val Vibrata	389.6	23.7	0.0	53.4	251.0	3139.0	0.0	12.5	20.8	13.1	56.7	30.2	10.8	15.0	0.9
Barletta	238.5	17.8	0.0	64.4	463.0	6166.0	0.2	13.3	75.2	15.6	29.5	54.8	6.0	25.0	1.1
S.M. Cavoti	276.7	18.6	0.0	38.7	39.0	570.0	0.0	14.6	43.6	11.0	55.0	34.0	7.7	7.0	0.7
Senigallia	362.6	32.5	0.5	82.3	139.0	1302.0	0.5	9.4	14.6	19.3	56.2	24.5	5.5	15.0	0.4
Putignano	193.8	17.9	0.0	80.9	230.0	2105.0	0.2	9.2	60.5	27.5	55.7	16.8	9.0	15.0	0.5
S.G. Ilarione	144.8	9.1	0.0	70.2	99.0	1492.0	0.4	15.1	143.2	11.6	48.3	40.1	12.9	11.0	0.9
Guardiagrele	894.4	37.3	0.0	38.2	22.0	249.0	0.4	11.3	15.9	8.2	91.8	0.0	6.2	10.0	0.2
Average	**359.7**	**22.4**	**0.1**	**62.8**	**172.0**	**2140.3**	**0.3**	**12.1**	**48.6**	**18.3**	**55.3**	**26.4**	**8.7**	**19.2**	**0.7**
Std Dev	*206.1*	*8.1*	*0.2*	*16.5*	*127.7*	*1790.0*	*0.2*	*3.4*	*38.6*	*13.3*	*15.3*	*17.3*	*2.4*	*10.9*	*0.3*
Italy average	*61.6*	*22.4*		*66.1*			*9.2*	*8.8*		*57.9*	*21.9*	*20.2*	*11.0*		*3.2*

Source: Author's calculations.

100

3.2.4.   The Determinants of IDs Performance: Factor Scores Regression

In the previous section, we presented a descriptive analysis of the characteristics of the 39 IDs in the different clusters. In what follows, ordinary least squares (OLS) regression analysis is used to assess whether the performance indicators are related to the factors obtained. For each of the most important factors, factor-score coefficients are estimated for each observation and then used as the independent variables in regression analysis.[5] As already mentioned, the obtained factors summarize the features describing the patterns of labour division and labour market in the IDs and their direct effect on population income.

The only economic performance indicators regressed on the factors obtained from the multivariate analysis according to their correlation values in 1991 are income, global productivity (sales per capita), export variation (between 1986 and 1991), and employment variation between 1961 and 1991. The only social performance indicator regressed is the unemployment rate. The variables related to variation in the number of firms and employees are linked to the specific patterns of historical development in IDs, which are only partially related to the kind of interfirm relationships observed in 1991. The estimated equations are the following:

$$inco91 = \alpha \; const + \beta_1(margi) + \beta_2(nonca) + \beta_3(diversi) + u_t \qquad (3.1)$$

$$inco96 = \alpha \; const + \beta_1(margi) + \beta_2(nonca) + \beta_3(diversi) + u_t \qquad (3.2)$$

$$saled = \alpha \; const + \beta_1(margi) + \beta_2(nonca) + \beta_3(diversi) + u_t \qquad (3.3)$$

$$exp91 = \alpha \; const + \beta_1(margi) + \beta_2(nonca) + \beta_3(diversi) + u_t \qquad (3.4)$$

$$unem = \alpha \; const + \beta_1 (margi) + \beta_2 (nonca) + \beta_3 (diversi) + u_t \qquad (3.5)$$

$$vale61-96 = \alpha \; const + \beta_1 (margi) + \beta_2 (nonca) + \beta_3 (diversi) + u_t \quad (3.6)$$

Here u is the disturbance term assumed to be normally and independently distributed with zero mean and constant variance. The factors are functions of the variables illustrated in Table 3.2.

The value of R^2 in all the equations (Table 3.5) is not particularly high, although it is acceptable for cross-section analyses. The Durbin–Watson statistic confirms the absence of correlation between residuals ($1.27 < DW < 1.65$, for degree of freedom = 34, significance points at 5 per cent). In equation (3.1) the coefficients β_1 and β_2, respectively related to the marginality and non-canonical factors, are significant at a level of 0.05, while the coefficient of the diversification/specialization factor is not significant at both the two significance levels of 0.5 and 0.25. Indeed this factor is almost never significant in all the equations. The most significant factor in the explanation of IDs' global productivity and unemployment is the first factor. The sign of the coefficient is negative for income and positive for unemployment. Autoregression of residuals excludes the presence of autocorrelation.

This result sustains the idea that a more concentrated structure is associated with a higher economic and social performance overall, while a relatively higher diversification or specialization is only a descriptive specification of the business structure not directly affecting performance.

Table 3.5 Explanatory 'factors' of industrial districts performance: Results of OLS estimations, 1991

Independent variables and results
No. of observations = 37

Equation and Dependent variable	Const	β_1	β_2	β_3	R^2	F	SE	DW
Equation (3.1) Income91	13.0 (46.6)	−0.50 (−2.6)*	−0.23 (−1.1)**	−0.05 (−0.2)	0.20	2.65	1.64	2.01
Equation (3.2) Income96	25.3 (36.0)	−1.2 (−2.5)*	−1.7 (−3.2)*	0.3 (0.45)	0.36	5.72	4.15	1.77
Equation (3.3) Sales per capita normalized (a)	162.2 (9.21)	−32.5 (−2.69)**	−2.2 (−0.17)	−12.85 (−0.83)	0.22	2.63	99.6	1.66
Equation (3.4) Var. Export '86–91	1.52 (4.7)	0.277 (1.21)*	0.54 (2.281)*	-0.35 (-1.16)	0.21	2.72	1.89	1.67
Equation (3.5) Unemployment rate	−1.50 (-3.3)	-0.02 (−0.10)	−0.10 (−0.63)	0.16 (3.84)*	0.32	4.92	1.23	1.59
Equation (3.6) Var. employment 1961-1996	420.1 (2.8)	117.5 (1.079)	292.9 (2.55)**	−194.0 (−1.4)	0.22	3.202	913.74	2.32

Notes:
t-statistics in parentheses.
*, **, stand respectively for 0.95, 0.99 per cent of significance.
(a) No. of observations = 31.
Source: Author's calculations.

Table 3.6a Performance indicators of (quasi) canonical industrial districts, 1991

	unem	inco 87	inco 96	M2	M2in	room	infr	saled	Expo 91	Expo 96
Santa Croce	8.6	14.5	25.0	106.6	35.1	5.0	62.6	1.0	1.8	1.4
Sant'Elpidio	10.7	13.1	27.2	109.7	34.9	4.6	-63.2	0.4	1.5	1.3
Prato	11.0	12.5	24.4	109.1	33.5	5.0	60.0	0.5	0.2	-0.4
Average	**10.1**	**13.4**	**25.4**	**108.5**	**34.5**	**4.9**	**19.8**	**0.6**	**1.2**	**0.8**
STD Dev	*6.7*	*1.2*	*1.3*	*6.2*	*3.5*	*0.3*	*102.2*	*0.3*	*0.6*	*1.3*
Italy average	17.8	13.3	28.8	94.1	33.0	4.3	100.0	1.0	1.0	1.0

Source: Author's calculations.

Table 3.6b Performance indicators of craft-based industrial districts, 1991

	unem	inco 87	inco 96	M2	M2in	room	infr	saled	Expo 91	Expo 96
Solofra	25.5	11.2	19.7	94.5	26.5	4.3	−184.9	1.0	1.3	3.2
Vigevano	11.0	16.1	22.7	88.8	35.4	4.2	30.1	2.0	−4.1	0.7
Carpi	4.7	11.2	24.4	108.8	39.2	4.9	103.0	0.6	−0.4	0.5
Bassano	5.8	13.5	26.8	118.9	38.5	5.2	27.7	0.6	1.9	0.6
Marostica	5.6	12.5	22.2	123.9	38.7	5.4	27.7	1.2	0.9	0.9
Civitanova	8.4	12.0	27.6	120.7	38.1	5.4	0.1	0.4	1.1	1.6
Pesaro	10.5	11.9	28.8	123.4	38.5	5.4	41.9	0.7	0.6	2.3
Guastalla	5.3	15.0	32.8	119.2	41.5	5.1	113.0	0.5	0.9	1.1
Desio	8.4	12.0	21.1	94.1	35.0	4.0	30.0	0.7	0.8	0.6
Poggibonsi	6.8	14.8	28.6	104.7	34.4	4.5	30.0	0.3	0.5	1.4
Montecat.	11.0	14.2	26.7	105.8	37.0	5.0	27.0	n.a.	0.2	0.8
Fermo	11.8	13.3	24.7	108.0	31.8	0.0	−60.0	0.6	1.5	1.3
Valpolicella	6.0	13.0	26.6	106.7	38.1	4.8	−17.0	n.a.	2.2	1.1
S.B. Tronto	11.4	12.9	24.0	104.7	34.4	4.5	−50.0	n.a.	1.8	0.6
Average	**9.4**	**13.1**	**25.9**	**108.7**	**36.2**	**4.5**	**8.5**	**0.8**	**0.7**	**1.2**
Std Dev	*2.5*	*1.4*	*3.1*	*10.5*	*2.5*	*1.4*	*47.6*	*0.5*	*1.5*	*0.5*
Italy average	17.8	13.3	28.8	94.1	33.0	4.3	100.0	1.0	1.0	1.0

Source: Author's calculations.

There is strong evidence for the hypothesis that when firms have more internal capabilities, collective performance is higher as one would expect from the large stream of literature surveyed. However, there are also signs that, among the four clusters, the LLMAs with a more structured pattern of labour division are those that achieve the better productivity rates and export growth.

3.6c Performance indicators of concentrated industrial districts, 1991

	unem	inco 87	inco 96	M2	M2in	room	infr	saled	Expo 91	Expo96
Arzignano	4.8	13.1	26.0	109.7	28.8	4.9	27.7	1.8	1.7	0.9
Sassuolo	5.7	12.8	31.5	122.6	38.7	5.4	103.0	0.8	1.3	1.1
Civitacastellana	19.0	12.0	17.2	91.4	31.2	4.2	−63.2	0.4	1.6	2.0
Cossato	6.2	15.3	25.8	97.8	39.7	4.5	30.3	0.9	1.2	1.8
Montebelluna	4.6	12.8	27.7	121.8	50.2	5.4	−27.0	0.6	1.1	1.0
Suzzara	6.0	16.0	27.2	120.7	41.1	5.0	−1.3	0.5	4.6	5.4
Cento	6.9	13.0	22.8	108.3	39.8	4.6	75.3	0.5	−0.8	0.8
Oderzo	5.7	12.4	26.9	125.6	39.5	5.5	−27.0	1.4	1.1	1.4
Schio	5.6	13.1	25.8	108.1	38.4	4.9	27.7	1.4	2.6	1.3
Palazzolo	8.0	13.2	23.3	104.7	34.4	4.5	14.0	0.8	−0.4	1.7
Castellarano	5.4	14.2	29.1	107.1	39.7	4.4	1.0	0.7	1.6	1.0
Average	**7.1**	**13.4**	**25.6**	**110.7**	**38.3**	**4.8**	**14.7**	**0.9**	**1.4**	**1.7**
Std Dev	*3.8*	*1.1*	*3.3*	*10.0*	*5.0*	*0.4*	*46.7*	*0.4*	*1.3*	*1.2*
Italy average	17.8	13.3	28.8	94.1	33.0	4.3	100.0	1.0	1.0	1.0

Source: Author's calculations.

Table 3.6d Performance indicators of marginal industrial districts, 1991

	unem	inco87	inco96	M2	M2in	room	infr	saled	Expo1	Expo6
Giulianova	14.0	13.8	25.1	101.1	33.2	4.8	−18.2	0.4	2.4	2.2
Ostiglia	6.0	15.4	26.2	118.6	46.3	5.0	−1.3	0.1	n.a.	n.a.
Val Vibrata	14.1	13.2	24.0	125.6	39.5	5.5	−50.0	0.2	1.8	1.2
Barletta	25.5	12.8	16.4	122.6	38.7	5.4	−125	0.7	7.7	0.4
Cavoti	18.2	7.6	13.6	96.9	32.9	4.7	−60.0	n.a.	7.4	−0.4
Senigallia	5.2	12.6	25.6	99.9	33.7	4.8	1.0	n.a.	1.5	0.1
Putignano	19.3	9.2	17.9	91.8	30.6	4.1	−125	0.7	0.7	2.5
SG Ilarione	4.8	11.0	22.5	106.7	34.5	4.7	−17.0	0.2	0.6	1.0
Guardiagrele	14.5	10.6	20.8	104.6	36.6	4.9	−40.0	n.a.	0.4	1.7
Average	**13.5**	**11.8**	**21.3**	**107.5**	**36.2**	**4.9**	**−48.4**	**0.5**	**2.8**	**1.1**
Std Dev	*6.7*	*2.3*	*4.2*	*11.3*	*4.5*	*0.4*	*45.3*	*0.3*	*2.8*	*0.9*
Italy average	17.8	13.3	28.8	94.1	33.0	4.3	100.0	1.0	1.0	1.0

Source: Author's calculations.

We now look at the performance of the different typologies. Table 3.6a–d shows that integrated IDs exhibit the best performance on average, in that they score high on unemployment, global productivity and per capita income (mainly in 1991). They also achieve good export performance, although the level is lower than in the case of marginal IDs. As regards individual indicators, the results are again varied.

Canonical IDs outperform the other with respect to the index of infrastructure, while craft-based or diversified IDs have a higher average size of dwellings. Marginal IDs are the most dynamic and overall they exhibit a variation in export that is much higher than the national average. These results point to the fact that good performance may be achieved even if the area does not comply with all the requisites of an ideal ID.

3.2.5.   Internationalization and Export Performance of Industrial Districts' Typologies

With the exception of export variation between 1986 and 1991 in craft-based IDs, the other typologies exhibit export performance much higher than the national average. The rate of variation is calculated in fact with reference to the national average for the same industry (classification by goods). This confirms the important contribution of IDs to Italian export performance. Notwithstanding the increase in the export absolute values, our IDs have declined in terms of international trade in the last period. From 1996 to 1999 the quota of world merchandise exports accounted for by our selected IDs (including specialization and ancillary industries) decreased by 27 per cent, while for Italy as a whole the quota dropped from 4.7 per cent to 4.1 per cent. The Italian trade in clothing, textiles, furniture, tannery and footwear, and therefore the industries in which IDs are specialized, contributed to this negative performance. The Italian quota of world textiles exports dropped from 8.7 to 8.0 per cent (20 to 22 in the EU), and clothing from 9.8 to 7.1 per cent (31.5 to 25.7 in the EU). The loss has been more localized in the European export markets than in American markets.

This trend inversion may be due to two distinct factors: in the more traditional (supply-dominated) industries where most of our IDs are specialized, the share of NICs' exports has constantly risen in the last few years. Countries such as China, Argentina, Portugal, India and Bangladesh have enlarged their international market share in footwear and clothing products. On the other hand, Italian IDs' loss of market share is also related to the less rapid growth of industries where they are mainly specialized. In this respect, the performance of 'specialized' industries, such as agriculture machines and mechanical engineering generally has been far better. In 1996, the provinces in which agricultural machinery IDs are located achieved exports of machinery worth more than 448 billion lira and more than 11 billions lira for tractors.

The average export performance of the various typologies of IDs conceal quite differentiated rates of variation, this pointing to possibly specific or idiosyncratic factors of explanation. Some of the more erratic cases may deserve a closer inspection. Carpi, for example, exhibits a very low rate of export variation in knitwear items between 1986 and 1991, strongly affecting the average performance of the craft-based IDs. The Carpi ID is strongly export-oriented – the average value of exports being 46 and 86 billion of lira per employee in 1991 and 1996 respectively – and this orientation dates back to the 1970s. The fragmentation of production in Carpi area, where few firms have direct links to international markets and thus often use traders, means that they are unable to cater to international, mainly European, clients requiring large batches and short delivery and reassortment times. The traditional distribution channels represented by traders seem more appropriate to the exchange of low-cost items, rather than those of better quality, since they assemble undifferentiated orders and deliveries for foreign brands. The presence of Carpi firms in marginal market niches makes them vulnerable to the competition raised by emerging markets in Asia, such as Bangladesh, India or China. Falling back on the domestic market is not a viable strategy since it does not ensure adequate volumes or margins. The poor performance of Prato is particularly striking when compared with other wool–textile areas like Cossato and Schio. The lower-quality level of Prato products prevented local manufacturers from preserving their market shares after the devaluation of the lira in 1992.

The IDs located in southern regions all show very high rates of growth in export. In Barletta, however, export performance, after a dramatic increase between 1986 and 1991, slackened in the following five years.

The export trends are also related to the strategies of international delocation enacted by an increasing number of firms in many of the surveyed IDs, either in northern and southern IDs. Delocation mainly concerns the upstream phases of production, such as the manufacturing of uppers for footwear mills, the preparation of semi-cured skins or some of the most labour-intensive phases of the clothing cycle of production. For all the tanning IDs, there are cases where distribution outlets overseas as well as tanneries, have been created, usually through joint ventures, either in countries producing hides and skins or promising growth in the leather goods industry. This explains, for example, why the quota of exports in semi-cured skin has decreased at the advantage of cured skin. The analysis of export and import data, geographical outlet markets and delocation strategies of IDs would provide richer information on their competitiveness, but would go beyond the boundaries of this work. The author is currently researching these areas with a view to future publications.

3.2.6. The Dynamic Performance of Industrial Districts Typologies: the Growth of Employment

As regards the dynamic performance of the four typologies of IDs identified, the results show that, on average, all of them grew more rapidly than the corresponding national industries between 1961 and 1996. During the sub-periods 1981–91 and 1991–96, employment growth was, on the contrary, slower for the whole sample, which indicates that processes of transformation were at work. More rapid growth is also displayed by export values in the two periods examined. However, differences emerge among the four typologies as regards both employment and firms' growth or exports. On average, between 1961 and 1996 employment growth was more rapid in marginal and integrated IDs (Table 3.7). In the former case, the sharp increase in employment was related to the younger industrial history of these areas, while in the latter it may have been due to the large economies of scale achieved by the industries belonging to this typology (ceramics, textiles, mechanical engineering). The large increase of firms in this typology relates to the presence of mainly vertically integrated firms after the Second World War. Overall, the patterns of growth displayed by these areas has much to do with their history, as the following chapter explains in more detail.

Table 3.7 Employment and firms' growth in the four typologies of IDs between 1961 and 1996

	Employment			Establishments		
	% var. 1961–96	% var. 1981–91	% var. 1991–96	% var. 1961–96	% var. 1981–91	% var. 1991–96
Canonical IDs	149.5	–12.5	4.9	161.3	–17.0	–1.6
Artisan IDs	131.1	12.7	–15.7	168.5	13.1	–23.0
Integrated IDs	311.2	22.4	–20.2	260.2	21.1	–11.7
Embryonic IDs	955.0	99.6	–18.8	120.8	65.8	–25.4
Italy average	*7.9*	*–10.7*	*–6.8*	*–3.1*	*–0.5*	*–0.1*
Average Italian IDs	n.a.	n.a.	–2.2	n.a.	n.a.	–3.0
Average Italian non-IDs	n.a.	n.a.	–10.2	n.a.	n.a.	2.2

Source: Author's calculations.

3.2.7.   The Evolution of the Industrial Districts Typologies between 1981 and 1991. A Brief Account

When comparison is made with the results of multivariate analysis conducted on 1981 data, it emerges that the tertiarization factor is less influential in this year, while a 'canonical' or agglomeration factor explains more than 27 per cent of total variance. The same cluster analysis repeated in 1981 displays a similar partition, but yields a larger number of 'canonical' IDs and a smaller number of concentrate IDs, which indicates that IDs are undergoing a process of evolution. The weight and diffusion of 'canonical' forms based on an extended division of labour was larger in 1981, and most of the areas in the typology of concentrate IDs in 1991, such as Montebelluna and Oderzo, were classified under the canonical type in 1981. In 1981, southern areas were located in two different clusters. This result evidences an ongoing evolution of IDs whereby 'canonical' features (inclusiveness, small firms and so on) tend to lose importance, while other characteristics of agglomerated areas, such as reintegration, emerge.

The comparison between different periods suggests that these typologies may mutate from one type to another. This may also imply that the typologies identified could be interpreted as different stages of a possibly continuous pattern of evolution. Marginal IDs may metamorphose into artisan IDs and then into canonical or integrated IDs. A bifurcation in the patterns of evolution emerges when the ID has reached a certain stage in exploiting economies of agglomeration; that is, a stabilization stage evidenced by a slow growth of enterprises or employees. In this circumstance, the ID may evolve towards either a canonical type, strengthening its specialization and the degree of labour division, or a more concentrated pattern where firms tend to reintegrate previously dispersed phases of production. Actually, we observed in all the IDs a process of concentration of supply that makes the hypothesis of a passage to a canonical model impossible to take for granted in the near future, in the light of current competitive pressures. Therefore a deterministic transition from one form of ID to another has to be excluded. Chapter 4 focuses on the dynamic properties of IDs.

3.2.8.   A Comment on Multivariate Analysis

An ideal factor analysis would have produced only one single 'pure' significant factor, and cluster analysis would have distinguished two groups: canonical and non-canonical IDs. By contrast, our results show the existence of a multidimensional space for analysis of IDs and local economies generally, which puts a question mark against the results obtained by Sforzi, as well as other authors. Closer inspection of Italian IDs shows that the empirical importance of the so-called 'canonical' ID is less relevant than one might expect. Hence, the lightness with which the notion of canonical ID is applied to all the agglomeration areas of SMEs is not justified. In other words, although one cannot avoid the use of the term 'ID' in a broader sense, what should be avoided is indiscriminately attaching the specific features of the 'canonical' ID model to any agglomeration of SMEs. This tendency is particularly evident when non-hierarchical or pairwise interfirm relationships, flexible specialization and cooperation are taken to be intrinsic to any non-scrutinized local agglomeration of SMEs.

The different patterns of labour organization identified by multivariate analysis do not perfectly coincide with either the industry or the geographical partition used to select our sample. In fact, areas specialized in the same industry belong to different clusters, which illustrates that technical features are far from constraining. However, when the specialization of these areas is examined more closely, it appears that, notwithstanding the common classification within an industry (even to a four-digit level of accuracy), the specific product specialization imposes different technical.

The explanatory factors of social and business structure obtained, even accounting for the ambiguity of the elementary indicators as stressed in Chapter 2, proved accurate in predicting the dominant kind of labour division in an area. They are highly effective in discriminating between different market/industry structures, although they may have failed to distinguish some subtle differences concealed beneath a similar distribution of firms.[6] They may also usefully be retained to discriminate between different patterns of learning in a cognitive perspective (Section 1.10). For this reason, deeper analysis of the organizational structure of IDs, as conducted in the following section, may reveal more details.

The results of the multivariate analysis obtained also raise the methodological question of their stability. We made some exercises to release some of the hypotheses assumed. We used, for example, a lower threshold of the correlation values and the results yielded an inverted ranking between factor 1 and factor 2. Some borderline cases, such as Solofra, Senigallia, Civitacastellana moved to a different cluster (marginal IDs).[7]

3.3.   INTERFIRM RELATIONSHIPS AND COOPERATION ALONG VERTICAL LINES

This section investigates the organizational structure of the IDs belonging to the same typology. A descriptive account of each area is provided on the basis of a variety of sources, including our interviews and original data. The categories of interdependence described in Section 1.7 are used to illustrate the different interfirm arrangements within the various IDs. From an organizational point of view, canonical areas are characterized by a two-way sequential interdependence whereby firms exchange information (bi-directional flows) and goods (unidirectional flows). Some of the canonical and craft-based IDs display these features, but much more common is sequential interdependence: more precisely, one-way interdependence, where each activity provides inputs to the other without a dense exchange of information along vertical lines. Reciprocal interdependence is common in cluster 4, where forms of intensive interdependence are apparent. This may come about between firms, but it is much more frequent among the internal R&D departments of the more innovative firms in the districts of Montebelluna and Sassuolo.

The IDs specialized in mechanical engineering industries also included cases of 'intensive' interdependence, which involves the joint application of complementary resources to a common activity in integrated manner. This typology also comprises cases of user–producer interactions for innovative activities. In contrast to these groups, embryonic IDs comprise areas where firms are linked by weak ties and, when they are linked, a sequential interdependence arises, with only one-way flows of goods between commissioning and final firms, often located outside the area.

3.3.1. Models of Labour Division in (Quasi) Canonical Industrial Districts

Prato (Tuscany), one of the most widely studied Italian IDs, specializes in wool textiles. The origins of Prato's specialization in wool textiles date back to the Middle Ages (Origo, 1957), In the second half of the past century, Prato specialized in the recycling of rags and remnants, used as a primary material for the production of woollen fabrics.

The structure of industry in Prato – as it appeared until the end of the 1980s – is one in which each firm performs only one or a few tasks in the textile *filière*. Some specialist coordinators, like the '*impannatore*' (Becattini, 1989), but also terminal firms and wool-mills, stand at the head of a long chain of operations, which ranges from carding to dyeing. The placing of final products on international markets is a function normally performed by 'buyers' in Tuscany (Cavalieri and Liberanome, 1989).

The *impannatore* purchases the raw materials, allocates the orders, and gives instructions to local specialist subcontractors on the basis of his or her own design, without owning any physical assets. S/he owns all the intermediate inputs across all the sequential stages, and s/he also markets the final output. Relationships between the *impannatore* and subcontractors are regulated by contracts of merchandise transfer. The product design stipulates the number and even the identities of the firms to which the work is to be assigned, and the extent to which the operations of the productive process are to be divided. This occurs interactively, because the *impannatore* collects information about what is technically feasible and suggests technical adjustments so that new processes or materials can be tried out by subcontractors. Terminal firms and wool-mills perform internally only a few operations and purchase intermediate inputs or subcontract out other specialistic functions on the basis of their own design (Casson and Paniccia, 1995). An extended vertical and horizontal division of labour is confirmed in the case of Prato.

Communication among all the stage-firms of the chain and between the final coordinators and their suppliers is ensured both by informal contacts and by codified instructions 'embedded' in the way semi-finished goods are supplied. In order to ensure high flexibility and short delivery times, which are crucial for Prato's competitive advantage, the area's production system requires 'empirical' rules of operation and communication. Rules are of particular importance for relations between customers and subcontractors. Instructions and technical specifications regulate the exchange of semi-finished goods in the district; they define behaviour, roles and the relationships between the actors involved in production; and they set objectives and criteria for performance assessment (Balestri, 1993). Among the many informal methods by which firms' performance are checked and their compliance with orders ensured, commissioning firms are free to visit their subcontractors to inspect the work in progress. These rules replace more standardized and formalized techniques and, at the same time, are something more than pure trust relationships.

Business relations have become difficult during the crisis that hit the area in the second half of the 1980s. Since this period, numerous artisan firms specialized in finishing, spinning and weaving were forced to shut down because of the 'unfair' rates charged by their subcontracting or client firms. Some customers failed to honour their debts or arbitrarily questioned the quality of the supply in order to obtain sizeable discounts (Maselli, 1993). Recently, one of the leading local trade associations denounced unfair practices by local entrepreneurs, and asked its members to declare the names of unfair entrepreneurs in order to enact sanctions against them (Unione industriale di Prato, 2000). As a result of the reduction in demand, the number of firms, weaving and finishers especially, has dramatically decreased. In the 1990s, new products, different from worsted or woollen cloth and based on new raw materials (synthetic fibres, viscose, flax, cotton, and so on) have been produced in the area (Bellandi and Romagnoli, 1993). Although, according to several surveys, firms used to be generally dependent on more than one customer, in recent years increasing numbers of final firms have tended to control their suppliers. In addition, in the past decade, the increasing complexity of coordination had led to the formation of more integrated firms or '*groups*' or 'networks' of firms.[8]

Santa Croce dell'Arno (Tuscany) specializes in the production of medium-to-high-quality cured bovine leather. The production cycle in leather tanning consists of 15–20 phases, of which at least half are subcontracted to task specialist firms (for example, the removal of hair and fat from the uncured skins, splitting the hide, flattening and drying). A distinction may be made between mechanical operations, requiring expensive and complex machines, and chemical ones, which generally do not require manpower. Task specialization mainly concerns the mechanical operations.

A major organizational change came with the emergence of networks of firms, which have been surveyed since the end of the 1980s. According to a study carried out in 1988 (quoted in Floridia, 1994), around 54.5 per cent of local firms were tanneries and 46.5 per cent were subcontractors. These mainly work for local tanneries. In 1996, more than 60 per cent of the turnover of the specialization industry was accounted for by tanneries. The networks of firms were estimated to be eight in the same year, controlling over 30 per cent of total local turnover.

Porto Sant'Elpidio (Marche) specializes in medium-to-high-quality leather footwear for women and children. It is among the highly specialized areas in our sample and in Italy. Just after the Second World War, the Marche region's solid artisan tradition in shoe manufacturing enabled each artisan unit to produce for the final market, integrating most of the intermediate stages of production. Each artisan unit was an autarchic entity, with few relationships with other firms. In the 1990s, the degree of specialization increased, as well as the density of linkages between firms. The industry structure presently comprises a large number of artisan manufacturers, often specialized in stage-production cycle, which work for local commissioning firms. These manufacturers can be divided into three kinds: subcontractors of specific components (for example, made-to-measure welts); subcontractors of standardized components (for example, soles, accessories); and homeworkers. Final firms, which account for more than 50 per cent of local turnover, sell their products, often under proprietary brand names, to the domestic market.

3.3.2. Models of Labour Division in Craft-Based Industrial Districts

Vigevano, in Lombardy, is presently an example of an integrated area specialized in both footwear (medium-to-high-quality shoes with leather uppers) and footwear machinery. In the footwear industry, the phases of production most likely to be subcontracted are the preparation of soles and heels, and the sewing–hemming phase. The latter is decentralized to a large extent because there are numerous highly skilled hemmers available in Vigevano as a result of the area's long-standing tradition in footwear manufacture.

The industry that produces footwear machinery has become even more important than the more traditional footwear industry in the area over the last thirty years (see Chapter 5). In 1996, employment in the footwear industry was 4 117 against 3 285 units in the mechanical engineering one (of which more than 2 300 in leather machinery manufacturing), while the area exported 40-billion-lira worth of shoe machinery against 23-billion-lira worth of footwear. The features of the local machine industry are described in more detail in Section 3.3. Since the severe depression that afflicted the area in the 1970s, local firms have shifted towards high-quality shoes. Leading Italian stylists have their headquarters in the area, although major processes of international delocation have taken place since the beginning of the 1980s. Apart from very important clients, most subcontractors are closely interconnected with local firms.

An extreme division of labour is apparent in Carpi, too, where a (modern) putting-out system is coordinated by terminal knitwear firms at the head of a subcontracting chain, which is rather shorter than in the Prato case and consists of a relatively smaller number of links. These knitwear manufacturers have concentrated increasingly on the financing and purchase of raw materials, the coordination of production, and the design and sale of garments. The vast majority of them rely on external networks of independent, mostly small, artisan firms to produce the garments. Unlike subcontractors in Prato, those in the Carpi area do not own the raw materials, nor are they responsible for product conception; they merely contribute the labour and machinery required to transform the manufacturer's raw materials in accordance with his/her explicit instructions. The majority of subcontractors have more than one client, and, unlike in Prato, no single firm controls its subcontractors entirely (Bigarelli and Crestanello, 1994a and 1994b; Brusco, 1982). In 1996, subcontractors accounted for 35 per cent of local production, while terminal firms accounted for the remaining quota of 65 per cent (Regione Emilia Romagna et al., 1998).

As regards the organizational structure of the area, relationships among firms form a close-knit or *star structure*: that is, one in which each firm has multiple horizontal (pairwise) and vertical (subcontracting) linkages with other firms. This pattern of labour division results from changes brought about by product technological innovations. The extent of the division of labour increased in the 1980s with the introduction of *pronto-moda* (henceforth: ready-to-make) production. Ready-to-make has partly superseded the traditional mode of production known as '*programmato*' by using a different production schedule and a different method for producing the sample collection. In 1996, more than 70 per cent of independent firms adopted ready-to-make production.

The relationship of local subcontractors with ready-to-make firms has grown increasingly close. About half the total turnover of local subcontractors comes from ready-to-make firms. Thus, considering that this new model is associated with smaller organizations, the degree of labour division has increased in consequence of the adaptation of ready-to-make in many subcontracting firms.

With the change in production processes, homogeneous production has been abandoned. In the 1980s, the range of products was constantly extended, quality was improved, and close attention was paid to the development of distributive retailing channels. Because of increased external linkages with other areas (new subcontractors were no longer located in neighbouring towns), there was little expansion within the boundaries of Carpi's LLMA.

Civitanova Marche and Fermo (both in the Marche region) specialize in medium-to-high-quality leather footwear for women and children. The degree of the division of labour varies slightly among these areas. On average, however, all these areas comprise a balanced proportion of commissioning independent firms and subcontractors, which ensures that about 70 per cent of work comes from within the area. According to a very recent survey carried out in Civitanova (Micucci, 1999), semi-finished goods and subcontracted work are generally realized autonomously as regards the supply/provision of materials and technical requirements, while product design is closely controlled by the commissioning firms. According to this survey, subcontractors tend to produce for more than one customer, but the degree of independence of these firms is lower than, for example, in Carpi, because the customer usually owns the more specific machinery and the hollow punch, while the subcontractor owns less specific machinery. Most of the firms are family-owned, and as the *ancy* indicator testifies, family members take part in management of the firm in supervisory, technical or support/staff roles. In most of the Marche districts specialized in footwear (but also clothing), firms out-source work from Italy to East European countries.

The LLMA of Pesaro (Marche) specializes in the manufacture of furniture. In the 1980s, a complementary production developed, consisting of furniture accessories and furniture made from materials other than wood, like marble, glass and metal. The area numbers more than 7 000 local units, and local firms are among the leading exporters of Italian furniture. Final firms are either vertically integrated or specialized in assembly and the intermediate and final phases of production; a few semi-mechanized firms specialize in the preparation of veneers. Stage-firms are very small, generally of artisan type, producing wooden components and semi-finished goods, frames, curved elements and poles; or they are mechanized firms specialized in wooden components (shutters, tables, boards, beds, chairs, as well as other items) or scaleboards. The furniture factories undertake product design internally and then assign the various stages of production to subcontractors. The components return to the contracting firm for assembly.

Generally, a furniture factory has two to three suppliers for each product. The producers of semi-finished goods are becoming less closely tied to the local production of furniture, and they sell their products internationally (Brutti and Ricoveri, 1988; Manacorda and Pattarozzi, 1990; Mezzino, 1985; Moussanet and Paolazzi, 1992; Quaglia, 1995; Omiccioli and Tamburini, 1999).

Desio (Lombardia) specializes in wood, metal, wicker and upholstered furniture (for living-rooms and bedrooms, and as garden furniture) and is located in an extensive area between Como and Milan specialized in furniture (the so-called 'Brianza'). This is one of the oldest districts in the sample, as well as in Italy, with origins dating back to 1800. Most of the local production is customized, and it is mainly oriented toward the internal market, although leading export companies operate locally. Export per employee in furniture items is low. As in the case of Pesaro, different models of labour division coexist in the area. On the one hand, there are firms that internally perform only the phases of cutting, sewing, covering and assembling, while they subcontract the finishing work (padding, polishing, and so on) to a wide variety of subcontractors. On the other hand, there are firms integrated upstream in the production of leather or downstream in the distribution stages. Subcontractors rely on their own competencies and design, and firms are often both independent producers and subcontractors at the same time. This explains the fragmentation of the industrial structure, where 73 per cent of firms are artisan in nature and 63 per cent of employees work for firms with fewer than 20 units. This fragmentation has led to considerably less automation of processes than in other areas; for example, the leading firms in Matera. The kind of production of these firms is therefore very customized. They provide good quality furniture for very specific family or office needs; a degree of specialization that protects them from the competition coming from big producers such as Ikea or the distribution chain Divani&Divani. Owing to the scant interdependence of firms – which are either final producers or autonomous subcontractors – forms of cooperation are very rare in the area. This lack of cooperation is also seen in the low degree of membership in employers' and workers' associations, and in the low proportion of voluntary associations. Evidence of networks of firms is also very scant in the area.

In Poggibonsi, in Tuscany, the core of the local furniture industry consists of a nucleus of (relatively) large firms that undertake all the phases of the production cycle internally, and that mostly produce 'blocked' bedrooms, living-rooms and kitchens. A new specialization in caravan manufacturing has developed more recently. Around these firms, a ring of independent artisans undertake customized operations or products. The most important final market for the Poggibonsi district is the domestic market. The area's long-standing specialization in the mechanical and glass and crystal industries, combined with the growth of furniture manufacturing, has shifted it towards the production of wood-working machines and tools, metal fittings for furniture and lighting fixtures (Bambi, 1998). More recently, it reverted to its specialization in caravan making – a relatively protected market niche – relying on the skills acquired from a well-established tradition of mechanical engineering. The district was formed in the first years after the Second World War, and it experienced, like all the other furniture IDs, its period of major growth during the 1950s and 1960s. The area's degree of diversification, which is considerable, increased during the 1980s in reaction to a decline in demand.

San Benedetto del Tronto (Marche), displays a high degree of diversification in manufacturing activities and also in services and tourism. Its textile and clothing industry does not take the form of a locally contained area, since the majority of manufacturing orders come from other regions, and design capabilities are not extensively embedded in local firms. The few final firms, however, account for around 50 per cent of local turnover.

Marostica (Veneto) – and part of the municipalities included in the adjacent LLMA of Bassano – specializes in the production of a wide range of ceramic products: tableware, gift articles, ornaments or lamp bases. The Marostica area consists of myriad small firms focused on cost control, which compete in market niches not (yet) affected by competitive pressures. As a reaction to the latter, local firms concentrated at the end of the 1980s on niche markets, where they could survive while preserving their managerial practices. The area suffered a reduction in employment amounting to about 23 per cent, and a downsizing of already small firms, the average size of which shrank from 9.6 in 1981 to 6.7 in 1996. Employment in 1996 is slightly lower than it was in 1971, while the number of firms has remained unchanged in the towns of their primary localization: Marostica and Nove. The spread of the industry to contiguous municipalities has not occurred, nor has an intergenerational reshuffle taken place.

On average, the owners of the firms specialized in ceramics perform the highly skilled operations, which require tacit knowledge, and deal with the ideation and design phase, such as cooking and stove-loading firing and kiln-loading, internally. There are no firms specialized in these activities; and the same applies to commercial activities. Conversely, decoration activities are performed by numerous specialists. According to Census data, none of the local ceramics firms is a limited company, and many of them prefer to maintain the status of 'artisan' firm even when they employ more than 25 people. According to our interviews, the local firms can be divided into three groups (Gurisatti and Vedù, 1993):

- (*small*) *integrated firms* that undertake all their principal activities internally (from modelling to commercialization) and only put out manufacturing services;
- *network firms*, or, in other words, collaborative groups between final and stage firms aimed at the exchange of orders: one of the firms will collect orders greater than its internal productive capacity and then allocate them to subcontractors or to other final firms specialized in finished goods, expecting the favour to be reciprocated. Because orders are differentiated, and because they comprise a wide range of products or quality which an individual firm cannot cope with on its own, they are spread around all the other firms in the informal group, the number of which is estimated at 15;
- *stage firms* specialized in the production of biscuit and in decoration. The former is a standardized activity, intermediate for numerous other firms.

The furniture industry in Bassano (Veneto) is characterized by a close specialization in the reproduction of antique furniture (period-style furniture). The high degree of manual ability required for production of this kind makes the industry closely dependent on artisan skills. The furniture firms only put out labour-intensive activities, in order to save on the relative costs. Little use is made of external suppliers for specialized tasks, while homeworking is much more common, given that the precision of specialist workers can ensure higher levels of quality. The fragmented nature of production and the artisan nature of local firms have increased in the past decade. Final demand was channelled to foreign markets by external buyers, as also happened in Tuscany.

Guastalla, a mechanical engineering area in the Emilia-Romagna region, belongs to the group of craft-based IDs, while the other mechanical areas are classified as integrated IDs, since their production structure includes manufacturers of agriculture machine components and tools, rather than engines or tractors. The production of the latter items involves, in fact, a different size of firms and skills unavailable in the rather fragmented industry structure of the area.

The area of Solofra (Campania) is specialized in goat-ovine leather. The area is characterized by vertically integrated tanneries run by second generation entrepreneurs who buy 7–8 per cent of their total sales from local subcontractors. Only activities having a less relevant quality content are decentralized. There are 178 vertically integrated firms (that is, 63.3 per cent of the entire supply) and 36.7 per cent subcontracting firms. There is no evidence of networks of firms in the area (Iannuzzi, 1995; Passaro, 1994; and interviews of members of *Unione Industriale di Avellino*, conducted by the author in December 1996). Notwithstanding the relatively large average size of firms, and of tanneries in particular, the degree of processes mechanization is very low.

3.3.3. Models of Labour Division in Marginal Industrial Districts

This cluster groups together most of the southern IDs, with the exception of Solofra. The least organizational complexity of the local industry is mirrored in the low proportion of clerical workers. As a consequence, the prevailing interfirm relationships concern only the exchange of semi-finished low added value inputs. Most of these areas, including Ostiglia, Senigallia and San G. Ilarione are on the 'periphery' of larger and more mature IDs engaged in mainly productive activities, while design and commercial functions are located internally within firms headquartered in external areas. This typology is therefore very close to the 'satellite industrial platform' type identified by Markusen (1996). In these areas, the larger commissioning firms internalize design and commercialization functions, while small firms are generally subcontractors relying on local or external firms. Generally speaking, firms in southern IDs are larger than the rest of the sample (and industry averages), which points to their greater inefficiency or less extended degree of labour division. If the real case is a higher level of vertical integration, then the phenomenon of irregular work in southern areas – as documented by many surveys and which emerges from our interviews with trade-unionists – must be taken into account. According to some scholars (Meldolesi, 1998), irregular work mainly concerns subcontractors rather than final firms, and thus simultaneously sustains the higher productivity of the latter and the survivability of the former. This would explain why southern firms appear to be more vertically integrated, when in reality they rely more on external workers. It is difficult, however, to gain a sound estimate of the diffusion of this phenomenon, and therefore to exclude the case of merely inefficient firms.

The area of Ostiglia (Lombardy) specializes in knitwear and mechanical engineering and is located only a few kilometres away from the knitwear area of Carpi. The area may be partly paired to southern areas, since industry plays a minor role in the local economy and the few industrial firms are generally subcontractors depending on external clients. The area is characterized by the presence of many small firms specialized in the same tasks – often with fierce competition between them – which work for or coexist with a few leading firms that tend to be vertically integrated and that have recourse to external firms to cover demand peaks. Subcontractors have been operating in the area since the 1960s, and originated from previous homeworking activities. The few leading final firms covering the complete cycle of production were founded during the 1970s, thanks to the decentralization process in the area of Carpi. The few firms that arose in the 1980s have delocalized their production to foreign countries. The labour force (generally female workers) suffers from having to accept lower wages and unhealthy working conditions.

The specialization of the area of San Giovanni Ilarione (Veneto) is very recent and dates back to the 1970s, when some exporters coming from the nearby area of Riviera del Brenta, procured low-quality shoes from homeworkers and small firms located in the area.

In Ascoli Piceno and Giulianova, both in the Abruzzi region, different product specializations can be found in the clothing and textiles industry: knitwear, clothing and shirt-making, and leather and footwear. These industries are characterized by hierarchical interfirm relationships between commissioning and subcontracting firms. Generally speaking, collaboration is not widespread within local industry and subcontractors do not take part in product design activities but simply execute work on design and requirements specified by the commissioning firm. According to a recent survey (Pizzi, 1998), 71.4 per cent of the sample firms state that the commissioning firm designs products in detail without leaving any refinements to subcontractors, while the remaining 28.6 per cent share in product design. Over 90 per cent work on raw materials provided by the commissioning firm. As a corollary to the scarce control over the core competencies related to the product, most of the subcontractors are commercially dependent on a single commissioning firm only and most of them receive orders from commissioning firms located outside the district. Stage-producers' production processes are mainly of an artisan nature that is appreciated by external commissioning firms since they can ensure a high product variability. In this respect, the area does not appear to be strictly self-contained. In the knitwear industry, final firms are generally small, though slightly larger than in the case of Carpi (on average they have less than 20 employees). Some of them are owned by non-local investors, who located to the area in the 1970s, supported by state aids. They put out all the phases of production, this largely comprising manual work such as semi-finished works, browdery, ready-to-make, and washing and dyeing.[9] Subcontractors, in this case, are mainly homeworkers. Unlike Carpi, there has been (at least, according to our information) no formation of firms' groups. This may be due to the smaller scale of the local knitwear industry as compared to Carpi. Not dissimilar is the labour division in the shirt-making sector, where firms (whether suppliers or *façonists*) sell a finished product to firms that then oversee its commercialization, or sell their product directly to a proprietary brand name. The former tend to be vertically integrated, while the latter sell their product to final clients and tend to put out large parts of their production stages. In this industry, there have been many cases of delocation towards Albania and Eastern European countries. In the clothing industry, as well, final firms resort to external suppliers for the stages of cutting, assembling, wrapping, and washing and dyeing; as a consequence, the proportion of *façonists* is very large. According to a recent survey (Fabbrini and Olivieri, 1999), over 60 per cent of the sample firms in Ascoli Piceno (generally the smallest), are subcontractors, while the remainder are commissioning firms. Some firms belong to a 'group' (six groups have been discovered). As cluster analysis suggests, families are very involved in both of these LLMAs. Only a few firms design products. The few designers replicate models of more famous stylists. These features also explain the low propensity to export of firms in the area, since the exporters are only the bigger final firms. A few firms delocated the simplest phases of production to foreign producers in Tunisia, Bulgaria and Taiwan (Fabbrini and Olivieri, 1999).

The two contiguous areas of Giulianova and Ascoli Piceno have experienced different forms of cooperation between workers and firms in the past. Between the 1970s and 1980s many cooperative firms, which collaborated in the exchange of orders, were established in the knitwear industry in Val Vibrata, but not in Giulianova. At the beginning of the 1990s, contrasts between the cooperative firms' strategy and management of their promoters (often allied with political parties), and subsequent bankruptcy depressed the local cooperation culture and native entrepreneurship. With respect to Giulianova, the rate of formation of new firms is lower (1995 data), according to the local trade unionist interviewed.

Barletta (Puglia) specializes in leisure wear shoes, a production that has been abandoned by all other areas in Italy. The local footwear industry hosts two main categories of firms: (a) large firms, which are highly verticalized and subcontract out to external firms only during peak production times. These firms are also reckless in terms of (cost) efficiency; and (b) small firms, either subcontractors or footwear mills, that have no clear specialization and that are undercapitalized. Suppliers are very specialized in the more standardized and repetitive operations, and realize large volumes of production mainly related to the production of uppers. These mills are relatively large, in relation to the national average, employing between 21 and 50 employees. Firms produce the same product and use the same technologies, and competitive relationships are predominant. Proximity has spurred imitative processes. Vertical relationships between firms are almost negligible, the firms being internally integrated. Automated equipment has been introduced in local factories and, as a consequence, the content of 'tacitness' in work has reduced. Goods produced in Barletta are homogeneous in terms of intrinsic and aesthetic characteristics. Homogeneity derives from the imitation mechanisms made possible by people's physical proximity and by the deverticalized structure of local industry. The innovative content of the product is embodied in the way hollow punches are created. These are dies for the models, supplied by footwear manufacturer designers, which, when applied to the presses, enable the cutting of uppers. Imitation rather than competition explains the diffusion of firms in an area where the tacit content of production is low.

Suppliers tend to work for only one client firm. Surveys of Barletta's area do not offer wide evidence of vertical cooperation. This may be due to the low degree of complementarity between local products, each firm doing similar things; as a consequence, substitution rather than complementarity is the prevailing relationship between products and hence competitive relationships dominate (Censis-Unioncamere, 1995; Paloscia, 1987; Viesti, 1995a, 1995b, 1996). Notwithstanding the low efficiency of local firms, export performance is positive, although unstable.

Putignano, in the Puglia region, specializes in children's clothing and bridal dresses for medium-to-high production. The proportion of independent and subcontractors is almost balanced, though is difficult to obtain realistic estimates since firms often perform the two functions at the same time (Comei, 2000; Viesti, 2000). Due to some financial difficulties in the last decade, most of the local firms reverted to subcontracting for commissioning firms located outside the region.

According to the results of cluster analysis, Casarano and Matera, too, are included in the typology of marginal IDs, although they are considered as illustrative units of analysis. These areas, which have not been considered to be IDs because the local proportion of SMEs is no greater than the national average, display a division of labour often considered to be typical of some local agglomeration of firms.

The area of Casarano (Puglia) is presently polarized between two types of firms that do not interact with each other. On the one hand, there are extremely big firms, such as Filanto, that are completely vertically integrated. On the other hand, there are many small firms that, like the large firms, are completely integrated or that work as subcontractors, generally for clients located outside the area (Corvino, 1988; D'Ercole, 1992).

The area of Matera (Basilicata) specializes in leather and cloth upholstery furniture. This industry has a cycle of production slightly different from the wood furniture industry, as described in the cases of Desio, Oderzo and Pesaro. The production stage can be subdivided into different operations: polyurethane moulding, filling-up, cutting and sewing of leather and clothes for coverings, assembling and control. Each of these phases of production requires a very low minimum-efficient size. In the area of Matera, many different organizational models cohabit, as well as different product specializations characterized by a different quality of raw materials for coverings. Some of the firms are vertically integrated; others only administer purchasing and quality control functions internally, putting out all the production activities; a third model is in between: moulding of polyurethane and filling-up are put outside, while cutting and sewing of coverings, assembling and control is undertaken internally. As in the case of tanneries, the cutting operation is completely manual: every piece of skin has its own 'history' and peculiarities, and it is only human care that ensures the quality of the cutting operation. CAD and CAM machines are used, instead of workers, since they perform cutting operations in a more efficient way for what concerns covering materials (as, for example, the cutting of overlapping clothes). Furniture firms (producers of sofas) also differ according to their internal layout, degree of internal informatization and mechanization (machines for moulding of polyurethane and for cloth cutting) (Belussi, 1999; Molinari, 1996).

3.3.4. Models of Labour Division in Concentrated Industrial Districts

This cluster groups together all the areas where a strong fashion or design-led industry (ceramics, furniture, textiles) is integrated with a complementary mechanical specialization.[9] These industries also host phenomena of technological innovation, concerning raw materials or final products, and the productive processes, more pronounced than in the other typologies.

The more highly educated workforces of these areas are matched by a high proportion of immigrants employed in lower-skilled jobs. Despite the high level of automation in most of the districts, there is still demand for very low-skilled labour willing to work in unhealthy conditions.

When the internal organizational structure of these areas is examined, it emerges that the most interesting feature is not simply the average size of firms. On average, a wider proportion of the firms in these IDs are larger than in the other typologies, but they nonetheless have less than 200 employees and are thus still classified under SMEs. What emerges from the qualitative analysis surveyed is that in these IDs there are firms that perform a leading role, either because they coordinate a long chain of operations, as in the textile IDs in particular, or because they adopt more innovative technologies, and managerial practices (for example, JIT) or tackle more sophisticated markets. In these areas, a virtuous interation between tacit knowledge, as resulting from processes of socialization that date back to the Second World War, and codified knowledge, introduced in the area by non-local actors, is at the basis of important tecnological innovations. Groups or networks of firms in these areas, and especially in Oderzo, Sassuolo and Arzignano, are a very widespread phenomenon, grouping together the local firms into unitary strategies that make these IDs more strategically integrated.

In Arzignano (Veneto), vertically integrated tanneries account for 39 per cent of firms, and subcontractors for the remaining 61 per cent. Although the number of medium-sized firms is still small, the structure of supply is hierarchical. A few relatively large tanneries organized into networks of firms (9 groups for 39 firms) control about 30 per cent of the entire local tanning output and employ around 2 300 workers through financial linkages with other firms. A few (17) medium-sized fully autonomous firms control 40 per cent of total local output and employ around 1 000 workers (Parri, 1994). Each unit in the group is headed by a member of the family, who has managerial and operative autonomy, although strategic decisions are taken by the family as a collective economic subject. Trust results from family ties but is reinforced by financial linkages. Putting-out appears to be more dependent on economic trends or fluctuations in demand. Pre-existing mechanical engineering firms have paved the way for the development of a cluster of firms specialized in the production of the machinery that fostered the mechanization of numerous tanneries throughout the 1970s. The pronounced growth of local firms can now be considered concluded, because environmental constraints have been imposed on the creation of new enterprises (scarce availability of land, and statutory waste restrictions whereby no firm unable to recycle its own waste is allowed to operate).

An entire wool production *filière* is present in Cossato. Well-known stylists like Cerruti, Piacenza and Pancaldi originate from this area, where they still maintain their manufacturing factories. Owing to such favourable localization factors as an abundant supply of water suited to textile production and a supportive industrial policy in the 1920s and 1930s, the province of Biella – where the Cossato LLMA is located[10] – was the birthplace of Italian industrialization (Secchia, 1960). Over time, the area has strengthened its specialization in high to medium-high-quality clothes. During the period of rapid growth between the Second World War and 1960–65, the area was characterized by vertically integrated enterprises. After a slump in demand in 1961–62, it underwent a process of fragmentation and the downsizing of large firms: internal shops became independent firms linked with other downstream units. However, the most important restructuring process began in the early 1970s, as a consequence, amongst other things, of a severe flood which destroyed numerous mills in the area. The industry is currently faced by severe challenges: a change in international competition (the emergence of new competitors with lower labour costs, together with a national increase in energy and labour costs, and a change in customer tastes). The result has been the disappearance of all factories with more than 500 employees and the emergence of firms of smaller size specialized in different stages of textile production. In 1981 the average size was smaller than in the previous Census year: 13.8 employees per unit.

From 1985 onwards, in the face of a further change in international competition and the introduction of raw materials other than wool, local firms decided to strengthen their specialization in high- or medium-to-high-quality production. As a consequence, the local firms' system acquired a new organizational structure. Groups of firms were established that consisted of different units enjoying operational autonomy but under the same ownership. These groups have targeted high-quality production, and secured an important share of the world export market in textiles. At the same time, firms once again began to integrate: in 1991 and 1996, the average size was 19.7 and 23.9 respectively. The Cossato networks of firms display a form of technical cooperation among firms belonging to different owners and specialized in different tasks along the production chain. Numerous firms are minority shareholders in the equity structure of local supplier companies.

Compared to Prato, Cossato has a number of firms with greater vertical integration, although the area underwent a process of disintegration in the 1960s. The industrial, rather than artisan, origin of Cossato, in which it differs from all the other textiles–clothing areas, explains the presence of a strong ancillary mechanical industry, which is not to be found in other areas. An exception is Carpi, where the artisan tradition combines with a well-developed mechanical industry, but in this case the strong mechanical vocation of the Emilia-Romagna region, in which Carpi is located, must be taken into account. A different product specialization, given that Biella specializes in high-quality clothes and Prato in medium-quality worsted cloth (and, more recently, woollen and new clothes), partly explains their slightly different labour organizations, but also their different models of internationalization and competitive strategies.

Schio is another example of an historical ID. Firms tend to be integrated and use highly mechanized, large-scale machinery, often not furnished by local suppliers.

Palazzolo sull'Oglio, in Lombardy, is another ID specialized both in textiles and clothing. Its origins are linked to the location in the area at the beginning of the twentieth century of a large firm, Marzoli, producing textile looms and a few other firms specialized in cotton spinning, like Cotonificio Ferrari and Filartex. The area gradually moved from a specialization in textile (cotton) manufacturing to mechanical engineering and clothing, and it is now, in fact, one of the most diversified areas in our sample. Subcontracting relationships are not very common, since the cotton-spinning mills tend to be vertically integrated, while clothing relies more on stage producers or *façonists*, mainly women or Chinese migrants. In the last ten years, the bigger clothing firms of the area have subcontracted out parts of their production to Eastern European countries such as Albania and Romania, while cotton textile firms have acquired intermediate products from north-African countries. Larger firms are often organized into formal or informal networks, with one unit specialized in the design of textile looms or spinning, and others in the production of critical components or in marketing. As a consequence, the degree of concentration of the local production in textiles and mechanical engineering is quite high. According to the estimates of the local trade association, the number of employees outside the district depending on local commissioning firms was 7000 at the end of the 1990s.

Montebelluna specializes in the production of sports shoes. During the past decade, the area has seen the formation of several large and medium-sized firms, each specialized in the production of a particular footwear item for a specific market niche. The businesses distinctive of local production display contrasting models of labour division. In the sector where technology is more important (plastic-based technologies), firms, often of multinational size, tend to be vertically integrated, rarely interacting with local small subcontractors. These firms are committed to technological innovation, particularly in relation to new types of sole (geotex) or new models of boots (with posterior entry), and they have their own R&D departments. Rather than exchange information or undertake technological innovation with local firms, these firms tend to establish networks with international companies (generally from the USA) and local institutions. Another group consists of large firms (like Lotto and Diadora) specialized in the production of soccer, tennis, jogging/running, basketball, and volleyball shoes. In the past, these firms were more deeply rooted in the local firms' system; now they prefer to decentralize abroad, emulating Nike's example of international networking. Irrespective of the location of their subcontractors, these firms have always orchestrated flows of goods and information from the latter. The third group consists of small firms specialized in mountain shoes and leisure shoes which out-source work to other small firms in the area. Linkages among these three different kinds of business, as well as internally to businesses themselves, are very rare, since competition tends to prevail. The first two groups of firms (in particular, the technology-based ones) are specific to Montebelluna and are not be found in other footwear areas in Italy (OSEM, 1995/6; Gandolfi, 1988; Corò, Gurisatti and Rossi, 1998).

Oderzo specializes in wood furniture. Unlike other furniture areas, firms rely more on automated processes of production, which ensure quality, flexibility and efficiency; as a consequence the number of small artisan firms is very limited. Four types of firms can be schematically distinguished in the area. First, there are furniture mills, often organized in the form of networks, which produce a wide array of furniture items (kitchens, bedrooms, and so on) and that take a leader position in the area by introducing technological, managerial and commercial innovations. Second, there are small groups of furniture firms, normally specialized in only one item (such as kitchen furniture) and adopting a follower strategy. There are almost 80 such networks in the area (which include the contiguous LLMAs). Third, there are subcontractors with a high degree of autonomy who sell their standardized items directly on the market to firms non belonging to the district. Finally, there are subcontractors, representing the weaker segment of firms that perform very specialized tasks (Guerra, 1998).

In Sassuolo (Emilia Romagna), as a consequence of major process innovations in the production of ceramic tiles, firms tend to be vertically integrated. The larger integrated firms are flanked by a system of decorators, small subcontractors specialized in small tile sizes, and firms specialized in glazing and grinding. As confirmed by secondary sources (Russo, 1985; Bursi, 1997) spontaneous or informal relationships with final subcontracting relations have been replaced by formal ones, and by the creation of networks or constellations of firms. The percentage of firms belonging to a group increased in 1996 and, according to an estimate provided by the association of ceramic tiles producers (Assopiastrelle, 1997), amounted to over 60 per cent.

Civitacastellana (Lazio) specializes in sanitary wares. The area presents a very peculiar form of limited company, the cooperative firm, where workers are at the same time employees and shareholders, though in the last decade external venture capitalists and some of the richest native families acquired equity shares in some of the local firms. This widespread diffusion of cooperatives can be related to the communist political tradition of the area (the so-called 'Stalingrad' of Lazio region), together with a desire for autonomy among workers, a scarce availability of capital funds and the manual and tacit nature of the production process and involved competencies. Workers have been very aware that they possess the 'core' competencies in the ceramics' manufacturing and have thus decided to exploit this to their advantage, rather than be beholden to a company boss. These cooperative companies, as well as the new joint-stock companies, rely heavily on their internal competencies and subcontract only a few standardized operations (Calza-Bini et al., 1996).

Local areas specialized in agricultural machinery (Suzzara) and in mechanical engineering (Cento), both of which are in the Emilia-Romagna region, exhibit a model of labour division somewhat different from those discussed thus far. The producers of final output (mototillers, motodiggers, small tractors, and such like) are small to medium-sized enterprises, and they buy components, specialized services and engines from external suppliers. The component suppliers are small to medium-sized firms generally dependent on more than one client: on average they have a higher degree of commercial autonomy than is the case in the textiles or clothing industry. Another kind of supplier consists of artisan production firms undertaking specialist work for the large number of firms located in the rich mechanical engineering region of Emilia-Romagna. The suppliers of engines are very large, often multinational, firms with internal R&D and commercial and marketing departments. They own versatile, very often automated, machinery. The structure described by this variety of linkages between final and stage firms has created a network: that is, a dense web of vertical and horizontal ties.

Notwithstanding the density of linkages among the producers of components, only very occasional cooperation linkages are to be found between the producers of final output and their engine suppliers, which guarantees innovation and, even more crucially, after-sales services to final customers. The leading role is played by the engine producers, which are large enterprises very often belonging to foreign investors. Whilst in the other areas surveyed the (price, technology or market) leaders are firms closer to the final market, in mechanical-specialized areas the leaders are the suppliers of engines.

By contrast, very close cooperation is found between producers of final output and their component suppliers. Here, the interdependence is higher; the innovation of, say, a brake-device in a tractor, may have several applications in all the other agricultural machinery produced locally.

Vertical cooperation is easier between machinery producers and users, because some sort of user–producer cooperation takes place. However, these interactions may in some cases be only hypothetical. These cases can be straightforwardly described using the scheme of the user–producer relationship (Lundvall, 1988, 1992). Innovations of an incremental nature require close communication between developers and users in a small group. In these circumstances, information exchange is especially easy because suppliers and customers have regular dealings with each other and have a good idea of their respective needs.

3.3.5. The Interaction between the Leading Industry and the Ancillary Mechanical Industry

The interaction between the users and producers of mechanical-based components or machines has proved beneficial in the past, as stressed by the literature, and the close complementarity between the Italian machinery industry and small firms specialized in fashion-led products even outside IDs has helped to shape the structural features of the former and its international competitiveness. The competitive characteristics of customized, flexible and inexpensive machinery has a great deal to do with the features of domestic demand expressed by the many small firms specialized in 'supplier-dominated' industries that have acted as proving grounds for manufacturers who have latterly become important exporters. The features of these 'users' has also fostered the introduction of 'incremental' rather 'radical' innovations, which can be exploited on international markets as well.

This virtuous interaction, however, has not held competitively in the recent past, once new electronic-based processes have been introduced in the industry. Now that electronic technologies have superseded mechanical ones, the user–producer pattern of cooperation has weakened. The producers of mechanical-based components are not suited to productive cooperation with a new electronic-based product.

In Vigevano, interactions between the footwear and shoemaking machinery industries have proved to be very limited. This is because the shoe manufacturers have refused to adopt new machinery, such as CAD systems, either because the new technologies require a reorganization of firms (new layout or new planning procedures) or the acquisition of new competencies and technical skills, or because they are too expensive. When a new CAD system engineered by a public research centre located in Vigevano was presented to the general public, the leading entrepreneurs in the area walked out of the demonstration.

Other experiences show that the local presence of a complementary industry is not always an advantage, because lock-in effects may occur. In fact, the emphasis on product innovation (new itemized or dedicated machines) by mechanical manufacturers may divert attention from more radical changes in process technologies. In this respect, German producers are more able to tap a demand for computerized, large-scale machinery because they are larger in size and are currently investing in system automation (CIM). In this case, belonging to a district is no help, because the footwear producers are too small for firms to be able to experiment with larger production systems. In addition, the splitting of investments impedes the undertaking of more ambitious projects. Smaller firms do not possess the capabilities and financial resources with which to buy and use the new machines engineered by their neighbours, which are instead sold to foreign producers. The small size of firms impedes achievement of the minimum scale at which innovative projects can be undertaken and research investments duplicated, while the imitation of neighbour's initiatives multiplies mistakes. However, this is not to rule out the possibility that the mechanical engineering industry will find its own way to achieve competitiveness.

Interaction between machine tools producers and users has seriously diminished in the past two decades. In Schio, for example, there are very important leading firms that buy their machinery, looms, bobbin-winders and washing machines from neighbouring European countries, while the local producers of looms, steam presses and shrinking machines sell abroad, often in Asia.

According to some interviews carried out in Sassuolo and Vigevano, tile makers and shoemakers, on one side, and machinery makers, on the other side, have a sort of love–hate relationship with each other. The former complain that machinery makers sell expertise acquired from working in Italy to foreign customers. Therefore, while the interaction between users and producers of machinery is virtuous in the first stage of development of the user and producer (or, in alternative: final and complementary) industries, this may not hold in a more mature stage.

Proof of the weak relationship between machinery producers and users in Vigevano is provided by export values, which are extraordinarily high for the former, as already mentioned on page 113. Nearly three-quarters of the output of machinery makers goes abroad.

3.4   THE INTERFIRM GOVERNANCE MECHANISMS IN INDUSTRIAL DISTRICTS

The description of organizational arrangements in the IDs highlights different forms of interdependence, ownership arrangements and coordination forms related to external and internal structural circumstances. The degree of competence differentiation seems to be a good predictor of the interfirm coordination mechanisms that can effectively be adopted independently of the level of organization, though it does not explain organization variety alone.

In general, coordination roles emerge when the number of units to co-ordinate is higher, organizational tasks are more complex and uncertain, and activities are more interdependent (Grandori, 1997). Coordination may concern flows of intermediate, instrumental or final products, as well as information flows sustained by different persons or entities with distinct (productive versus commercial or technological competencies) specializations, as well as by the same individual or entity (firm). Inspection of the coordination modes of interfirm relationships provides useful information on the patterns of labour division in our sample, and helps answer the research questions already raised as to whether IDs are networks, and to what extent relationships among firms are regulated by trust via cooperation. Before addressing such a question, it may be worthwhile to look at the subjects or mechanisms performing or ensuring coordination in IDs. We reviewed the following:

1. spontaneous mechanisms of interaction: the proximity of firms enables subcontracting out to nearby specialized firms, provided the latter are competent, without the need for a contract;
2. specialist co-ordinators, such as the *impannatore*, the buyers in Tuscany or southern IDs, the manufacturers in Carpi, or the exporters in San G. Ilarione;
3. firms at the head of a chain of complementary activities (for example, a textile *filière*) (Montebelluna, Sassuolo, Prato);
4. groups or networks of firms, whether formal or informal.

Generally speaking, when national and international demand has shifted in recent decades towards a greater degree of complexity, variability and volatility, more formal coordination mechanisms or integrated organizations have emerged. Networks of firms and leading firms with an interconnecting role have gradually replaced the informal mechanisms of coordination that were more common during the 1970s.

Co-ordinators may also stimulate innovation because they are connected to international markets for the distribution of final goods or the procurement of inputs or machinery. The scarce diffusion of international 'buyers', like those very active in Tuscany, also explains why local systems in the Marche region – including Pesaro – have not been oriented towards export markets since the beginnings of their development. Middlemen and commercial agents – very often from other regions – have played a major role in allocating orders in southern Italy IDs. This is another reason why southern firms are more internally integrated than those in areas where the mediators – for example the *impannatore* – are 'embedded' in the local environment and therefore able to reduce coordination and information costs. Hence, it is no coincidence that some of the IDs located in the southern regions of Italy display a positive export performance.

Coordinators have often performed an innovatory role, since they have introduced or spurred new processes and managerial practices (for example, the adoption of certification procedures or company-wide quality control: CWQC) or discovered new market niches. They perform a role of 'catalysts' or 'bridges' for all the firms they coordinate. Because imitative processes are very common in IDs, their actions and strategies are adopted by other local firms.

Price and informal communication may regulate the vertical relationships between firms when production processes are not particularly sophisticated and demand has a limited degree of uncertainty. Instructions given on the first occasion may hold for subsequent orders, since demand is not affected by high variability in products and quantity.

Where vertical linkages between firms are very scarce – as in the cases described above for Southern areas – specialists have no role to play in production coordination. The majority of firms in IDs are linked together because they make use of the same pooled resources, such as the services supplied by local trade associations or chambers of commerce, trained workers, or local reputation. In these cases, the most efficient coordination mechanisms used to achieve common results and mutual benefits are rules and procedures prescribing some types of action and forbidding others, and common staff supporting common services. Consortia constitute another typical case of pooled interdependence. We reviewed, in particular, export and purchasing (raw materials or energy) consortia, finding that they are aimed generally at promoting a common brand, financing participation in an exhibition, or reaching a critical mass to purchase critical resources. Notwithstanding the fact that most of the times the members of a (marketing) consortium usually belong to the same informal network, they have often been unstable.

3.4.1 Structure and Functions of Networks of Firms

A general phenomenon, although one of varying extent and mixed with other strategies, is the formation of either larger or vertically integrated firms at the head of a group of subcontractors or final firms. A few firms have moved into leadership positions by tightening their relations with a handful of reliable subcontractors and firms specialized in complementary activities for the supply of a diversified range of products. This phenomenon is known in Italy as a '*group*' of firms, though we prefer to call them networks of firms.

As we have seen, networks of firms play an important role in the areas analysed. A fairly recent work has highlighted the importance of networks of firms in the overall Italian economy (Barca, 1994). A network includes companies under the decisive influence of a single person or group of persons (a 'coalition') as regards strategic decisions, if not day-to-day management. A network enables the *principal* to count on various units that can easily be run by one or a few individuals acting as delegates (*agents*). It also gives the principal constant access to information about the results of the unit, and enables him/her to maintain control over strategic decisions.

A network may also perform two further functions. First, it may associate one or more managers without losing control as minority shareholders. Second, each son or daughter of a family may be placed in charge of a single company, thus preventing conflicts among relatives and training them in the business by allocating responsibilities according to age and skills.

Networks of firms in our IDs perform both these functions. To be stressed in particular is the functionality of networks of firms *vis-à-vis* cumulative learning, and especially learning-by-doing: especially in the tanning industry, and, to a lesser extent, in the other fashion-led industries. Technological capabilities in these industries are tacit and individually embodied: that is, they are tied to the skills and routines engendered in a worker or firm.[11] The more artisan nature of tanning activities in Santa Croce as compared to Arzignano may explain the differing nature of the networks of firms in these two areas. It seems, although more evidence is required, that family *delegates* are less common in networks of firms in Santa Croce than in Arzignano. In fact, in the Santa Croce networks of firms, former workers can be found at the head of operating units, while this is rarely the case in Arzignano, where family ties seem to be relatively more important than trust based on long-term relationships ('repeated games'). Networks are rarely found in southern IDs, which testifies to the different nature of their production processes, these generally being more standardized or organized internally into larger integrated leader firms.

The various units of the network may be specialized in different phases of the *filière*, exploiting their complementarities, such as those between textiles machinery and textiles manufacturing, or in differentiated products covering the full range of supply; for example, from low quality to high quality, or from men's clothing to women's clothing. Indeed, groups are formidable instruments with which to pursue diversification strategies, because each firm in the group covers a niche market, while the group as a whole places a complete range of items on the market. The specialization of the units may also concern managerial functions, with some units specialized in manufacturing and others in marketing, pre- and post-sale services or finance. Generally, it is the parent firm that specializes in tertiary functions.

Groups may also be viewed as an efficient solution to labour poaching (Section 5.3), or to the exit of trained workers or technicians, which might otherwise impoverish a firm's internal capabilities. When a worker threatens to leave his/her job, the employer may deter him/her from leaving by offering legal autonomy, albeit formal, as the administrator of a unit belonging to the group, and/or a share of its capital stock. Offering a stake to the worker is less common in most IDs; in fact, family-based groups tend to prevail.

The case of a worker with overall and even managerial experience is different, in that s/he is more likely to create a firm in competition with the one s/he has left. In this case, involvement in capital stock is more frequent. Groups can be viewed as the natural evolution of coordination mechanisms in local embedded industrial systems or as the product of self-organized processes of ID evolution. As such, they may suffer from the same risks of inward-looking attitudes that affect independent firms. In recent years, despite the flourishing of groups in many areas, difficulties have arisen. Groups based on financial and family considerations, without a clear strategic plan and an effective innovatory role, have suffered from financial or market crises.

The extent to which the group may represent an effective organizational form for the present evolutionary pattern of IDs depends on the nature of the control exerted by the principal on the different units in the group and on its overall competitive strategy. As already mentioned, the principal of a network of firms may exert a loose or tight control over the day-to-day management of the various units. Concerning the units specialized in production, the principal may impose (or just agree to) the adoption of a more standardized production process, and more automated machinery allowing a lower degree of variation, but a higher level of quality. S/he may also decide to abandon small market niches – where a single unit was previously focused – and switch to larger bands. The organizational choice may then be variously combined with a different positioning on the market.

In the textile IDs of Cossato, Schio and Palazzolo dell'Oglio, most of the firms linked to groups owned by worldwide famous stylists have focused on high-luxury bands or high fashion. These groups have integrated some of the more competent and qualified subcontractors in the district area, at the same time subcontracting out – often to small firms in other regions or countries – the components or phases of production more labour-intensive or low quality, securing an important market share within international trade. This has been possible whilst also preserving the autonomy of the single units. In other cases, groups have targeted medium-to-low market production, by compressing the autonomy of the units of production and striving for survival against TNCs or illegal workshops closer to home that compete more successfully on these markets.

The diversity in the internal organization of networks and in their competitive strategy means that we can preclude the possibility that the rise of groups in many IDs merely represents a return to hierarchy. A correct interpretation of the phenomenon that concerns us requires more thorough research aimed at discovering whether or not the new forms of organization (the networks of firms) imply a naïve replacement of tighter hierarchical control exerted by the principal of the network) on the activities of the different units joined with a standardization of the production. We believe that the answer, and a well-founded prediction on the viable evolution of IDs, is that the organizational forms and competitive strategies of the most dynamic actors of the districts will intermingle; a feature that warrants further research.

3.5   TOWARD A CONCLUSION: INDUSTRIAL DISTRICTS BETWEEN COMPETITION AND COORDINATION

The mechanisms of coordination thus far analysed proved effective in integrating the locally widespread goods, information or technologies and in relating the local system of firms to international markets. In those IDs where the coordinators appear more active in involving local firms in strategies of innovation, in the search of new markets and in the adoption of new managerial practices, the overall performance results were more successful, this pointing to a more efficient and interconnected structure of coordination.

IDs exhibit a coexistence of various organizational forms: consortia and coordinators at the head of a sequential chain of operations may coexist within the same ID. Indeed, where organizational variety is low, as in those IDs where firms are mostly subcontractors, the weaker these areas are, the more vulnerable the competitive advantage becomes. At a fine-grained level of analysis, it may be possible to find different – apparently conflicting – rules of governance coexisting in the same ID, such as price, power and conflict governing relationships between commissioning firms and subcontractors, final firms and clients, employers and workers. Concerning vertical relationships between firms, the replacement of a formal agreement or the integration of subcontractors into formal or informal networks suggests that trust is not always an efficient mechanism of regulation. The cases examined prompt criticism of the above-mentioned 'ideal–typical divide' between market and hierarchy and show on the contrary that the features of a network – that is, the coordination processes and structures that an interfirm coalition may employ – are not necessarily 'intermediate' with respect to those of firms and markets. Within each ID, coordinating actors, ownership arrangements and rules of governance are highly varied and come in different mixes and intensities.[12]

The integration of conception and execution into one firm, and therefore firms' 'autonomy', is a distinctive feature of a large proportion of enterprises in the various types of IDs, with a lesser incidence in marginal IDs. We make the point, however, that is not autonomy by itself that is crucial for competitiveness: it is rather the firm's ability not to stand alone but to relate with other firms and institutions as sources of ideas, best practice and information to make these firms successful. Moreover, the firms' linkages do not all need to be contained into the ID.

An analysis focusing on individual leading companies or groups of coordinators, and then looking at their linkages with other firms and their ability to upgrade a large set of connected firms, would be more predictive of IDs' performances. A comparison of the roles performed by these coordinators in the IDs, presenting similar socio-economic conditions such as those identified by our multivariate analysis – and therefore within each typology – would permit a better assessment of the viability of IDs in the future.

Many of the local markets prove to be characterized by 'contestability' conditions. The description of an ID's markets in terms of degree of contestability (Chapter 1) also sheds light on how cooperation arises. Customers do not rely on trust alone: they periodically test the market and solicit bids from other subcontractors, or proximity enables them to check whether their suppliers are offering prices close to costs. The fact that relatively low levels of asset specificity characterize these transactions makes subcontractor switching fairly easy. At the same time, the ease with which customers can compare the offers received with prevailing prices in the neighbourhood fosters the development of trust and the creation of stable exchange relationships.

The extent of the local reservoir of competencies affects the degree of contestability of markets, but competence is a necessary but not sufficient condition for control; the 'large number' factor – that is, the large availability of phases specialists – plays a role as well.

Whereas the birth of leading industries has been spurred by burgeoning entrepreneurship, leading firms or customers are well aware of the costs of each individual phase of production. Price bargaining remains intense in most of the areas. In Carpi, suppliers regularly document their costs, even to the point of opening their books to the manufacturers with whom they have long-term relationships (Lazerson, 1995). According to our short survey of the leading trade organizations in craft-based IDs, collective agreements on the rates for subcontracting work are not common, because firms prefer to engage in individual bargaining and do not trust a collective agreement, which may be unable to take full account of the specificities of the work subcontracted.[13] In the Emila Romagna region, where the artisan associations have the largest number of members in Italy, artisan firms proved unwilling to sign any agreement that would have put them in a situation of competitive disadvantage with firms located in other regions where a system of collective bargaining (for fees or wages) is uncommon.

Among stage-producers or subcontractors in most of the IDs surveyed, and especially in the 'marginal' ones, the fierce competition among firms in the periods of declining demand inhibits the adoption of more advanced processes or quality improvements. For example, in the footwear industry, either in Tuscany or Marche IDs, there is a fierce competition between uppers' manufacturers and homeworkers specialized in hemming. In the sewing phase, especially, the search for better quality is not satisfied by more advanced machinery, but rather by contracting the work out to more skilled workers, principally homeworkers. As a consequence, the attempt by the manufacturers of uppers to shift towards more qualified productions in order to obtain larger mark-ups may be hampered by the shoe factories' use of homeworkers. In other words, homeworkers are used strategically by shoemakers to curb the power of upper's manufacturers. Subcontractors cannot easily resort to investment strategies in specific assets, since the customer owns the more specific machinery and the hollow punches, while the subcontractor owns less specific machinery. When the rent left in the subcontractors' hands is nil, their resources for investment in new tangible or intangible assets are at risk. In southern IDs, subcontracting firms are either less efficient, or they receive a price that is not sufficient to cover their costs. In some cases, the rewards accruing to a subcontractor firm in a dependent relationship with its commissioning firms do not permit investments in new machines or competence building, while, because of the nature of the relationship, the opportunities for learning are very scant.

Our findings, however, may not mean that firms have to gain their independence or that a fragmented structure is preferable. Indeed, in those IDs dominated by larger and leading firms, the overall system of firms is growing rapidly. What makes the difference is the leadership position of these larger firms.

Not all IDs show conditions of *fair* competition. In Prato, Palazzolo and Vigevano many examples of unfair competition behaviour have been referred to those we interviewed, and others are documented in surveys such as Balestri and Toccafondi (1994). In the new scenario of decreasing demand a process of disruptive competition is taking place. There are cases where (a) some entrepreneurs imitate one or more items within a rival's sample, or (b) spread false information about commercial soundness and such like about their rivals. The pioneer firms that first diversified their production have been followed by other firms, which offered low prices in order to grasp an increasing limited demand. This activated a progressive race towards continuous price reductions, which ultimately eroded the profits both of pioneer firms and of followers. In the new context, easy communication among firms turned into a diseconomy for the district economy rather than being an advantage as in the past.

NOTES

1. Since some variables, for instance the rate of association (*asso*), were not available in 1991 or, conversely, others, such as *famy* were not in 1981, we inserted the same variable with the same value in that year. This ensured that the analysis was based on a coincident number and the same kind of variables.

2. The analysis was carried out by a French programme: *Systeme Pour l'Analise de Donnée* (SPAD).

3. Essentially, hierarchical techniques may be divided into *agglomeration* methods, which proceed through a series of successive fusions of the N entities into groups, and *divisive* methods which partition the set of N entities successively into finer partitions (Everitt, 1981). As the two methods are equivalent, we chose the agglomeration one.

4. This finding suggests that it would have been more appropriate to use the concept of 'functional area' for empirical testing (see Section 2.2).

5. In 1981, we test the relationship between the factors and income only, as the other performance indicators were not available.

6 The factors obtained also prove less predictably accurate when an area has a lower degree of specialization. They therefore encapsulate the social structure associated with all the manufacturing industries, rather than the main one alone.

7. Further details may be obtained from the author.

8. Accounts of the organization of 'groups' of firms are provided in Section 3.4. In contrast to Paniccia (1998), we here prefer to call them networks. Other authors prefer to call them constellations of firms (Lorenzoni, 1990).

9. This holds for the areas specialized in agricultural machines that are integrated with other mechanical and metal-working industries.

10 In the interviews, as well as in the survey on Cossato, it was very difficult to distinguish between Biella and Cossato, which are contiguous LLMAs. Indeed, in 1992 all the municipalities in the two areas were merged into the new administrative province of Biella.

11 The degree of tacitness may be too subjective to determine, and the concept is highly elusive. A meaningful measure might be the average time taken to train a skilled worker. However, in an ID where a dense interchange of information exists between firms and population, learning also occurs outside the walls of a factory or outside a regular contract of work.

12. In this respect we strongly agree with Grandori and Soda (1995) and Grandori (1997).

13. We restricted our survey to the larger craft-based and canonical IDs, namely Prato, Carpi, Desio, Santa Croce, P. Sant'Elpidio, Fermo, Pesaro and Solofra. A short questionnaire was conducted by telephone.

4. The Growth and Decline of Industrial Districts

4.1. INTRODUCTION

Having presented evidence of the organizational variety and on the static performance of different types of IDs, this chapter focuses on their evolutionary patterns. First analysed are the natural and historical factors that have boosted the take-off of specialization industries in the sample of IDs. In this regard, a distinction is drawn between supply-side and demand-side factors explanatory of IDs' formation. Then discussed, using correlation analysis, is the relationship between proximity and industry structure (degree of specialization and vertical integration), on the one hand, and growth on the other, in the period 1951–96. The industry growth of the areas in the sample is compared with the national average in order to find evidence that employment in IDs grow faster than those located in non-agglomerated areas. Also explored are the reasons why some IDs grow more rapidly than others, given similar external demand and technological conditions.

The question of the strength of agglomeration forces cannot be separated from the question of the pattern of growth. Do IDs have a life-cycle? The evolution of IDs is examined in the light of a view of the processes of growth as based on endogenous forces of agglomeration. At this stage of research, and considering what is presently available in the form of official statistics, it is difficult to test a local growth model, either endogenous or neoclassical. The data collected by industry censuses, and the information that we gathered from case studies, enable the identification of some regularities in the general change that has come about in the patterns of labour division and interfirm relationships. The data are analysed using a 'hypothesis-generating' approach. The results point to a positive relationship between within-industry external economies and firms' and employment growth in the first stage of an industry's development alone, while the former factors lose their importance as soon as the industry achieves maturity.

Analysis of the structural factors that give rise to various patterns of labour division permits reappraisal of the role played by vertical cooperation in most of the areas examined.

4.2. THE INDUSTRIAL DISTRICTS AS ENGINES OF GROWTH?

The year 1951 was taken as the period when the 'initial conditions' were set, although less accurate figures for some industries in the break-down of the 1951 Census data meant that 1961 data had to be taken into account. [1]

In Tables 4.1 and 4.2 the rates of growth (as a percentage) of the specialization industry in each ID are calculated as index numbers (1961 = 100), and they are divided by the indexed rate of growth of the corresponding industry at the national level. The data offer evidence that, on average, the sample of IDs grew more than the corresponding (specialization) national industries between 1961 and 1996. Moreover, the difference between IDs' and national average rates of growth is underestimated, since the latter for each industry also comprise ID areas but the rates of growth for non-ID areas alone are not available. This offers wide evidence that IDs in the post-war period have been a formidable engine of employment growth and have served as an incubator of the formation of new firms.

The typologies identified in the previous chapter may have a predictive value as regards short-term performance, but they are unable to discriminate clearly among different patterns of development. Apart from the cluster of embryonic IDs, which groups together all the areas in which development started in the 1970s, the more mature IDs are scattered among the three typologies, which do not distinguish between old and more recent IDs. Similarly, it does not emerge that IDs belonging to the same industry have the same pattern of growth. [2] This indicates that even different points of departure may have converged on a similar pattern of labour division in the 1990s, or conversely, that, starting from common initial conditions or facing similar technological or market conditions, IDs then follow idiosyncratic processes of growth. For this reason, the sample was divided into three groups according to their average values in 1951. On inspection of the size of the leading industry in 1951, just after the Second World War, three groups can be distinguished according to average values of employment. The first group, the smallest, includes the oldest IDs – those which date back to the beginning of the last century or that were the sites of the Italian industrial revolution in the 1800s. They employed on average more than 17 000 employees. The group of 'post-war' IDs comprises those whose specialization industries already averaged 2 000 employees in 1951, while the younger IDs grew in the 1970s. Figure 4.1 shows the different patterns of development of these three groups very clearly. The group of historical districts grew at a steady rate, while the younger ones expanded dramatically. The group of post-war IDs display intermediate rates. [3] A process of convergence, also considering the income variable, is far from having been reached.

Table 4.1 Employment growth (*) in selected IDs between 1961 and 1996

	51–61	61–71	71–81	81–91	61–91	61–96	91–96
Arzignano	0.5	1.5	1.3	1.2	2.4	3.3	1.3
Santa Croce	1.8	1.5	1.0	1.0	1.6	1.8	1.1
Solofra	2.2	1.4	1.6	1.0	2.3	2.8	1.1
Vigevano	1.4	0.6	0.8	0.5	0.3	0.2	0.9
Porto S.Elpidio	2.6	1.5	1.6	0.9	2.0	1.9	1.0
Casarano	1.5	1.3	3.5	1.4	6.7	6.9	1.0
Bassano	0.4	5.3	2.1	1.0	10.9	12.3	1.1
Marostica	0.9	1.2	1.2	0.9	1.4	1.0	0.8
Sassuolo	1.6	3.4	1.1	0.8	3.0	3.1	1.0
Civitacastellana	0.8	1.3	2.2	1.0	2.9	3.0	1.2
Cossato	1.0	0.9	0.9	1.1	0.9	1.0	1.1
Prato	2.1	1.2	1.3	0.9	1.5	1.7	1.2
Giulianova	1.7	1.4	1.6	1.1	2.5	1.9	0.9
Ostiglia	0.3	1.3	4.5	1.3	8.1	2.3	0.7
Carpi	3.3	2.5	1.4	1.0	3.4	1.5	0.7
Ascoli Piceno	1.2	1.8	1.7	1.4	4.2	3.3	0.9
Montebelluna	5.3	1.2	1.1	1.9	2.6	3.1	1.2
Civitanova	1.8	2.0	2.2	1.0	4.4	4.8	1.1
Barletta	0.7	1.3	1.4	4.6	8.3	7.5	0.9
Pesaro	3.4	2.1	1.1	1.3	3.0	3.0	1.0
Suzzara	0.5	1.4	1.4	1.1	2.2	1.8	0.9
Guastalla	1.1	0.9	1.4	1.0	1.3	1.1	0.9
Cento	0.9	1.2	1.7	0.9	1.8	0.7	0.4
Matera	0.3	0.2	9.4	7.8	12.1	16	1.3
Desio	1.0	1.2	0.9	1.1	1.1	1.0	0.9
Oderzo	2.0	2.9	0.9	1.3	3.3	5.7	1.7
Poggibonsi	2.6	1.8	0.7	1.0	1.3	1.1	0.8
Schio	1.0	0.9	0.9	1.0	0.8	0.7	0.9
S. B. Tronto	0.6	1.0	3.5	1.7	5.7	3.0	0.6
S.M. Cavoti	0.2	0.9	2.7	3.9	9.9	10.4	1.2
Palazzolo	0.6	3.8	1.0	1.3	4.9	1.7	0.7
Senigallia	0.4	1.6	1.8	1.5	4.5	4.2	1.1
Putignano	1.8	1.4	0.9	1.0	1.2	0.9	1.0
S.G. Ilarione	0.5	17.5	2.2	1.2	44.0	50.4	1.2
Montecatini T.	1.2	1.2	1.7	0.6	1.3	1.2	1.0
Fermo	3.6	1.7	1.6	1.1	3.0	3.2	1.1
Guardiagrele	1.4	1.5	1.2	0.4	0.8	1.5	1.9
Valpolicella	1.2	1.7	1.1	1.5	2.8	3.2	1.3
Castellarano	1.7	5.2	1.9	1.2	11.3	11.3	0.9
Average	*1.1*	*1.2*	*1.1*	*1.0*	*1.3*	*1.3*	*1.0*

Note:

(*) Index numbers of growth deflated by the corresponding national index.

Source: Author's calculations.

Table 4.2 Firms' growth (*) in selected IDs between 1961 and 1996

	51–61	61–71	71–81	81–91	61–91	61–96	91–96
Arzignano	0.5	1.4	1.7	1.0	2.5	2.9	1.2
Santa Croce	1.8	1.5	0.8	0.9	1.0	0.9	0.9
Solofra	1.0	1.8	1.3	0.7	1.8	2.6	1.5
Vigevano	1.0	1.0	1.4	0.7	1.1	0.9	0.8
Porto S.Elpidio	1.8	1.9	2.2	1.1	4.6	4.5	0.9
Casarano	0.7	1.4	1.1	0.7	1.0	2.1	2.0
Bassano	0.3	4.2	2.6	1.3	6.9	8.0	1.1
Marostica	1.1	1.7	1.9	1.0	3.0	2.0	0.7
Sassuolo	3.4	2.1	1.2	0.9	2.3	1.9	0.9
Civitacastellana	1.1	1.2	2.0	0.6	1.5	1.4	1.0
Cossato	1.9	1.6	1.1	0.8	1.4	1.0	0.7
Prato	8.1	1.2	1.1	0.8	1.1	0.8	0.7
Giulianova	1.1	0.9	1.2	1.2	1.2	1.3	0.9
Ostiglia	0.2	0.6	2.6	1.0	1.6	1.2	0.8
Carpi	0.6	3.3	1.8	0.7	4.2	2.4	0.6
Ascoli Piceno	1.2	1.1	1.0	1.6	1.6	1.8	1.0
Montebelluna	0.4	1.5	5.0	1.3	10.1	10.3	1.0
Civitanova	0.8	2.6	2.7	0.5	3.8	9.5	2.3
Barletta	0.7	0.9	2.0	2.5	4.2	4.5	1.0
Pesaro	1.0	2.3	1.4	1.6	2.5	2.5	1.0
Suzzara	0.1	1.9	0.7	1.2	1.6	1.3	0.8
Guastalla	0.1	2.0	1.5	0.8	2.3	1.6	0.7
Cento	0.1	2.1	3.1	0.5	3.6	1.8	0.5
Matera	0.3	0.5	0.9	3.3	0.6	0.9	1.4
Desio	1.4	1.1	0.8	1.1	0.5	0.4	0.8
Oderzo	0.3	2.6	1.9	1.7	4.3	5.1	1.2
Poggibonsi	0.8	1.9	0.8	1.6	1.1	1.1	0.9
Schio	1.2	0.7	1.4	1.1	1.0	0.7	0.7
S. B. Tronto	0.9	1.0	1.1	1.3	1.5	1.2	0.7
S.M. Cavoti	0.4	1.2	0.6	2.2	1.7	2.2	1.1
Palazzolo	0.3	1.9	1.3	1.4	3.6	2.4	0.7
Senigallia	0.7	1.1	1.0	1.4	1.6	1.6	0.8
Putignano	0.8	2.2	1.1	1.3	3.2	4.1	1.1
S.G. Ilarione	0.4	1.8	5.4	1.9	17.9	18.7	1.0
Montecatini T.	0.5	1.8	2.5	1.0	4.3	4.2	0.9
Fermo	1.0	2.2	3.0	1.2	7.4	7.5	0.9
Guardiagrele	0.6	0.6	1.0	1.2	0.8	1.2	1.4
Valpolicella	1.7	1.8	1.2	1.1	2.3	2.3	1.0
Castellarano	1.6	3.6	2.5	0.7	6.6	4.1	0.6
Average	*1.4*	*1.3*	*1.3*	*0.9*	*1.2*	*1.0*	*0.9*

Note:
(*) Index numbers of growth deflated by the corresponding national index.

Source: Author's calculations.

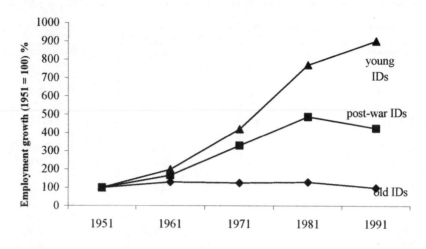

Source: Author's calculations.

Figure 4.1 Patterns of growth of selected industrial districts, 1951–96

4.3.   THE RELATIONSHIP BETWEEN ECONOMIES OF AGGLOMERATION, COMPETITION AND GROWTH

As mentioned in the survey of the literature, the economic rationale of IDs resides in external economies and economies of agglomeration. Along Marshallian lines, the agglomeration of firms and people produces both static and dynamic external economies. Growth is to be expected where firms are concentrated. The specialization of capital or human resources and the diffusion of knowledge in an agglomerated area produce increasing returns, which attract new entrants (entrepreneurs) and increase the number of employees (growth of incumbent firms). Another hypothesis put forward in the literature on IDs concerns the existence of intra-industry externalities. The growth of one specialized industry engenders the birth of other firms specialized in the production of complementary products or services, or in instrumental goods (machines and tools).

Knowledge spillovers among firms in an industry or among households in a city have been renamed recently 'Marshall–Arrow–Romer (MAR) externalities'. After Marshall, Arrow (1962) presented an early formalization, and a paper by Romer (1986) further contributed to an approach that predicted regionally specialized industries which grow faster because neighbouring firms are better able to learn from each other than geographically isolated firms. In contrast, Jacobs' theory (1969) predicts that industries located in areas of high industrial diversification will grow faster. The MAR theory also predicts, like Schumpeter, that local monopoly is more conducive to growth than local competition, because local monopoly restricts flows of ideas to others and thus enables externalities to be internalized by the innovator. When externalities are internalized, innovation and growth accelerate (Glaeser et al., 1992). This view contrasts with that of other authors (Asheim, 1994; Bellandi, 1992, who maintain that local competition, as opposed to local monopoly, fosters the pursuit and rapid adoption of innovation. Generally speaking, however, the externality hypothesis cannot be tested, because it is difficult to distinguish technological externalities from more traditional Marshallian ones; a point also made by Krugman. Moreover, whilst technological externalities may be considered substantial in areas like Silicon Valley or other technological IDs (Saxenian, 1994), our sample mainly consists of traditional industries, where spillovers largely concern tacit know-how or a combination of context-related and codified knowledge.

The relationship between agglomeration and growth in Italian IDs and elsewhere has not been studied extensively. The few works available (Cainelli and Leoncini, 1999; Forni and Paba, 1997) fail to use an appropriate unit of observation (they refer mainly to the Italian 'province'). The study by Cainelli and Leoncini shows that employment is negatively related to either specialization or variety, which suggests the presence of interfirm rather than intrafirm externalities. External demand measured by employment growth at national level, and competition – as measured by average size of firms – are instead very significant. The results confirm neither the MAR nor Jacobs' hypothesis. Either specialization or variety has a negative impact on growth. Conversely, Italian development (at the provincial level) is apparently related to the spillovers of agglomeration due to competition among firms in areas characterized by modest specialization and high inter-industry variety. These results, however, have much to do with the used specification of the models and variables, the spans of analysis and the econometric methods used.

Should methodological improvements be made, a critical concern will be whether the relationship between the proximity of firms and people can be expected to remain constantly of the same sign and intensity, or whether some sort of lifecycle of development operates in agglomerated areas. This hypothesis has yet to be tested in the empirical literature.

After showing that IDs grow more than non-IDs, in what follows we shall examine the various factors that may be responsible for the different rates of growth achieved by IDs. We shall rely on the hypothesis that externalities, including spillovers of (tacit) knowledge, are affected by proximity and by the market structure. To verify the MAR versus the Jacobs approach, we shall look at the correlation values among rates of growth, average size of firms and degree of competition (measured by the number of firms in the localized industry).

Employment growth may derive from either the extent of entry or the growth of incumbent firms. The stock rather than flow nature of ISTAT data precludes distinction between these two effects.[4] We shall therefore assume that the entry/exit of firms and the increase/decrease of employment are of the same proportions in each period of observation.[5]

As regards the relationship between employment growth and economies of agglomeration, the correlation values are illustrated in Table 4.3. Growth has been calculated for each of the ten-year inter-Census periods, between 1951 and 1991 and between 1991 and 1996, and for the longer period 1961–91. For each decade, the relative growth indicators have been correlated to the explanatory variables at the beginning of that decade. Similarly, the rate of variation in the period 1961–96 has been correlated to 1961 variables. In order to avoid a 'size' effect – that is, a high percentage variation linked with very small absolute variations – the growth indicator *vale* has been calculated in logarithms. Also, the variables with the highest standard deviation, such as *finh*, *firm* and *empl*, have been calculated in logarithms in order to compress a scale effect.

The first thing to note is that growth reacts differently to the same factors in different periods of time, since the sign and the value of correlation are not the same for each of the four ten-year periods considered. The year 1981 appears to be a turning point in the relationship between growth and the agglomeration and competition indicators, given that the signs of correlation – though not always significant – are the same for all the variables between 1961–71 and 1981–91, but not between 1951–61 and 1991–96. The variable *size* is weakly significant owing to its lower variance.

Table 4.3 Correlation values among employment growth, agglomeration, specialization and competition, 1951–96

Growth Indicators	Agglomeration and competition indicators					
	Ln(*finh*)	Ln(*einh*)	HH	Ln(*firm*)	Ln(*empl*)	Size
Lnvale 51–61	−0.2	−0.3	−0.2	0.3	0.3	0.0
Lnvale 61–71	0.2	0.2	−0.2	−0.1	0.1	0.1
Lnvale 71–81	0.4	0.5	−0.4	−0.2	−0.5	−0.3
Lnvale 81–91	0.5	0.6	−0.4	−0.4	−0.5	−0.2
Lnvale 91–96	0.0	0.0	0.2	−0.2	−0.1	0.2
Lnvale 61–91	0.4	0.4	−0.5	−0.2	−0.3	−0.2

Source: Author's calculations.

The results also show that specialization,[6] density of firms and stock of firms and employees are negatively (or insignificantly) related to growth over the period 1951–96. Positive feedback in agglomeration processes may therefore not be expected to persist. Indeed, beyond a certain point congestion reduces the attractiveness of an existing agglomeration for new entrants – particularly if the specialization industry is entering a maturity phase in which technological or market opportunities are almost fully exploited. Growth in the period between 1971 and 1991 is also negatively correlated with the variables measuring the degree of competition (*firm*) and average size of firms (*size*). Overall, these results highlight the marked dynamism of the less industrialized areas in the sample. When the correlation values are calculated for each of the three sets of IDs divided according to their age of formation, the results are slightly different).

According to these results, the correlation values between growth and agglomeration are high for the first years until 1981 for both old and post-war IDs, and negative for young IDs. A specular situation characterizes the decade between 1981 and 1991. The correlation signs of the variable related to employment (*empl*) seem to suggest that the role of agglomeration and specialization is stronger or positive only in an ID's (and industry's) first stage of development, while it declines in importance when the industry reaches maturity. Similarly, in the period of an ID's maturity, a high rate of specialization or a large scale of industry is not a necessary condition for growth. The maturity of an ID coincides with a stage at which fewer new firms are born and the growth externality for incumbent firms perhaps no longer operates. However, even if employment decreases, this in itself does not necessarily imply decline; rather, it may simply imply stabilization at a particular size (Baptista, 2000). Since a decrease in employment may derive from a rise in productivity rates, it can also be paired with the growth of more structured firms, thus signalling that processes of organizational restructuring are at work.

We may therefore conclude that neither agglomeration nor specialization factors induce one industry to grow faster than others: the history of the area has to be taken into account. In our sample, a distinction has been drawn among areas the origins of which date back to the 1970s, others which arose just after the Second World War, and a further few which began two centuries ago. The correlation values may therefore be appraised with respect to each of these groups separately. Any test of the MAR versus Jacobs hypothesis requires preliminary verification that the sample selected is homogeneous with respect to the age of formation of the industry under investigation.

The correlation values between the growth of the leading industry and the growth of ancillary industries provide a first insight into the effects of dynamic economies of agglomeration on other industries (inter-industry externalities). The results show a weak although positive relationship (Table

4.4). Generally speaking, however, specialization has been more pronounced than diversification: the Herfindhal index increased by more than 45 per cent between 1961 and 1996.

In the same period, one finds that the growth of the specialization industry has instead a marked ability to drive the development of machinery manufacture, at least in those locations where the latter was present in 1951. This result seems to confirm that an increase in the downstream industry (the user) induces the upstream industry to produce on a more efficient scale by enlarging the market for the machines and tools that it uses. It is also interesting to note that the positive correlation is more pronounced in the period 1971–81; that is, when the externalities of specialization were more developed in the more mature IDs – those in which metalworking activities had been present since 1951. This period also coincides with the most rapid growth periods for most of the IDs (see Table 4.2). A strong complementary mechanical industry in IDs specialized in consumption goods is not a constant feature of the sample, which indicates that the full range of external economies may not develop despite the strong agglomeration or specialization of an industry. Even areas characterized by a high density of firms and employees, or by specialization in fashionwear production, have been unable to attract or to stimulate the formation of an industry for instrumental mechanical goods. This is true of localities in which there has been no mechanical engineering tradition in the past (starting from the 1951 census year), cases in point being the IDs located in the Marche or most of the southern regions. The cases where a mechanical industry specialized in the production of instrumental goods for the specialization industry has developed comprise all the historical IDs (Cossato, Vigevano, Desio, Prato, Schio), Pesaro – which has a long-standing shipbuilding industry – Poggibonsi, Palazzolo and all the Emilian IDs, which are located in a region

Table 4.4 Correlation values between rates of growth in the specialization industry and correlated industries, 1951–91

Growth indicators in logarithms	Ancillary industries (*)	Mechanical industry
1961–71	0.0	0.1
1971–81	−0.1	0.4
1981–91	−0.1	0.3
1951–96	0.1	0.4
1961–91	0.1	0.5

Note:
(*) Ancillary industries have been specified in Chapter 2, note n. 9.

Source: Author's calculations.

with a solid mechanical tradition.

The rate of diffusion of mechanical industry has been rapid in these areas, perhaps also because of cooperative interactions between the users and producers of the same machine.

4.4. PATTERNS OF GROWTH AND INTERFIRM EVOLUTION IN INDUSTRIAL DISTRICTS

4.4.1. Prerequisites of Industrial Districts' Formation

This section analyses the origins of industrial development in IDs by examining the mechanisms of skills formation and entrepreneurship diffusion. It therefore focuses on the 'supply side' of entrepreneurship in IDs, and on the 'demand-side' factors that have favoured the take-off of IDs in Italy. According to the historical evidence available, and in the light of the indicators of growth, proximity and specialization that have been calculated, the areas studied display distinct patterns of entrepreneurial development.

Investigation by historians and sociologists of Italian IDs has well documented the specific historical circumstances in which IDs located in the central and northern regions first arose. The present study covers a sample of IDs located throughout Italy and therefore points to a broader set of conditions or prerequisites that explain the formation of IDs in northern as well as southern Italy. For non-Italian readers, it may be useful to summarize the 'push' factors of entrepreneurship in order to point to the possible reproducibility of IDs in other national contexts.

Important social changes took place in Italy between 1951 and 1961, together with rapid industrialization. The most important social change was the disappearance of the metayage system of land-tenure (share-cropping) that had prevailed for centuries in Emilia-Romagna, Marche, Tuscany, Umbria and Veneto. Metayage, large estates ('latifondo') and small-scale farming were the prevailing land tenure systems in Italy before the Second World War. Under the first system, the farmer used the owner's land and gave the owner half the crop in return. On the large estates the owner hired wage-earners to cultivate his or her generally extensive landholdings, while in the third system the owner of a generally small estate was also the farmer. The large-estate system was very widespread in the *Mezzogiorno* until the agrarian reforms enacted in 1950.

According to some scholars (Paci, 1982), the origins of the large entrepreneurial class in Marchisan industry, and also of its marked flexibility, lie in the metayage 'extended family' (see also Section 5.2). In fact, former metayers became used to acting as capitalists. Since they were obliged to share their crops with the owner, the metayers developed such entrepreneurial qualities as a rational and acquisitive mentality, and a penchant for saving and accumulation. In their race with the owners, they were forced to refine their managerial abilities, making the most efficient and flexible use of the human resources available in their large families. According to Census figures (ISTAT, various years), in 1951 there was a proportion of 27.5 per cent of extended families in north-eastern regions (27.1 per cent in the Marche region, 22.6 in Emilia, 22 in Veneto) compared to a proportion of 15.1 in Campania or 10.9 per cent in Puglia.

Apart from its effects on industrial or capitalist skills, the system of land tenure and its subsequent reform had effects on accumulation. Once many of the landlords – whose estates were often worked by ten to twenty sharecroppers – were freed from the old system, following the agrarian reform in 1951, they unified their lands into a single capitalist farm. Some of the minor landlords, almost all of whom belonged to the urban bourgeoisie, preferred to keep their farms as second-string businesses run by salaried managers. All the remaining proprietors, large and small, sold their land to the peasants. These sales, which were in some cases preceded by a period of rental, selected out a broad stratum of highly skilled peasants. In the southern regions, agrarian reform had different effects, because the importance of large and medium landed property remained unchanged; the small properties freed by migration have in practice remained unsold and have often been left uncultivated (Brusco, 1982).

Besides metayage, another prerequisite for the emergence of IDs has been the extensive presence of the handicraft activities traditional in all the villages and urban centres of these areas where the local bourgeoisie spent their rent, fuelling demand for high-quality consumption goods. Brusco (1982) has also emphasized industrial factors as well; for instance, the large manufacturing firms in the Emilia Romagna region that fuelled the technical skills of many self-employed metalworkers some decades later.

Let us now examine IDs' patterns of development with respect to our sample, which includes southern areas that arose on a different basis from those considered by the literature so far. By and large, after the Second World War the pool of resources and the heritage of knowledge, abilities and skills were diversified in the areas considered in the sample, mirroring differences within the various macro regions of Italy.

Most of the areas in the sample sprang from artisan traditions, although of differing depth (all the clothing, footwear and furniture districts in the Marche region, Desio, Palazzolo, Vigevano, Montebelluna, Bassano, Santa Croce, Arzignano, Prato, Carpi, Solofra and Barletta). Industrial origin, linked to the existence of large mechanical engineering factories at the beginning of the twentieth century or just after the Second World War, is typical of all the Emilian districts (Cento, Guastalla, Sassuolo, Suzzara and Castellarano), as Brusco has pointed out. Other areas, notably Civitacastellana, Ascoli Piceno, and Palazzolo, were also once sites of large firms which transmitted the knowledge that proved so valuable for industrialization after the post-war period. The other areas resulted from a combination of an artisan tradition and the presence of big firms, or else they developed on the initiative of entrepreneurs or traders. These 'pioneers' were either local (as in the cases of Matera, Putignano and Casarano), or came from neighbouring areas, from where they moved in order to exploit less costly inputs, labour or land (for example, Giulianova, San G. Ilarione).

In some cases, the manufacturing tradition was not strictly related to the specialization that prevailed in the post-war period, but it proved eminently suitable for different items of production. Arzignano specialized in silk manufacturing and silkworm breeding, but in the wake of the crisis that hit the silk industry between the two wars, the silk factories were forced to close down. Given the large numbers of workers and the availability of water, they were encouraged to reorganize and to convert into tanneries. The Carpi knitwear industry and the mechanical IDs flourished in an area where most workers were employed in hemp preparation, straw processing and straw-hat manufacture. Poggibonsi, by contrast, developed an important industry of caravan construction, relying on its tradition in both furniture and metalworking. This seems to indicate that the underlying 'competencies' of one territory may explain its specialization for a longer period of time.

4.4.2. Three Distinctive Growth Patterns of Industrial Districts
Three different and quite generalizable patterns of development can be distinguished in the sample. They can be labelled as follows:

- artisan;
- industrial (due to the existence of 'incubating'[7] industrial firms);
- pioneering or Schumpeterian (due to the initiative of immigrants or pioneers).

Although a commercial or agricultural background to entrepreneurship is also apparent, we only mention the main sources here. The first two patterns involve knowledge and skills embodied in a myriad of individuals; in the third case skills are embodied in only one or a few individuals, who then create or stimulate the formation of organizations (by imitative processes) in which their expertise is diffused and transmitted to their collaborators.

Self-employment motivations appear to underline the formation of new firms in all the IDs, stemming from the desire either to exploit experience acquired in a previous job as dependent workers or to gain independence. The desire of many entrepreneurs for independence was fuelled by the diffusion among the local population of anarchic or communist ideologies, either in the Tuscany and Emilian districts, or in Civitacastellana, loath to accept subordinate employment. These individual motives, combined with the favourable local conditions already mentioned, led to the creation of numerous firms, often family-owned or run as cooperatives.

The patterns just described display the 'push' factors of entrepreneurship, rather than its 'pull' factors. Historical facts bolstering the growth of IDs have been the post-war crisis of the large manufacturers specialized in war production or large-batch mass production; and the rapid growth of either domestic or international demand. The post-war period is an appropriate starting-point for evaluation of the 'initial conditions' of industrial development in IDs. At that time, Italy embarked on a rapid and extended process of industrialization, which substantially increased per capita income and led to the number of employees in manufacturing industries in 1951 having doubled by 1971. The post-war phase of 'Ricostruzione' (Reconstruction) engendered large demand for consumption goods like clothing, ceramics and furniture, which many areas with a long tradition in the manufacturing of house and personal goods could rapidly satisfy. This growth opportunity also arose thanks to the withdrawal of competing European countries from traditional industries.

After the Second World War, firms in the various sectors spread through imitation and also thanks to relatively easy access to the sector (limited financial impact, low environmental restraints, available land and raw materials, and so on). Spin-offs by ex-workers occurred, in some cases allegedly encouraged by the manufacturers (tanneries, wool mills, and so on) themselves, who provided work or granted the use of machinery to the new enterprise. In her post-war history of Prato, Dei Ottati (1994) documents loans of capital by large woolmills in Prato, but the literature confirms that this practice concerned most IDs, including those in the southern regions.

The boom years for most industries came with the 1970s (Table 4.2) when firms in clothing and furniture IDs recorded growth in relative terms of 256 and 140 per cent, and employees increased by 92 and 54 per cent, respectively. Lower, but nevertheless remarkable rates of growth, were achieved by machinery, textiles and furniture IDs.

Of the classic factors of localization, the availability of natural resources (the abundance of water in all the tanning IDs and in Biella-Cossato or Schio, kaolin in Sassuolo, marble in Valpolicella, and so on) or closeness to important final markets (for example, Rome for Civitacastellana, Venice for Bassano-Marostica, Milan for the Brianza area) explain the birth of numerous IDs. These factors initially contributed to the specialization of areas, but not to their growth in following years. In most cases, the development of industry freed itself from the initial localization conditions and agglomeration forces, together with more specific historical circumstances, so that entrepreneurial patterns of development came to the fore. This observation seems to support, although in a very anecdotal manner, the 'new economic geography' claim about the cumulativeness of the processes of development. The theory of entrepreneurship is better able than the theory of localization to explain the evolution of IDs, since the growth factors were endogenous to the places in which the agglomerated industries first arose.

When international demand increased after the Second World War, different places had a different heritage in terms of industrial firms and related capabilities, while the sources of seed finance for the new ventures were not available in all the locations due to a different history and rural contractual arrangements and infrastructures. This explains why not all the areas have shared evenly in the process of growth.

Industrial skills varied considerably across Italian territory just after the Second World War. While the northern regions included areas of centuries-long tradition like Biella, Brianza and Schio (where the Italian industrial revolution took place), no comparable area existed in southern regions. This finding may contrast with some recent contributions showing that in 1951 southern areas hosted an even higher number of IDs than northern ones and that these districts disappeared in the following decades as a result, according to the authors, of competition by other IDs located in northern and central regions of Italy and the loss of human capital in the South following massive migration (Brusco and Paba, 1997; Cersosimo, 2000; Viesti, 2000).[8]

Our point is that the southern IDs we considered were on average weaker than northern ones, and this rather being a bias of our sample (we did not analyze all the southern territory) may highlight another feature of the *vexata questio* of southern development. On average, IDs located in central-southern areas had 130 plants and employed 866 units in the leading industry in 1951, with an average workforce of fewer than six employees. The corresponding average in northern Italy was 453 plants and 2 185 units with an average plant size of 10.7 employees. While areas in the north were typically diversified in several manufacturing industries, southern areas were notable for their almost complete lack of mechanical industries (Tables 4.5 and 4.6). The lower average size of businesses in southern IDs testifies to their structural weakness in comparison to the north and highlights the unevenness of industrial development in Italy. This is not to overlook the fact that even in northern regions, such as Ostiglia and S.G. Ilarione, there were rural areas lacking robust industrial firms.

It is, however, true that the performance of our IDs also worsened in the following decade. The number of industries engaged in the production of consumption goods (textiles, clothing, footwear, food, wood and furniture) decreased by 15 per cent between 1951 and 1961, compared to an average increase of 30 per cent in the northern IDs included in the sample. The areas included in the sample, however, can be considered the more successful cases in the south, given that they prospered in following decades, while most of the other IDs surveyed by Brusco and Paba disappeared.

Understanding of this process may offer an instructive lesson for less industrialized regions or countries in the world. As described by Cersosimo (2000), at the beginning of the 1950s, the southern Italy economy was largely a closed market. The local production of consumption goods was geared mainly to local demand. The low per capita income of the local population and an inadequate transport network meant that the southern market had little attraction for producers and sellers located in other parts of Italy. Between 1951 and 1961, a number of important events changed the initial conditions and had a pronounced effect on development in the years that followed. New roads were built, per capita income increased due to national transfers and remittances by emigrants, and consumption by the southern population came increasingly to resemble that in the northern regions, as a result *inter alia* of the spread of new media like radio and television. Within a decade, the opening up of the southern market pushed out those local artisan manufacturers unable to compete with cheaper and more effective products from northern Italy.

A lesson to be learnt from Italy's experience that is applicable to less developed countries seems to be that a protectionist policy for a nascent industry may be effective. This implies not a protectionist policy in itself, which would have isolated the south from external trade, but a selective policy intended to strengthen local seeds of industrial development and favour commercial openness in a gradual manner. This 'wisdom of hindsight', however, may be difficult to apply to southern Italian areas in their present state, since the factors in the competitiveness of Italian economy, and its role in the international division of labour, have profoundly changed. Moreover, there is no guarantee that 'enclaves' of traditional industries based on cheaper productions in an integrated national context of more sophisticated consumption models can be sustainable. Two solutions might be envisaged in this regard. One coincides with the promotion of the artisan content of production linked to local culture and history in competition with more standardized products, although the value added of these activities will not be high. A second alternative is to foster a model of industrialization in Mediterranean or eastern Europe countries that acts as a vehicle for the diffusion of models of consumption similar to those followed by Italy. The experience of Italy may prove useful for countries at different stages of development and with different rankings in the international division of labour. A profitable exchange of information and resources within Italy, as well as between Italy and other countries, can be imagined in this regard.

Table 4.5 Diffusion of industries in selected northern and central industrial districts in 1951

	Leading industry			Mechanical industry (*)	
	Local units	Employees	Average Size	Local units	Employees
Arzignano	19	361	19.0	11	382
Santa Croce	315	154	4.9	3	84
Vigevano	1153	8874	7.7	48	658
Porto Sant'Elpidio	359	1160	3.2	1	5
Bassano	131	480	3.7	115	2518
Marostica	44	1036	23.5	12	97
Sassuolo	23	2353	102.3	237	990
Cossato	205	23963	116.9	12	133
Prato	777	21315	27.4	13	239
Ostiglia	18	27	1.5	5	52
Carpi	99	316	3.2	23	380
Montebelluna	376	1811	4.8	9	159
Civitanova	191	484	2.5	5	56
Pesaro	164	520	3.2	187	1095
Suzzara	354	1918	5.4	234	1300
Guastalla	550	1029	1.9	123	493
Cento	302	1393	4.6	121	848
Desio	3700	15000	4.1	335	7511
Oderzo	73	238	3.3	60	323
Poggibonsi	165	473	2.9	160	707
Schio	79	7258	91.9	94	1830
S.B.Tronto	410	555	1.4	91	188
Palazzolo	224	1587	7.1	141	2889
Senigallia	277	441	1.6	11	50
S.G. Ilarione	31	48	1.5	2	6
Montecatini T.	1687	7576	4.5	43	421
Fermo	243	362	1.5	155	283
Valpolicella	39	600	15.4	78	310
Castellarano	4	107	26.8	2	38
TOTAL	**12012**	**102825**	**8.6**	**2331**	**24045**
Average	*414*	*3546*	*8.6*	*80*	*829*

Note:

(*) Includes machine shops.

Source: Author's calculations on ISTAT (census data).

Table 4.6 Diffusion of industries in southern industrial districts in 1951

	Leading industry			Mechanical industry (*)	
	Local units	Employees	Average Size	Local units	Employees
Solofra	78	342	4.4	1	1
Casarano	215	413	1.9	4	5
Civitacastellana	35	1138	32.5	1	1
Giulianova	41	106	2.6	5	10
Val Vibrata	297	405	1.4	4	9
Barletta	326	701	2.2	1	35
Matera	74	160	2.2	1	25
S.M. Cavoti	121	154	1.3	1	1
Putignano	191	656	3.4	149	230
Guardiagrele	102	154	1.5	1	2
TOTAL	**1480**	**4229**	**2.9**	**168**	**319**
Average	*148*	*423*	*2.9*	*17*	*32*

Note:
(*) Includes machine shops.

Source: Author's calculations on ISTAT (census data).

4.4.3.   The Patterns of Development of Centre-Southern Industrial Districts

As already mentioned, almost all the southern IDs, with the exception of Solofra and those with a smaller number of employees in 1951, are clustered in the typology of 'embryonic IDs' in 1991 (Chapter 3). The specific circumstances and the driving forces where these IDs have organized and then developed according to different entrepreneurial patterns warrant discussion, since they may offer insights for foreign scholars interested in the promotion of IDs.

The recent development of these areas, together with other historical circumstances, explains their prevalent specialization in mass production, the inefficiency of their mechanisms of local accumulation or their generally more vertically integrated structure.

Civitacastellana (ceramics) acquired technical competence from the location in the area since the nineteenth century of medium-sized firms attracted by positive localization factors (the availability of inputs and proximity to the large market of Rome). Artisanship was strong in the past, although at the beginning of the century there were no native entrepreneurs in the area; most of them came from abroad or from other provinces. After the Second World War, many ex-workers created their own enterprises, which heightened the specialization of the town of Civitacastellana, although the surrounding area saw little diffusion of entrepreneurship.

The development of the footwear industry in Barletta was consequent on the founding of large footwear firms in the 1960s which exported to US markets or on the transformation of artisan firms that survived after having grown to more industrial size. The Barletta area was favoured by external investors, both because of its good geographical position and because of its already existing artisan tradition. However, the origins of entrepreneurship in the area need to be differentiated, since investors were either local and external landowners, or else traders (wholesalers or retailers), typical of an area that has traditionally been commercially oriented. This factor may partly explain why local production gradually became mechanized and specialized in large batches (mass production). Proximity was a more efficient vehicle for the diffusion of technological innovation embodied in machinery than for the diffusion of tacit knowledge.

A similar pattern is apparent in Matera (furniture), where a Mr Natuzzi, after serving an apprenticeship in Brianza – the area in which the furniture ID of Desio is located – returned to Matera and founded a firm (whose distribution chain is presently known with the brand name Divani&Divani) that is now a case study in many Italian books on management.

The history of Putignano, too, is linked to the name of an entrepreneur, Cesare Contegiacomo, whose first company, created in 1906, incubated many of those who would become owners of local clothing mills in following decades (Comei, 2000; Viesti, 2000).

The pioneer route may be an interesting although unpredictable opportunity of development for less developed regions or countries. The pioneers in Matera or Casarano acquired their knowledge in contexts different from their native ones. When they returned to their home towns and invested in their own factories, they played an important role in diffusing information and encouraging workers to create their own enterprises.

In the remaining southern areas of Ascoli Piceno, Giulianova, Guardiagrele and San Marco dei Cavoti, an artisan tradition in shoe manufacturing or dressmaking began in the 1940s, which was then – unlike in other cases – reinforced by decentralization or by the establishment of northern or even multinational companies in the following decades. Ascoli Piceno and Giulianova, in particular, saw the arrival of large manufacturers (for example, Maglificio Gran Sasso, Casucci Jeans) in the 1950s, attracted by the area's favourable natural and institutional localization factors (financial incentives), with controversial consequences for ensuing development (see Chapter 3). These firms grew until they became leaders of their sectors. From the outset, they pursued a policy of decentralization, which subsequently extended to include subcontracting firms, which, in their turn, commissioned work from other firms of smaller size.

As already mentioned in Chapter 3, firms in southern IDs tend to be relatively larger and more vertically integrated. The recent historical manufacturing tradition or specialization of southern IDs may also explain why they increasingly specialize in large batches of production rather than in high-quality and distinctive products.

Neither Casarano nor Barletta have gained a reputation in Italy for a particular quality of their products. These areas specialize in the production of more standardized items that do not require high worker skills, given that they comprise a lesser amount of tacit knowledge and can be produced by mechanized processes. Casarano has followed a different pattern of expansion than many. In the 1950s a substantial number of young workers – today at the helm of the largest firms in the area which also achieved leading positions nationwide – moved to other regions of Italy rich with job opportunities, such as Vigevano. Anticipating the large-scale migration from the area throughout the post-war period, they acquired their shoemaking skills. On their return, they imparted vital impetus to the area's specialization in shoe manufacturing. It is interesting to note how local networks based on personal relationships have proved successful in directing migration towards the same destination as in the past, and how this process has positively influenced the area's development. Convenience factors in the area were the ample availability of labour, especially female – because male workers were migrating – able to supplement their low wages with agricultural work (and public subsidies) and variable working hours.

The minor reliance of final firms on external suppliers has more to do with minor externalities than with the cultural propensities of the local population, as held by the canonical literature. The emphasis placed here on a historical heritage of skills and abilities enables a reappraisal of the role of cooperation and the 'mutual trust and knowledge' deemed crucial for the growth of IDs. If we regard cooperation and trust as a self-sufficient explanation for economic development in areas of the centre-north, we must then state that the lack of real entrepreneurship in the south is mainly the result of distrust and 'amoral familism' (Banfield 1958, quoted in Putnam, 1993). Instead, it seems that a more complex interrelation of diverse factors is at work. Opportunism does not seem to play a great role when one has to rely on others' ability or competence to fulfil a task. Take, for example, the case of one firm trusting another to succeed in a certain innovation, perhaps because of the proven record of the latter. Contingencies might prove more complicated than expected. The trusted person thus fails to honour the contract not because of opportunism but because he or she wrongly estimates the difficulties and skills required. We do well, as suggested by Luhmann (1988), to distinguish between *confidence*, stemming from ability, and *trust*, based instead on underlying disposition or motivation.

The 'stock' of skills and knowledge – that is, its level when a process of demand growth starts – affects the model of labour division and the overall evolution of local systems of production. In the case of southern IDs, the infrequent use of external workers seems due more to a lack of confidence in the abilities of third parties than to a fear of opportunistic behaviour. The scarce availability of competencies and technical skills makes the entrepreneurial activity more risky and increases the cost of information for economic actors, two factors both underlined in orthodox explanations of vertical integration (see, for example, Perry, 1988).

There are various constraints imposed on the process of evolution of IDs by historical contingencies, which make predictions – for the purpose of economic development planning – a risky undertaking. Even if two areas have similar initial conditions or face common exogenous (demand and technology) circumstances, they may evolve along a different pattern. By way of an initial conclusion, vertical cooperation among firms specialized in different phases of production is influenced by different historical and technical factors. The spread of skills affects the willingness to assign part of the production plan to external firms. Moreover, the availability of capital funds is a prerequisite for the formation of new firms.

4.4.5. The Hypothesis of the Industrial District Life Cycle *à la* Stigler

Thus far we have looked at the evolution of IDs in terms of employment and firms' growth only. Another question that has emerged recently in the literature on IDs is the existence of a life-cycle where the different stages of development correspond to different degrees of labour division. At a macroeconomic level, it is important to gauge whether or not the different phases of the economic cycle affect the degree of vertical integration of IDs. As is widely known, the Stigler model prescribes that vertical disintegration is the typical development in growing industries and vertical integration in declining industries (Stigler, 1951). In a further refinement of this model, Adelman (1958) adds the rate of growth of demand as an explanatory cause of the degree of vertical integration during different phases, while other authors have claimed that technological factors are more influential. Stigler cites external economies as a factor facilitating the disintegration of an industry but he definitely concentrates on the 'pull' or demand factors of growth. The data available on the evolution of ID industries between 1951 and 1991, however, hardly lend themselves to use in a life-cycle model. Although more recent census data are broken down at a four-digit level, the comparable data for the period 1951–91 recently issued by ISTAT (1999) are at a two-digit level of classification and therefore do not permit us to test whether the degree of labour division has varied during different phases of the economic cycle. Moreover, the model would require data on the added value or production achieved by the manufacturing industries, data which have been available only since the 1990s. It is true that the size of an industry in terms of employment in an ID gives clues to the degree of labour division, but it may not be taken as an accurate measure, considering also that informal relationships of control may exist between firms specialized in different industries. We have already mentioned the considerable role of effervescent demand in the 1960s in fostering the formation and growth of IDs, but the positive phase of the economic cycle coincided with different stages of development within our sample of IDs. We had evidence that a common phase of development does not have similar effects on all IDs. A phase of demand growth may coincide with a shrinkage in the number of firms in a more mature ID, and an increase in a southern ID. This has consequences for the effectiveness of economic policies since it points to a regionally/locally diversified impact. However, caution is necessary when the relationship between the economic cycle and structural adjustments in IDs is analysed, because the demand relevant for an ID may have a different dynamic to that of the specific groups of products in which the ID is specialized.

In many cases, IDs do not alter their internal structure and degree of vertical division. Instead, they increase the number of specializations that are locally present. In Marostica, the use of external suppliers has changed only slightly over time. In Desio, the organization of production, the features of entrepreneurs and the relationships among firms have remained almost unaltered, and no form of vertical division of labour has developed. Very small firms began as autonomous, non-limited companies, and so they have remained. The start-up of ancillary productions like upholstery, metal and marble has completed the range of locally available products but it has not altered the local model of labour division. At the beginning of the 1990s, many firms specialized in tailor-made furniture, while some started to work as subcontractors (Censis – Unioncamere, 1995).

Product or process innovations have changed the degree of labour division and interfirm relationships in some areas. The various patterns of labour division to be observed in Sassuolo since the Second World War have emerged as a consequence of the introduction of technological innovations in the production process. The area has moved through three different evolutionary phases characterized by the introduction of new process technologies since its initial investment in ceramics after the war. The same applies to the district of Montebelluna.

In Barletta, technological and product changes have spread very quickly among the local population because of frequent imitation: product specialization, first in leather uppers, then in coloured shoes and, latterly, for the technology of 'high-frequency' (water-jet injection) (D'Ercole, 1992).

In the restructuring of the production process following the introduction of particle-boards in Pesaro, furniture mills have outsourced many intermediate stages of production or reverted to commercial rather than manufacturing activities. In the 1980s, the emphasis shifted to higher quality. In order to more effectively carry out quality control, some operations, such as japanizing and painting – that seriously affect the quality of the final product and that previously were carried out externally – have been reintegrated. Thanks to the introduction of automation systems, which guarantee more direct and efficient control, the specialized phases (of sectioning, drilling, flanging/curling) have been reintegrated as well. This strategy has been pursued by larger furniture factories in particular, while smaller ones have recently transformed themselves into commercial firms because of difficulties in adapting to new technologies.

As for the hypothesis of an ID life-cycle, not all the cases confirm the existence of a cycle divided into distinct phases of a similar length and in a predetermined sequence. It is indubitably true that IDs evolve, but some IDs do so more rapidly and others more slowly. Growth patterns do not necessarily confirm the Stiglerian hypothesis: a growth of demand does not always coincide with decentralization or a stabilization of demand with centralization, although we are far from a rigorous testing of this model. Enterprises have thrived in some areas as a result of the demand for subcontracting work by firms located in other regions. Entrepreneurial patterns are dissimilar and this may affect subsequent development.

In some areas, like Barletta, Desio, or Putignano, firms have reverted to subcontracting, after a phase in which they worked on their own designs. Where this has occurred, firms display much higher levels of competence than in the previous phases, but they are far from being commercially autonomous.

The introduction of ready-to-make articles in Carpi decreased firms' size even further, while in Sassuolo the introduction of third firing increased the degree of verticalization. The speed with which innovations are introduced varies in the sample, and even within IDs specialized in the same industry. The furniture-manufacturing areas of Oderzo and Pesaro were very quick to introduce technological innovations, while Bassano and Desio stuck to their original specialization. Montebelluna is not a comparable case: its product specialization is unique in Italy, and therefore its rate of innovation cannot be compared to that of other footwear areas.

Comparisons among areas yields such a variegated picture that it may be hazardous to generalize on patterns of development, not least because the impact of common external technological or demand factors has differed among the various areas. A particular discriminating factor among IDs, however, seems to be their age of formation.

4.4.6. A National Network of Industrial Districts?

In view of the large number of IDs in Italy, and in some regions in particular, one may wonder whether they are not in some way connected. Actually, a web of relationships concerning the exchange of goods, information and human resources exists between the IDs located in different regions, to the point that we may envisage a national, rather than merely regional, network of IDs. The emerging industrial area of Matera buys leather from Arzignano, rather than from the closer area of Solofra, because the former is better suited to the specific needs of the local product specialization (bovine leather). Shoemakers in the Veneto region buy leather from the more high-quality artisans of Santa Croce dell'Arno, rather than from Arzignano. Manufacturers in Carpi purchase yarn from textile firms located in the distant areas of Biella and Cossato, rather than from the closer area of Prato. It is obvious, therefore, that proximity to another ID is not in itself an advantage for purchasers if the latter area does not meet specific requirements. Indeed, such proximity offers economies of purchasing to firms located in other regions, often in ID areas.

Apart from these inter-territorial linkages, a 'fetch and carry phenomenon' is apparent between northern and southern areas, where the latter inherited and renewed the traditional specialization from northern areas. Some products or specializations located in northern regions have migrated to southern regions in the last two decades. This change is also evidenced by export performance: exports of fashion goods have declined in northern IDs to the advantage of mechanical engineering exports, while they have increased in southern IDs.

Three factors may be cited in explanation of this process:

1. diseconomies of agglomeration in northern areas due to pollution effects and the lack of industrial premises or land;
2. a decrease in transportation costs between northern and southern regions;
3. a lower cost of labour per employee due to low unionization and a different equilibrium in the labour market in southern regions.

The migration of production towards southern areas is the case of the IDs of Fermo and Porto Sant'Elpidio, which are currently specialized in men's, women's and children's shoes, made from various materials, whereas until the 1970s they specialized in leisure footwear manufacturing. Such production has been almost completely abandoned and is now carried out in Southeast Asian countries or in the Barletta and Casarano areas, which are much more competitive because of cheaper labour costs.

Subcontracting firms in Giulianova, Ascoli Piceno, Guardiagrele and S.M. Cavoti receive some of their work orders from firms located in Biella, Brianza or Tuscany.

In Carpi, local independent firms have subcontracted some of their production outside the district since the 1980s. The majority of non-local subcontractors are based in Veneto and Lombardy (Mantua), where different labour-market conditions help reduce labour costs. Other reasons are unrelated to costs and prices, but instead concern the quality of services provided by workshops outside Carpi.[9]

Northern and southern areas are also linked by flows of migration; in fact, most of the industrialized areas in the north have attracted individual workers from the south. Owing to high labour demand in northern regions, this phenomenon was much more pronounced between the 1950s and the 1970s than it is today. The demand for unskilled labour in the north is now better satisfied by immigration from non-EU countries, while workers from the south tend to be uninterested in unskilled jobs. Immigrants are more willing to accept wages and conditions of life which, although poor, are superior to those available in their home countries, while this is not the case for the southern population.

NOTES

1. It has to be remarked that census data in 1951 are classified according to a less detailed code. For example, different industries are paired together as if they are one (wood and furniture, clothing and footwear, metalworking and machine shops), whereas they are rightly separated in the following Census year.

2. The data supporting this proposition may be derived from Tables 4.2 and 4.3, when the specialization industry of each ID (see Figure 2.1) is considered. A clearer illustration may be obtained from the author.

3. Young IDs: Solofra, Casarano, Bassano, Giulianova, Val Vibrata, Civitanova, Barletta, Matera, Oderzo, Poggibonsi, S.B. Tronto, S.G. Cavoti, Senigallia, Putignano, S.G. Ilarione, Fermo, Guardiagrele, Sant'Ambrogio di Valpolicella.

Post-war IDs: Arzignano, Santa Croce, Sant'Elpidio, Montebelluna, Marostica, Sassuolo, Civitacastellana, Carpi, Suzzara, Guastalla, Cento, Palazzolo, Montecatini T., Castellarano.

Historical IDs: Vigevano, Prato, Cossato, Desio, Schio.

4. ISTAT does not provide data on firms' birth and death rates. Hence, application of the concepts used, for example, by the ecological perspectives not possible. These data, however, are available from other sources, though for a shorter time span.

5. Data on firms' birth and death rates are not available for the entire sample, so it is not possible to apply any of the concepts of the ecological perspective.

6. It is useful to remember that the variable *HH* varies in the interval between 0 and 2000. The lower its value, the higher the degree of diversification; the higher its value, the higher the degree of specialization.

7. The term clearly refers to the image of 'incubator' plants used in the context of the theory on

new firms' formation. See, among others, Storey (1982).

8. This form of behaviour is not new in the area. As Brusco noted as early as 1982, 'the relationship between Modena and Reggio, on the one hand, and the neighbouring provinces on the other appears to be that of the metropolis to colony, and the two together constitute a single system' (1982, p. 171).

5. A 'Differentiated' Policy for Industrial Districts

5.1. INTRODUCTION

This chapter draws a conclusion on a workable industrial policy for IDs based on the results of our research, while, at the same time, integrating the contributions and findings of others. The features of a workable industrial policy are envisaged taking into account, first, the social and meso-institutional transformations that have occurred in IDs in the last two decades and then the available instruments of industrial policy at the national and local level. The critical social transformation that emerges from our analysis concerns the educational structure of local population, the increasing proportion of immigrants in some IDs and certain other features regarding so-called human and social capital (Coleman, 1988). Among social institutions, we consider families, schools and local banks. We reviewed, in outline form, how the institutional framework of IDs has changed in the last decades, falling short from an in depth analysis that would go beyond the remit of this book.

In the previous chapter we offered evidence that positive economic and social performance are often tied in some typologies of IDs. Here, we take a more critical view on the future competitiveness of IDs by looking more closely at some of their social and institutional features not yet mentioned. This analysis completes the picture and reveals that alongside organizational change within and between firms, some very critical transformations in people's expectations and in the social structure may influence the future viability and resilience of existing IDs. New social and economic configurations within IDs might not necessary be less competitive, provided that a coevolution of social and organizational change takes place.

The following section outlines some common social features of the IDs' sample, on the basis of the descriptive statistics and other evidence that identify the critical strengths and weakness of Italian IDs. Among these are the potential decay of social cohesion due to new cultural attitudes of young workers and incoming immigrants, an increasing tendency towards international delocation of part of local production, and the entry of foreign multinational companies (MNCs), together with substantial problems of inadequate training and education at the local level, shortage of modern infrastructures and a spoilt natural environment: all of which raise major challenges for the future of IDs.

5.2.   COMMON SOCIAL AND INSTITUTIONAL FEATURES IN INDUSTRIAL DISTRICTS

5.2.1.   Local Identity and Migration Phenomena

The presence of immigrants is a typical and distinctive feature of the most industry-oriented IDs, the local labour markets of which are close to full employment.[1] The presence of immigrants reaches considerable proportions in all the districts located in the centre-north of Italy in 1999. These IDs appear to be the most attracting areas for immigrants in Italy (the statistics do not count unofficial or not-resident immigrants) (Table 5.2). Indeed, districts have been receptive to immigrants since the Second World War, but the latter predominantly originated from the nearby countryside or southern Italy. Immigration from outside the European Union, however, falls into a different socio-economic context, coinciding with a change of jobs and the self-promotion expectations of the local population, in particular of women and young people.

Immigrant workers mainly take lower-paid and lower-skilled jobs that are also often unhealthy. The relative indicator (*immi*) is able to shed further light on the nature of production processes by pointing to zones of customized or standardized production that use unskilled labour.[2] The complementarity between migration and national employment in some IDs – as opposed to the crowding out effect observed in the labour markets of other countries – and the constant attraction of immigrants from foreign countries to most of the more industrialized IDs are indicative of new social equilibria and possible evolutionary patterns in IDs. At this stage of the development of both IDs and immigration phenomena, immigrants may create – together with the phenomena observed in the USA and France (Borja, Freeman and Katz, 1992; Tribalat et al., 1991) – downward pressure on wages in ID labour markets by hampering the technological upgrading of local production and related worker education levels. Social integration would also be questioned, requiring new mechanisms for the local regulation of informal work practices and tax evasion, or the provision of social services for new citizens.

In areas with the highest presence of immigrants, the social and economic (factory) integration of the first wave of immigrants from former Yugoslavia and Mediterranean countries can now be considered concluded. Indeed, some worker representatives in local trade unions are non-Italian nationals, and these immigrants are generally well integrated into local society as regards access to schools, public housing, and generic social services. The question arises as to whether immigrants from foreign countries will continue the local traditional specialization, given that the Italian younger generation are increasingly less attracted by their parents' jobs and are, on the contrary, oriented towards new professions. Generally speaking, communities of immigrants may inject new skills and practices into manufacturing, or even introduce new specializations, and revitalize local production by offering a new basis for local reputation and competitive advantage. In this respect, both the expectations of and attitudes to work and the qualifications of migrants have to be taken into account. The former are closely influenced by the nationality of immigrants (not so much as regards their cultural attitudes as their motivations), and by patterns of migration in terms of travel financiers and regular or irregular entry.

In the absence of systematic evidence on these matters, we may examine the particular case of Chinese migrants in 'historic' districts like Prato and Schio, and in other textile areas like Carpi and Palazzolo sull'Oglio. In the textile workshops, entire family groups are employed to meet orders in a very short delivery time. Immigrants from certain regions of China come to Italy not just to earn a wage but also to accumulate capital and to set up their own enterprises. A family that forces one of its members to emigrate must resort to illegal forms of human trafficking, which are risky and usually expensive. Moreover, the immigrant has a duty to provide economic security and prestige for himself and his/her supporting family. To this end, the immigrant integrates into the Chinese socio-economic enclave in the recipient country, comprising a system of enterprises managed by compatriots. By working for his/her relatives, who are often the main financiers of his/her emigration – at a low wage – the immigrant may gradually redeem his/her debts, and without interest. Relatives cover the newcomer's expenditures, pay for his/her food and accommodation, and obtain legal status for him/her. This 'pattern' of emigration explains why working conditions in Chinese workshops are often informal, while their Italian competitors, which instead pay regular wages, taxes and social contributions, accuse them of exploiting their workers and of practising some sort of social dumping. In the Prato district, such practices, but also those of native entrepreneurs, vitiate the climate of fair competition that the local trade associations strive to promote (Unione industriale pratese, 2000). The Carpi ID currently comprises around 300 clothing workshops, mainly 'dressmakers' owned by Chinese migrants, which have strengthened the area's specialization in the phases of sewing. Large Chinese communities specialized in clothing are also present throughout the Veneto region, and in the areas of Palazzolo and Carpi.

While the first generation of Chinese migrants has realized its ambition of setting up its own enterprises, less evidence is available on the attitudes towards self-employment of other nationalities and the social mobility of the thousands of immigrants employed in lower-skilled jobs in tanneries or mechanical firms in places like Emilia Romagna or Lombardy. It is difficult to predict what such attitudes will be because present occupations in most of the cases preclude the acquisition of entrepreneurial skills. Moreover, the barriers against entry into self-employment are today much higher than they were ten or twenty years ago, and the competition is stronger. Consequently, a process of entrepreneurial diffusion along the lines followed in the past, only this time driven by migrants, is unlikely today.

Younger immigrants, who moved into these areas in the wake of the success achieved by first-wave immigrants, are faced with problems of integration. The local social and institutional context is unable to provide them with either regular jobs or adequate housing, with negative consequences on 'community' identity and cohesion. Immigration therefore raises a double challenge for IDs. When migrants are integrated into the local labour market, they often accept lower positions and wages, thus offering economic incentives for the less innovative firms. Capital may therefore be diverted towards less efficient, labour-intensive and lower-paid activities. Secondly, if immigrants are not integrated into the local community, or if they stay out of the regular labour market, their possible diversion toward irregular or illegal jobs may be detrimental to the local community's social cohesion. Immigration by better-qualified workers, say electronics experts, who can be more easily included in production processes, is on the contrary an insignificant phenomenon in Italy and in IDs.

5.2.2.   Shortage of Qualified Workers and Labour Poaching

The shortage of native workers in IDs concerns less qualified and more highly qualified jobs alike. All the areas in the sample suffer from a shortage of skilled workers, a problem which engenders 'labour poaching': the offering of higher wages to the most highly qualified workers employed by rival firms. Staff poaching practices are a form of unfair competition that distorts the 'good' competition that should characterize a canonical ID and thus represent one of the most pernicious forms of non-cooperative behaviour. In most areas, larger or leading firms often manage to 'steal' workers from other small firms by offering better work conditions and wages. This behaviour is commonplace in numerous areas, including canonical IDs. Even though entrepreneurs may be friends in constant informal contact, they do not refrain from labour poaching, which in fact is a tacitly accepted 'rule of the game' in the local community.

The phenomenon of labour shortage derives from local training mechanisms, that can be described as follows:

1. Because of the evolution of international labour division, growing numbers of firms in IDs have moved to niches or specializations with higher quality content (for example, Cossato, Porto Sant'Elpidio and Montebelluna) that require more complex or uncommon skills. As a consequence, mere infrafirm mobility (task rotation) no longer suffices, and workers, on average, lack the education to manage more complex technologies and information or to formalize methods of work (certification procedures or company-wide quality control: CWQC).
2. One of the more traditional forms of training – apprenticeships in crafts firms – has vanished in many areas. Moreover, the mechanization of industrial processes in some IDs has altered the pattern of socialization. In Civitacastellana, the handmade production typical of the 1980s enabled workers in factories to emulate their more experienced workmates and to strengthen friendships or solidarity ties, whereas the introduction of automation in recent years has given rise to a machine-dominated work rate, a noisier environment, and fewer opportunities to talk or work collectively. Socialization now takes place outside the mill or factory in places (discotheques, bars) where intergenerational meetings are much less frequent.
3. Other traditional ambits of training and learning like the family, whether extended or otherwise, have lost their importance. The children of entrepreneurs frequently suffer from an 'orphan syndrome' (Ginsborg and Ramella, 1999) caused by the absence from home of both their parents, engaged in strenuous jobs. In addition, owing to more rational urban planning and the evolution of the industry itself, factories are no longer located in the 'house's backyards'. Factory work now takes place at a distance from the family and therefore becomes less 'familial' to the younger generation.
4. According to many trade unionists, the shortage of skilled labour induces employers to ask for extra hours of work (overtime). Some employers complain that their workers sometimes enjoy better standards of living than they enjoy themselves because of the high wages paid. Overtime induces a lower need to hire new personnel and therefore impairs the socialization of young workers in the production process and work mobility.

5.2.3. The Quality of Human Capital: Education and Ageing in Industrial Districts

The educational structure of the population in district communities is another critical point in relation to IDs. Our sample is characterized by levels of higher education below the national average, and by an education profile of the local population concentrated on low degrees of qualification. Less clear

Table 5.1 Education levels in industrial districts, 1991 (percentage values)

	High	Comp	Illi		High	Comp	Illi
Arzignano	14.4	76.0	9.5	Suzzara	19.1	68.5	12.4
Santa Croce	15.8	69.0	15.1	Guastalla	29.2	67.7	13.1
Solfora	14.0	63.2	22.8	Cento	21.4	66.3	12.4
Vigevano	19.9	69.4	10.6	Matera	28.5	54.0	17.4
Porto S.Elpidio	15.2	67.7	17.1	Desio	20.7	69.6	9.4
Casarano	13.7	59.9	26.3	Oderzo	17.8	68.5	13.7
Bassano	20.4	69.5	10.3	Poggibonsi	18.4	64.9	52.8
Marostica	15.9	74.1	10.0	Schio	20.6	71.0	8.4
Sassuolo	20.0	66.9	13.2	S. B. Tronto	22.9	59.9	17.2
Civitacastellána	16.6	66.3	17.1	S.M. Cavoti	13.3	58.3	28.3
Cossato	15.4	75.2	9.4	Palazzolo	13.9	77.2	8.9
Prato	17.9	69.0	13.0	Senigallia	24.6	62.1	13.3
Giulianova	20.8	60.2	19.0	Putignano	3.4	61.8	34.8
Ostiglia	19.4	68.5	12.1	S.G. Ilarione	8.6	77.3	14.1
Carpi	21.2	66.0	12.7	Montecatini T	16.8	70.1	13.1
Ascoli Piceno	24.8	59.0	16.2	Fermo	24.3	58.8	16.9
Montebelluna	16.9	71.7	10.7	Guardiagrele	17.6	57.2	25.2
Civitanova	21.3	62.9	15.8	Valpolicella	19.2	70.9	18.7
Barletta	14.8	62.5	22.8	Castellarano	15.9	66.4	17.7
Pesaro	27.1	59.8	2.1				
Sample's				*Italy's*			
average	*18.5*	*66.3*	*16.2*	*average*	*22.4*	*63.2*	*14.4*

Source: Author's calculations on ISTAT (1995a).

is the evidence on levels of illiteracy, which are highest in southern areas (Table 5.1; indicators *high, comp* and *illi*). The data show that mature IDs with an extended industry based on small independent firms and an inclusive labour market have large numbers of residents who have completed compulsory schooling. They also reveal that the growth of the specialization industry between 1961 and 1991 was negatively correlated with the variation in the number of higher-educated people.[3] This may be explained either by the low vocational content of the Italian higher-educational curriculum or by the strong attraction exerted by the local labour market over the younger generation. Young people – whose activity rate in industrial activities is higher than the national average for the sample as a whole – prefer to start work early and thereby gain economic and personal independence, rather than postpone entry into employment by attending a higher-education course.

Table 5.2 Education levels by group of age in industrial districts, 1991 (percentage values)

	drop (a)	qual34 (b)	qual44 (c)	qual19 (d)		drop (a)	qual34 (b)	qual44 (c)	Qual19 (d)
Arzignano	14.7	24.3	15.7	18.6	Suzzara	38.0	36.7	25.4	17.7
Santa Croce	29.2	32.2	20.2	15.5	Guastalla	13.9	36.1	24.5	17.5
Solofra	21.0	27.2	17.6	16.4	Cento	28.8	40.9	28	19.8
Vigevano	14.8	38.1	24.5	19.5	Matera	18.4	37.7	26.3	20.8
Porto S.Elpidio	18.2	29.8	18.1	14.4	Desio	12.2	35.9	23.1	19.6
Casarano	20.9	35.2	24.7	19.4	Oderzo	32.0	31.7	18.5	16.3
Bassano	12.0	26.4	19.4	15.5	Poggibonsi	37.6	40.4	26.9	19.1
Marostica	10.1	19.1	16.3		Schio	8.9	32.9	24.0	18.1
Sassuolo	33.9	33.6	23.2	18.6	S. B. Tronto	14.8	37.8	26.8	22.4
Civitacastellana	29.3	32.2	22.2	17.7	S.M. Cavoti	23.2	35.1	27.1	22.1
Cossato	20.9	35.2	24.7	19.4	Palazzolo	15.1	25.6	17.6	14.1
Prato	32.1	32.1	23.4	17.7	Senigallia	45.5	47.8	33.6	23.8
Giulianova	37.8	40.6	28.8	21.9	Putignano	22.8	30.3	20.9	18.0
Ostiglia	39.5	38.9	25.6	17.4	S.G. Ilarione	18.7	14.7	10.2	8.4
Carpi	36.0	35.0	21.8	16.6	Montecatini	30.2	31.7	23.0	16.6
Ascoli Piceno	12.6	44.4	33.9	25.7	Fermo	11.4	43.6	33.2	24.1
Montebelluna	29.0	28.6	19.3	16.0	Guardiagrele	22.0	35.1	27.1	22.1
Civitanova	38.6	41.6	28.6	21.8	Valpolicella	12.5	31.3	20.9	17.6
Barletta	31.6	26.9	20.3	16.6	Castellarano	28.8	40.9	28	19.8
Pesaro	9.3	44.9	33.3	25.9					
Sample's average	*23.6*	*34.2*	*23.8*	*18.8*	*Italy's average*	*15.4*	*38.8*	*29.3*	*23.1*

Notes:
(a) Proportion of people with higher schooling; (b) proportion of people with compulsory schooling; (c) rate of illiteracy; (d) schooling drop-out in the group aged 15–42; (e) diploma qualification in the group aged 19–34; (f) diploma qualification in the group aged 35–44; (g) diploma qualification in the group aged 19 and over.

Source: Author's calculations on ISTAT (1995a).

These results are largely to be expected when considering a local economy chiefly dependent on manufacturing specialization, where the tacit nature of production – mainly based on artisan skills and on a culture of adaptation – does not require the high codification skills that may be related, albeit simplistically, to a higher level of education. Yet multivariate analysis shows that between 1981 and 1996 changes did occur, and particularly in some areas, thereby contributing to the evolution of IDs. As well as average rates of education, the indicators of education in different age classes may provide a clearer picture of the attitudes and expectations of the younger generation. The data show that in at least half of the sample areas, young people are more oriented than their parents were towards educational qualifications. The school drop-out rate in the 15 to 42 age group is much lower than in the older groups, although it is still much higher than the national average (Table 5.2).

However, the impact of intergenerational attitudes towards education on the performance and evolution of IDs is ambiguous. Indeed, education may be a factor that distinguishes between successful and unsuccessful IDs. On the one hand, the more complex internal organization and sophisticated technologies of firms, or the introduction of ICTs, require higher codification skills and therefore higher educational levels. More educated entrepreneurs or employees and more successful/innovative firms are synchronous phenomena closely related to the possibility that the intergenerational transfer of small-firm ownership in IDs will coincide with an entrepreneurial class of more highly educated people at the head of their parents' firms. Some entrepreneurs' sons or daughters take master degrees in business administration or technology and then return to their home factory to innovate their parents' traditional management style and strategies. However, there are also cases where they are entirely uninterested in their parents' occupations and work ethic. On the whole, it appears that young people with higher qualifications are more oriented towards activities unrelated to the traditional specialization of their area. This is evidenced for the sample as a whole by the low correlation value between high levels of schooling and the presence of firms specialized in business services. In areas like Marostica-Bassano (ceramics), the enstrangement of the younger generation from the traditional specialization of the areas in which they live is already manifest, giving rise to a downsizing and decline of the specialization industry. In other areas, the next decade will decide whether the social and industrial systems can coevolve on the basis of local resources. Those areas that fail to produce a more highly skilled local workforce and upgraded human resources are bound to lose their competitive advantage.

Another typical feature of most northern and central IDs, which partially relates to immigration phenomena, is the pronounced ageing of the population. This tendency is associated with a fall in birth rates indicative of changes in the status of women, the family structure, and lifestyles; changes that may have pernicious consequences for the viability of local labour markets. The structural lack of labour in these areas is also related to the age structure of the population. Not only are young people increasingly less attracted to the occupations of their parents, and not only is heavy, unskilled and poorly paid work increasingly performed by immigrants, but the younger age groups are shrinking in size because of a dramatic decline in the birth rate.

Table 5.3 Socio-demographic features of industrial districts: immigration and population ageing

	Proportion of immigrants in the population (1991)(*1000)	Proportion of immigrants in the population (1999) (*1000)	Proportion of people aged 14 and under	Proportion of people aged 65 and over
	Sample's data			
IDs (average sample)	7.8	22.0	15.2	15.9
Centre-North IDs	8.2	28.9	13.8	17.0
South Italy IDs	4.7	9.9	18.5	14.3
	Italy's average data			
Centre-North IDs	11.7	28.9	13.9	16.7
South Italy IDs	5.4	9.1	20.1	12.9
ITALY	9.4	22.0	14.6	15.3

Source: Author's calculations on ISTAT (1995a; 2001).

5.3. SOCIAL AND ECONOMIC (INTERMEDIATE) INSTITUTIONS

5.3.1. Social Institutions

Among social institutions, we consider here families, schools and local banks. The data presented (Table 5.4) confirm that the extended family typified IDs located in the Emilia-Romagna, Tuscany and Marche regions during the post-war period, but that it was less commonplace in the remaining regions. By 1991, the proportion of extended families had dramatically decreased in all the IDs considered, although it was still above the national average in areas where it had been greater in 1951. Given that large families were a typical component of the entrepreneurial model of metayage regions, which also provided entrepreneurial skills together with a flexible workforce and unified budgeting, one may ask what the functional

Table 5.4 Types of family, proportion of housekeepers and level of education of women, 1991

	Proportion of extended families	Proportion of mono-nucleus families	Proportion of housekeepers in the female population aged 14 and more	Proportion of higher educated females
Canonical IDs	17.3	13.9	24.9	23.0
Craft-based IDs	15.7	14.2	30.3	26.1
Integrated IDs	11.4	14.6	26.0	25.0
Marginal IDs	12.7	12.2	35.9	33.8
Italy's average	12.6	15.5	31.2	29.9

Source: Author's calculations on ISTAT (1995a).

equivalents were in the areas where different families types or land-tenure systems prevailed. As shown in the previous chapter, the growth of entrepreneurship in regions like Lombardy and Veneto or the southern regions of Italy has followed different paths, which indicates that different mechanisms of capital accumulation have been at work, with subsequent effects on the organization of businesses. Firms in southern IDs rely more closely on informal work, and ancillary workers are much less frequently employed in family businesses, while in many other cases larger firms financed by the richest families in the area then subcontract work to other firms, triggering a process of diffusive investment. Indeed, the lack or weak presence of functional equivalents for the extended families and the metayage system helps explain the comparative rarity of small businesses in southern areas. For some communities of migrants (Chinese, in particular) in IDs, the family is still the main source of finance start-ups, equipment, information and informal apprenticeships.

The prevalence of the traditional extended family structure has diminished in IDs, while mono-unit families, such as single-parent families, are on the increase. This also mirrors a change in the role of women, who exhibit higher levels of schooling and higher activity rates. In the sample, women aged 14–29 are, on average, better educated than their male counterparts (Table 5.4). On the other hand, it would be foolish to argue that the profound socio-economic transformations that have concerned Italy in its entirety have not affected the ID communities. The implication when assessing the competitiveness of Italian IDs is that one of the main institutions devoted to the transmission of values and skills has profoundly changed, while it is impossible to foresee which new institution will take over the family's functions, preserving social cohesion in a modernized socio-cultural context.

As sociologists have pointed out with regard to the Poggibonsi area in particular, the transmission of skills linked to the area's manufacturing specialization, or of values like attachment to work and a willingness to work hard, is severely questioned by young people, who in certain cases reject their parents' lifestyles (Ginsborg and Ramella, 1999). Long working hours and factory labour are disliked because they reduce the time that can be devoted to the worker's family or hobbies, and they impair the quality of life. In some IDs with high levels of illness linked to air pollution – tanning districts, for example – factory work is associated with disease.

It is incumbent on sociologists to identify the new institutions that will replace the traditional ones. For our purposes here, suffice it to point out that one of the institutional underpinnings of IDs is changing, and this raises new challenges for the economic sustainability and permanent identity of these areas.

Besides the family, schools also transmit values, technical expertise and knowledge, and in this area, too, there have been significant changes. Besides the well-known cases of Prato, Biella or Reggio Emilia, since the early 1960s even suburban areas like Solofra or Montecatini T. have seen the establishment of specialized tanning and footwear schools, respectively. We assessed the presence of technical schools in over 60 per cent of the IDs surveyed. Some of them played a key role during the developmental phase of local industry, becoming one of the central structures around which an ID (for example, Brianza) defined its manufacturing specialization. However, in the last few years two tendencies have been apparent in all the areas examined: (a) increasing unemployment rates among graduates from such schools, or rather a mismatch between the subsequent job and the qualification obtained, and (b) a significant decrease in enrolments. It is rather difficult, in fact, to distinguish between the two phenomena, which are consequential on each other in that they are intertwined. The decrease in enrolments is a sign, like the others cited above, of the alienation of the younger generation from the area's traditional occupations. Secondly, local firms demand skills that differ from those imparted by the training programmes offered by the schools. Related to this, owing to a perverse selection mechanism, it is precisely the less motivated and less able students that enrol in these schools. Action has been taken to structure school curricula so that they reflect the skills requirements of firms (for example, through work placements in companies during the school year), but the results have been unsatisfactory so far.

One of the best known disadvantages of small firms is their more difficult access to credit. According to Becattini and other scholars in IDs, the crucial resource of credit for continuous development is ensured by the 'benevolence' of the local credit system. In contrast with the traditional hostility of banks to small firms which are generally disadvantageous as compared to large ones, local banks in these IDs have given a vital support for the development of the district (Becattini, 1990). Banks rooted in the local economy, often small with only a national diffusion, direct local savings to the local demand of investments rather than diverting them elsewhere, therefore contributing to a locally rooted virtuous circuit of accumulation and investment. Transactions costs related to the assessment of the moral and entrepreneurial qualities of people asking for loans is made easier by proximity relationships. The hypothesis of embeddedness of local banks in IDs (Becattini, 1990), that is the question whether the banks that operate in IDs are fully integrated into the socio-economic network, has been recently tested (Baffigi et al., 1999). A local bank *b* is assumed to be embedded in an ID if two conditions are met (double concentration condition):

1.   *b* concentrates its loan in the ID (concentration of lending);
2.   *b* holds a large market share in the ID's credit market (concentration of credit market).

The authors discovered that only 58 out of the 199 IDs designated by ISTAT satisfy the two criteria. These IDs include the best known and oldest district areas (Carpi, Biella, Prato and Vigevano). This suggests that district banking localism tends to be stronger in more mature IDs (Baffigi et al., 1999). Therefore, local embedded banks are not a typical feature of all IDs. Even once the resilience of local banks has been assessed, this does not ensure them being effective and supportive for local businesses. Local banks have proved to be more selective in commercial loans in the last decade due to a profound transformation of the Italian financial system, which witnessed numerous merger and acquisition operations. In the present context what is required is the availability of long-term investments or equity capital, based upon a joint review of the firm's business plan and commercial prospects – not just its short-term financial performance (see also Amin, 1997 on Emilian IDs).

5.3.2.   Economic (Intermediate) Institutions *versus* National and International Institutions

As regards economic institutions, professional associations and trade unions have changed into the providers of services as they have increased their memberships. These institutions have supplanted central or local public support policies in many areas. One lesson to be learnt from the cases surveyed is that IDs have flourished in the absence of a supportive national policy. The factors accounting for the take-off and subsequent development of IDs cannot be reduced to industrial policy or plans for local development, although some influence cannot be denied in certain cases (for example, Biella in the past century). A more active role has been played by local and 'intermediate' institutions, although these differ markedly among the areas examined.

Service centres are to be found in historical IDs especially; particularly in Emilia Romagna, Tuscany and Marche; which confirms that the presence of a 'red' political subculture fostered the growth of SMEs, as argued by Trigilia (1990). The Veneto region, in which 'white' coalitions have ruled the regional administration and municipal councils for over forty years, has been less interventionist. These results are coherent with the index of infrastructure endowment calculated (Chapter 3).

By virtue of some sort of institutional imitation process, *'centri servizi'* have arisen everywhere on the initiative of local chambers of commerce, regional councils and employers' associations. In the 1980s and 1990s, these service centres became the keystone of regional and local industrial policies. However, they did not always prove crucial for the development of these areas. Employers (non-artisan, especially) complained that the services were ineffectual and the centres too bureaucratic, while the officials working in the centres accused entrepreneurs of being myopically self-reliant.

In Sassuolo, notwithstanding the existence of large public-funded centres for innovation, leader firms tend to have their own internal service structures, or when they require specialized consultancy services they use national or international consultants, amongst other things, to ensure confidentiality.

An alternative situation is represented by cases in which 'intermediate' institutions – genuine products of local society like employers' associations, chambers of commerce or trade unions – have supplied a diversified range of services: specialized ones, like R&D, training and education for a few more innovative firms; and more standard services for the vast majority of firms, such as accounting (especially for artisans) and financial services, economic information (on fairs, foreign markets), goods-purchasing services, management consultancy services, as well as catering facilities, medical care, and the like.

In recent decades, local trade associations and trade unions, even in the IDs where they are stronger (variable *unio* in Table 3.6, Chapter 3) have been subjected to fiercer competition. Political upheavals, together with more stringent demand for more specialized services and better wage and work conditions, respectively, have removed consensus from the traditional associations, fostering the development of new groupings with a more corporativist nature. The evidence shows that the 'institutional density' of the areas surveyed has been differentiated: local employers or artisans, as applicable, do not wield strong representative power everywhere. In most of the southern areas and in northern areas like Marostica or Ostiglia, private professionals assist local entrepreneurs with bookkeeping, taxation, recruitment, and other matters. The fewer the members, the less the number and effectiveness of the services supplied, which suggests some sort of economy of scale in the provision of services. This observation prompts the question as to whether it is the institutions that support the success of an area, or whether it is the specialization and agglomeration processes operating in the phases of full development that strengthen the local institutions. This is a question best dealt with in sociological terms and on which there is little to add here, apart from pointing out that statements to the effect that the 'institutions are an essential ingredient for ID's success' (Piore, 1990) are, at least as regards the past, entirely unfounded. This notwithstanding, there exists strong demand for institutional responses more effective than in the past. Before listing possible measures to meet this demand, it is advisable to decide which is the more appropriate level of action: local or national. This question has also arisen in the lively debate on new regionalism (*federalism*) in Italy and Europe.

5.4.   A NATIONAL VERSUS A LOCAL INDUSTRIAL POLICY

The variety of industrial structures and institutional arrangements within each administrative partition, either regional or provincial, suggests that local rather than national institutions or collective/organized actors have greater awareness of problems (and of possible solutions). Local institutions are the most suitable actors, given that they are a direct expression of local society, and are thus able to articulate local needs, highlight the deficiencies to be remedied, and single out the pernicious processes that must be prevented . On the other hand, local actors are unable to supply solutions if they can only rely on their own financial resources or competencies. Regional, and especially local, authorities are highly differentiated with respect to institutional *expertise*. In addition, there are some issues that extend beyond the local dimension – such as pro-competitive policies, interregional infrastructure and so on – which must be addressed by national institutions.

A move by the former Italian government supports the idea that an interactive process of problem identification, proposal, action and monitoring between local and national institutions is the preferable solution. The *patti territoriali*, or 'territorial pacts', are a case in point. These are agreements between local private and public actors (companies, local agencies, trade unions and employers' associations) on the implementation in subregional areas of coordinated and integrated infrastructural and production schemes to enhance local development. The interventions envisaged, besides private and public funding mechanisms, are the streamlining of administrative procedures, and special contracts between companies and employees or between companies and banks, with a central (governmental) agency coordinating decentralized policies. By defining the criteria for evaluation and selection of (competing) projects, and by monitoring and comparing results across the country, this agency stimulates a virtuous circle of competition and imitation, and the most successful initiatives are rewarded and cited as examples to be imitated by other local operators. This in turn reassures the proponents of the successful project, thereby increasing their power of persuasion with respect to reluctant or more pessimistic local partners, and offering benchmarks for other local actors. Moreover, the procedure for submitting a project, and the subsequent process of comparative evaluation, involves a process of common learning. Some of these pacts have been 'signed' in ID areas like Casarano, Barletta and Matera (including a larger number of contiguous municipalities): that is, 'embryonic' IDs. The measures approved are targeted on consolidating the local system by promoting the localization of new activities within the local productive *filière*. Although the pacts play on that intriguing equilibrium between competition (between regions) and collaboration (among local actors) (Barca, 2000), which is one the distinctive features of canonical IDs, they have not been signed in IDs more than in non-ID areas. One of the reasons lies in the inter-industry nature of the initiatives eligible for support, but the variety of 'local' regulation modes, in terms of active institutions and administrative practices, also explain their varied success (Messina, 2001).

5.5. A NATIONAL POLICY FOR INFRASTRUCTURE AND NETWORK INDUSTRIES

Apart from the technical role of national institutions in IDs' policy, a national industrial policy addressing the cost of network services such as telecommunications, electricity, gas, water and transport may have a major impact on the cost functions of small firms in IDs. At the same time, a policy oriented towards the provision of interregional infrastructures is also necessary in order to facilitate the exchange of goods, knowledge and information with other regions or countries.

The rise in energy costs during the 1970s due to the oil shock increased the costs of textile and ceramic firms in particular, although firms reacted by adopting energy-saving technologies. The effects of the recent and still ongoing rise in oil prices on small firms have not yet been assessed, although they may have been substantial given that Italian electricity prices are the highest in Europe for small industrial customers. The competitive disadvantage of small firms in Italy, those consuming between 30MWh and 2GWh per year, ranged between 36 and 55 per cent in 2001 (January), when prices reflected the peak in imported oil prices. The disadvantage for SMEs consuming gas is lower, although prices are well above the weighted European average (Aeeg, 2001). An even greater impact on the viability of small firms in IDs may have been exerted by the cost and the rate of diffusion of ICTs, although in this case the obstacles to their use are also cognitive rather than merely economic. A national policy for the liberalization of the industries concerned – which are presently subject to weak competitive pressures – may prove helpful for the competitiveness of firms in IDs.

The level of infrastructure provision varies within the sample (variable: *infr*). The least infrastructured areas are located in the south, but examples of inadequate physical infrastructure can also be found in northern areas; for instance, Fermo, Porto Sant'Elpidio, Montebelluna and Suzzara. In Arzignano, Montebelluna, Vigevano, and Marostica especially, industrialization has proceeded with scant respect for the urban and natural environment. The problem of transport infrastructure is particularly serious in the Veneto region and, according to local employers' associations, the situation worsened in the last decade after many firms extended their commercial linkages with external and foreign areas. The best equipped areas can be found in the Emilia Romagna region. The infrastructure indicator is significantly related to income (0.77) and with the rate of unionization (0.42), and weakly with the presence of a political subculture (0.31). This result shows that the political stability and strength of a local political party or coalition have not always been able to ensure the general availability of public goods. This is confirmed for the LLMAs located in Veneto, and may therefore be generalized to the whole region, where a dominant Christian Democratic Party – until the political upheaval caused by the 'Mani Pulite' (literally: 'Clean Hands') investigation – has failed to ensure basic services for the local population. The less 'localistic' and interventionist nature of this culture, as opposed to the 'red' administrations in Emilia Romagna and Tuscany, has been documented by many social scientists and is confirmed by our findings. Regional policy makers (local councils, for example), have provided (or negotiated with the national government) infrastructures (transport, industrial premises, and so on) in some localities only, while in others, such as Veneto and all the southern IDs, local industrial policy has not been incisive.

5.6. A DIFFERENTIATED AND 'PHASE-BASED' INDUSTRIAL POLICY

5.6.1. Differentiated Policies and Development Strategies for Industrial Districts' Typologies

The acknowledgement of the variety of IDs is another reason to ask for decentralized policies, but other implications derive from this consideration. Our analysis showed how IDs are different, even if they are specialized in the same industry and react non-unanimously to the same economic trend. Critical features and potential weak points of entrepreneurs are differentiated according to whether they are commissioning/final or stage firms. The direct implication is that policy interventions should be differentiated as well. The kind of solutions and available policy tools in a district such as Prato are necessarily different from those applicable to a marginal ID, like Barletta or S.M. dei Cavoti. The strengthening of competitiveness in Prato, where a large variety of specializations, skills and competencies may easily be found locally, may be obtained by recombining different firms and opening the district to external firms. This may not apply to marginal areas where the advantages of agglomeration have still to be produced. We therefore envisage selective policies, or rather strategies – as explained below – for each typology of ID. Below are described, in very general terms, the aims and instruments of the various strategies of development, emphasizing, in particular, the role of the policies targeted to attract foreign and external direct investments (Ashworth and Voogd, 1990; Wells and Wint, 1990) in the four different typologies. The reasons for this emphasis is explained below.

For marginal IDs that are in a phase of rapid growth, industrial policy has to be directed towards the enlargement of final markets and the full exploitation of economies of agglomeration in order to consolidate the nascent manufacturing specialization.[4] The connection with final markets, consisting of commissioning firms or distribution channels, has to be strengthened in order to permit the consolidation of the financial structure of local firms and the activation of processes of accumulation and investment. The districts that mainly consist of subcontracting firms need to encourage firms in the development of certification procedures and quality control methods. The market strategic objective should be that of tapping the demand for subcontracting works coming from national or international leaders. The instruments developed in the realm of (passive) internationalization (export insurance schemes, export consortia) might be appropriate for this, though these tools have to be revised, taking into account new ICT opportunities.

In light of the observation that a complete network of activities will not emerge if the local population does not possess the required competence and knowledge, a selective intervention should identify those activities that are not present in the local texture (bottlenecks) and favour their emergence. This may be done either through favouring technological and commercial transfer from the (few) leading commissioning firms located in the district or from northern or external firms, through locally attracting firms that have the required competencies. In this respect, it may be pernicious to attract firms to the district that have a level of technological specialization higher or inappropriate in comparison to the average level of the indigenous firms, since a vicious mechanism of deprivation may occur (Cantwell, 1989).

For those areas like Casarano or Matera, and to a lesser extent Putignano and the Val Vibrata (Ascoli Piceno), where a few larger leading firms exist, spin-offs may be publicly supported by financing the loan of machinery to former employees who have moved to self-employment, or by funding training courses within the incubator firms, as well as by developing a more effective banking system. In-house training for workers, subcontractors and suppliers should be supported as well. Specialized courses could be financed either by the regional council or by employers' associations, or out of European Union funds (for example, the European Social Fund). The (possibly gradual) regularization of the illegal work widespread in these areas is another specific measure required in southern IDs. Though this practice yielded competitive advantage in the past, its resilience may seriously impair the take-off of the area because it may delay upgrading policies of firms, which mistakenly believe that a cost-cutting strategy may help them to survive. It may also act as a form of unfair competition against legal firms, and, even more crucially, delays the access to more innovative finance (including listing on the Stock Exchange) and adoption of formalized certification procedures, for those firms that rely on informal suppliers. Further, it should be noted that the presence of informal work in southern IDs has not impeded significant processes of delocation to nearby European countries, such as Albania and Romania. Insisting on a policy of labour-cost containment may not therefore ensure the sustainability of firms in the medium term.

For craft-based IDs, a local strategy of development should be directed towards reinforcement of the competitive advantage of the area by supporting innovation and innovative actors. Selective incentives should be directed towards these innovators. This would permit either to enhance the technological content of their product or their degree of customization in order to compete in high quality market bands. The strengthening of the main specialization should not be a strategic objective, since these areas are sufficiently diversified to ensure jobs and income to the local population.

Where the innovating actors are public institutions (universities, research centres), these should be able to provide 'useable' innovations to local SMEs. This implies that likely innovations should not be created in a context far from the user firm, but the phases of innovation (planning, demonstrating and piloting) should be coordinated with and within the SMEs. Public funding should be supplied to projects and services concerning cross-sectors and pervasive technologies (for example, logistics and TLCs). Education and training policies also have to be fostered, although they are very difficult to devise for SMEs: on the one hand, training courses offered by external agents (for example, regional councils) are often non-tailored to the specific needs of small firms. On the other hand, as documented by several surveys (ISFOL, 1995; Russo et al., 2000), small entrepreneurs are often unable to predict their likely training needs in a time horizon longer than one year, this making the planning of programmes very challenging. Moreover, SMEs have such tight resources' constraints that they cannot second production employees without disturbing production, even for the time needed to attend a course.

Attraction of new ventures in the specialization industries of these areas, and even more importantly in the cross-cutting industries, the promotion of catalysts and, in particular, the internationalization of those commissioning or final firms that can activate a flow of exports for their local subcontractors (*filière* effect) or strengthen the reputation of the area, may also produce a large impact.

For canonical IDs and integrated IDs, that have already reached a stage of full exploitation of economies of agglomeration, action must be finalized to open the local texture of firms to new markets and technologies. Given that the measures targeted towards technological upgrading envisaged for the previous typology are valid, a special emphasis should be placed on product rather than process innovations and on the pervasive technologies (for example, logistics, TLCs). 'Technological windows' on what is happening in the industries contiguous to the one in which the ID is specialized are particularly effective, since those of a limited size are far away from or simply unconnected to the places where the innovations are developed, that will soon impact on the processes used by SMEs or the products that compete with them. The conversion of tacit or codified knowledge in the specialization industries towards new uses should be favoured. A case in point is represented by the competences sustaining the ceramic-tile industry in Sassuolo. The local ceramic tradition in the area has already found and may find in the near future a fruitful usage in the production of 'technoceramics' for the aero-spatial or electrical transmission industries. The enrichment or 'contamination' of the local 'savoir-faire' and their competitiveness in these typologies may be sustained by:

- attracting new firms able to relate the local contexts and the

specialization industry to the international centres of production of
new ideas and knowledge in the same or contiguous industries;

• reaggregation of independent firms in stable organizations (for
  example, networks of firms) able to offer an integrated range of
  customized products in a high market band (see Section 3.3.7);

• development of internationalization strategies aimed at exporting not
  only final and intermediate goods, but also patterns of consumption
  sympathetic with them;

• promotion of international technological programmes.

The (local) financial system should be redirected towards the provision of
funds for investment in technology. Apart from the more traditional loan
consortia developed since the 1970s in most IDs, concentrated and canonical
IDs should benefit from credit institutions for particular aims: for example,
listing on the Stock Exchange, new national or international ventures, and
firms' capitalization. Education and training policies are fundamental for
these IDs, since these can redirect the local population's cultural orientation.
In the present technological context, coinciding with the diffusion of
microelectronics and ICTs, the ability to convert cognitive routines is a great
challenge, but this policy may be directed especially towards the younger
generation, obtaining simultaneously the result of entrenching them in an
open local context, and opening their horizons to the wider world.

It should be noticed that the more a district is in an advanced phase of
development, the more pregnant with possibilities becomes a policy aimed at
attracting foreign or generally external firms that may be of a high level of
technological competence and not necessarily specialized in the same
industry of the district. Virtuous circles and mechanisms of 'cumulative
causation' may in fact be prompted when the host economy offers
technological and organizational resources not distant from those of the
investing firms (Cantwell, 1989).

A substantial difference between the policies for marginal IDs and those
envisaged for the other typologies resides in the fact that in the latter case the
strategies devised concern the core of firms' strategies and are designed to
redirect objectives, strategies, learning mechanisms, practices and
organizational structures, whereas for marginal IDs actions should be
targeted on the local environment. It is evident that the above-mentioned
interventions do not have to be activated by private or public institutions;
instead they can be better defined by intermediate institutions by means of a
programme of persuasion and training prior to the provision of more tangible
services. The institutions' patterns of action should emulate those of
spontaneous catalysts or coordinators. Trade associations, for example, can
use their websites to provide a forum for the exchange of ideas, for the

advertising of success stories, for the promotion of best practices, or to organize benchmarking groups and meetings. These websites may become portals where enterprises can find opportunities to market and procure goods, recruit personnel, build their reputations, and also receive ideas and stimuli for change in a virtual process of learning. The same applies to trade unions, which can enhance the match between labour demand and supply by compiling databases, or promoting local-level learning and training schemes.

The activism of these intermediate institutions should not undermine the need of public intervention, through appropriate fiscal or financial instruments or infrastructure projects.

For all the typologies so far surveyed in this phase, with the partial exception of marginal IDs, amenities and the quality of life of the local environment assumes a crucial role in attracting and sustaining more dynamic actors. In this sense, industrial policy should transform itself into a territory policy concerned with urban, environmental and cultural aspects.

In those marginal IDs located in areas where phenomena of 'organized crime' is present, the upgrading of civic life is essential and therefore a policy of legality and security may well accompany the growth of the local industry.

The variety within IDs, as related to the emergence of internal networks or integrated firms, points to selective policies aimed at encouraging and fostering the most dynamic actors. To the extent that the function of these actors 'out of the scale' of IDs does not damage the collective performance or the welfare of IDs – as our first results show – they should be sustained by policy measures. The presence of a leading firm as an orchestrator of flows of goods and information in local areas may in fact be a point of strength rather than of weakness. Our results also show that IDs perform better when they have a more integrated industrial structure, with firms playing an interconnecting role, providing new ideas, techniques, best practices and technologies. Therefore, these firms or networks should be sustained and encouraged to disseminate their knowledge locally. Supporting or locally attracting the innovative actors, either at organizational or technological level, may trigger off such pathbreaking events or may redirect the trajectory of development in a way that IDs, due to their self-organized nature, are not able to produce spontaneously.

It is of paramount importance that such policies be devised locally through partnerships between leading firms, local associations of employers, trade unions and councils, though within a national framework that assigns main objectives and rules, therefore avoiding inconsistency at the national level or, even worse, disruptive competition.

The policies, or generally the strategies, so far envisaged for Italian IDs are very different from those popular in the 1980s or more recently, where the idea of service centres conquered the attention of many policy makers.

The provision of services such as marketing, credit access, accounting, export assistance or insurance helped to overcome the diseconomies associated with small size in accessing critical resources. All these policies were based on the assumption that the limits of small firms in an agglomerated context were related only to the high costs of some external resources, and not to their core activities.

It is now time to let the entrepreneurs be aware of the fact that this traditional knowledge, the intangible resources on which past successes were based, may no longer be enough to meet future competition. Consequently, an awareness of what is happening inside their own area (industry) and related environments, but outside their own social confines, could directly influence their work patterns. Conversely, it is necessary to defeat the entrepreneur's traditional mistrust of (often) public institutional organisms (though such initiatives do not have to be prompted or financed exclusively by public entities), while it is important to overcome the small entrepreneur's self-reliance. Self-reliance is often an outcome of the little time available for small entrepreneurs, which prevents them from attending training courses or making these available to their employees.

Networking or 'contamination' of IDs, in order to extend their sources of knowledge and stimuli to change is essential. If the agglomeration of many SMEs in bounded places has historically represented a protection against the diseconomies of small scale and, at the same time, a propellant for the SME's virtue, in the present scenario small firms might suffer from isolation even if they are 'integrated' in an ID. As mentioned earlier, the ID as an organizational model helped to overcome the diseconomies associated with small size in access to critical resources, but the new competitive challenge now finds the ID isolated, inward-looking and locked in to its industrial trajectory, rather than connected to the centre of production of new ideas and knowledge. These attitudes and risks involve both firms and networks of firms or single 'coordinators'. In quite a few cases groups have proven to be financially weak and founded on the basis of non-strategic motivations that hardly ensure their viability in the long run.

In those IDs dominated by fashion-led industries, information problems may be overwhelming because neither the firms nor their environment may have the capabilities needed to diffuse and interpret new knowledge. Because the producing firms are relatively small and the population of customers is diverse and geographically dispersed, while the distribution channels are controlled by very large and international department stores, the costs of spreading and acquiring information on innovations might be beyond the resources of both suppliers and buyers. Moreover, the places of conception of new fashion trends are often located outside Italy or Europe. The new sport products for jogging, trekking or mountain-biking are more related to

American rather than European life styles and, therefore, the 'Italian taste' may not in the future play as important a role as that underlined by Porter (1990).

According to a suggestion by Langlois and Robertson (1995), information 'impactedness' can be reduced if the developer of an innovation and the user are in the same organization (although 'organizational failures' have to be taken into account as well). Users can make producers (and innovators) aware of specific commercial needs to which they should devote attention. Following this reasoning, those firms belonging to a group may be connected to a variety of hubs representing different niche markets and thus providing relevant information. One unit of the group may be specialized in marketing and international market access, while others may focus on production or engineering. However, the group may not by itself be able to answer to a demand for information and knowledge. It must be networked to other sources of information and capabilities as well. Many groups have risen on the basis of financial and family motivations, by compressing the autonomy of the units coordinated, and hence failed. They are still a spontaneous answer to the local texture of firms affected by the cultural traits of the firms and of their environment. It is here that the need for a strategic policy intervention appears, either to help those firms excluded from successful groups or to connect existing groups to international or strategic networks. All the initiatives that aim to connect the firms within IDs to other actors, transnational firms, universities or research centres that operate on a larger scale, can help to revitalize the competitiveness of IDs.

5.6.2.   A Phase-Based Industrial Policy for Industrial Districts

A differentiated policy may be devised either for different typologies of IDs or for different stages of development. Provided that IDs go through different stages of development, appropriate and specific policy instruments and objectives may be envisaged for each of phases. Actually, as said earlier, the different typologies correspond to a certain extent to different phases of development, though there is no automatic transition from one type to another. The recommendation given for marginal IDs may be valid in general for the first phase of growth in any ID, while those identified for craft-based IDs may apply to a phase of take-off or consolidation. For canonical and integrated IDs we pointed to policies aimed at revitalizing a process that has attained full exploitation of external economies, and these can be applied to new IDs. Therefore a differentiated policy may have the same content, either if applied to different typologies or if applied to different phases of development.

The only phase we have not considered is the first phase of incubating an

ID, while many existing Italian IDs have comprehensively moved on from this stage, which, in Italy, may be placed in the 1950s. It may nonetheless characterize the industrial development of IDs in other countries, such as, for example, Eastern Europe countries. In this stage, industrial policy should not be intrusive but should accompany spontaneous mechanisms of competence activation and exert a sort of 'maieutic' art, to make explicit and diffuse the underlying tacit knowledge and competencies owned by the local population. With respect to Italian history, artisan or industrial backgrounds have constituted the humus for entrepreneurship, but within other national contexts the incubator institutions or processes may not coincide, but rather consist in large firms' or universities' centres of excellence. Those cases of industrial specialization in one industry pioneered by former migrants warrant a specific focus from developing regions (see Chapter 4). The countries from which major migratory flows have originated should act as incentives to emigrants to return home once they have acquired knowledge, skills and capital.

The objective at the initial stage of an IDs' formation is to exploit the potential of the area and to enlarge the number of operators included in the emerging local specialization. Demonstrative actions aimed at generating a common and public awareness of the process of development are useful in helping to promote imitative processes and to create a sense of belonging to a common 'epos'.

Where large firms constitute the main typical breeding environment of new technical skills, workers spin-offs may be publicly supported by financing lending of machinery to former employees that become self-employed or funding training courses within the incubator firms. Public formation may be directed towards the activation of professional schools specialized in the emerging specialization of the area for the young generation or in ad hoc training courses organized according to the needs of the firms. In most of the larger IDs, technical schools have arisen spontaneously and have contributed to the formation of a new class of technicians, though their role nowadays is challenged. Good urban and industrial infrastructures are an obvious but critical prerequisite of this form of development, as for any other. Although the incoming and exit flows of produced goods may be not retained massive, logistic bottlenecks may seriously block the take-off of an area, especially if they impede the tapping of an increasing national or international demand.

Mechanisms of capital accumulation should be favoured at a local level. Therefore, any supportive financial system that can ease credit access for new entrepreneurs is welcome. In Italy, a banking system inclined to finance any industry-related loan application (provided it be supported by adequate personal guarantees) rather than genuinely promising ventures has dramatically blocked, *inter alia*, the development of entrepreneurship in areas where local mechanisms of capital accumulation were very weak.

However, the above prescription may appear highly theoretical since it is very difficult to assess which stage of development an ID falls in, especially in transition periods. Even accounting for the cyclical nature of an ID's development, it is difficult to interpret trend changes, since the length of each stage is not known. Rather than worrying about IDs' stages of development, policy makers should pay careful attention to the trend factors that have the largest impact on structure and performance of an ID. Critical resources should be identified and areas of vulnerability (for example, dependence on imported energy inputs) should be carefully monitored in order to engineer in advance policies of defence and reply.

5.6.3. Marketing Industrial Districts

The entry of new firms, whether domestic or multinational, represents a groundbreaking event, capable of introducing a new rationality of action and producing a new pattern of division of labour among local firms. The cases of TNCs' entry into IDs have been very limited so far and restricted – with respect to the areas examined – to Montebelluna, Palazzolo and some of the Emilian agricultural machinery districts.

Given that change may originate from outside, improving cooperative relationships and building networks that reach outside of the region may prove more productive for some localities than concentrating on indigenous firms.

Employing the work of Wells and Wint (1990), a marketing policy for IDs should be defined with respect to the following facets:

- type of inward investment to select (greenfield, merger or acquisition, brownfield);
- target countries, industries and firms;
- product to market.

The wide diffusion of family ownership in IDs may dampen merger and acquisition patterns of entry, to the benefit of greenfield investments. Whether such investments become less frequent in the international market for reasons explained elsewhere, we may expect an increase in the other forms of entry as soon as problems of intergenerational passage come to the surface.

Identification of the industries to target should derive directly from a careful analysis of the local industrial structure and its likely bottlenecks. The target, however, should be defined according to more specific criteria than the mere industry classification and be related, for example, to the internal organization of TNCs (see, for example, the classification provided in Birkinshaw and Hood, 1995), best practices adopted and level of technological complexity, each of which is more suitable predictors of the foreseeable degree of integration of an industry with its local environment. The final element considered here for the definition of a marketing strategy is the ID product. The availability of diffused competencies and knowledge, as well as other typical economies of agglomeration, are a strong factor of attraction for some typologies of international investments, as an already mature literature has suggested. However, these factors may be not sufficient if professionals in the firms that IDs have to attract are very sensitive to other less tangible features of the localization environment, such as quality of life, education level or civic attitude. An unpleasant local environment does not make it easy to attract highly qualified human capital, such individuals preferring more attractive places if they are to relocate. It is not by chance that Silicon Valley arose in California.

The enacting of marketing policies requires an upgrading and thorough transformation of economic and social structures: a higher degree of education of workers, potential partners and overall increased population, a qualified urban and natural environment and more effective infrastructures.

The attraction of investors relies on a set of instruments, like financial and fiscal incentives, the provision of industrial premises, seamless procedures of authorization, and so on.

The critical problems of low educational levels and unsuited training must be resolved with respect to both the demand and supply of labour and training, respectively. Central and local institutions may provide more tailored programmes of education or training, but individual firms, together with other firms or local trade unions, should be able to identify their needs, while the population should change attitudes toward education, and invest more heavily in education. The entry of new actors/firms, with their repository of knowledge and competencies, may require new skills and create new (managerial) professional roles, contributing to new knowledge and new cultures, the presence of which in the local context – because of proximity – may stimulate new ambitions and moves towards higher levels of education and training.

NOTES

1. The correlation values for the sample as a whole show that the presence of immigrants (*immi*) is negatively related to the unemployment rate (−0.50) and to the inactivity rate (*inac*: −0.42), and positively to manufacturing rates (*manf* and *mane*, respectively 0.46 and 0.42) and the presence of small firms (0.47). Population Censuses yield data on the number of migrants (foreign residents and the current population at the town level) but not on their geographical

origin. However, we may confidently assume that they are mostly extra-EU citizens, since those from EU countries generally tend to settle in the 'art cities' or tourist resorts, while only a few of the areas in the sample are of this type (namely, S.B. del Tronto, Giulianova and Senigallia). Moreover, the date on which the censuses was carried out, 31 October, is not a high-season period for the places near the coast. Instead, areas like Montecatini T., which comprises the health spa of Montecatini where most foreigners are employed in the tourist industry, have been assigned the average *immi* value for the LLMA in which they are located.

2. Correlation value between *immi* and *C3* is 0.47.

3. Data are not presented here, but may be requested from the author.

4. The absence of the producers of tools or machinery in the local area may not be a real bottleneck considering the experience of more mature IDs (see Section 3.5).

6. Conclusions and Research Implications

6.1. THE ORGANIZATIONAL VARIETY OF INDUSTRIAL DISTRICTS

This book delivers an articulated view of IDs characterized by distinct patterns of labour division and institutional arrangements, evolutionary paths, and overall by a different width of agglomeration economies. The factor analysis carried out on 1991 data produced several ways of describing the 39 IDs concerned, while the results of the cluster analysis conducted on the same data yielded four different typologies of IDs in Italy, namely, 'craft-based', (quasi) 'canonical', 'integrated' or 'concentrated', and 'embryonic' or 'Schumpeterian' (Chapter 3).

A variety, rather than simply a marked division between 'canonical' and 'non-canonical' IDs, came to light. The 'canonical' IDs, as identified by Sforzi and other scholars, were clustered in different groups in 1981 and 1991. This is a logical consequence of the quantitative and comparative approach employed. The use of quantitative indicators enabled differentiation among Italian IDs, which an external and superficial observer would have taken to constitute a homogeneous whole. It emerged from the study that the empirical importance of canonical IDs is not particularly significant, not even in the so-called 'Third Italy'. Only a few areas fit the model of canonical IDs, these being the best known and most thoroughly studied ones. Areas like Prato or Santa Croce, which have been extensively analysed in the literature, are more of an exception than a widespread form of socio-economic organization, even in Italy. This would suggest that the international literature should be more cautious in its treatment of IDs, using the term 'ID' only to denote agglomerations of SMEs in a few or complementary industries within limited areas. This would prevent the simplistic extension of the very specific features of the 'canonical' ID to any agglomeration of SMEs.

Overall, the sample of IDs exhibits excellent economic and social performance compared to the national average. Average productivity, the level of per capita income and the average size of dwellings are higher than the national average, while unemployment is lower. When compared with non-ID areas, employment growth in the post-war period has been more pronounced in our sample. More dubious, however, is export performance in the first half of the 1990s. The indicators that define an ID; namely agglomeration, specialization in one particular industry and a concentration of SMEs; depict these areas as more successful on average than non-IDs' areas, while the additional features comprised in the canonical model do not appear to be necessary conditions.

Economies of urbanization and the creation of ancillary industries do not always result from agglomeration processes. Ancillary industries or urbanization economies have not arisen everywhere. The full range of external economies can only be observed where particular historical contingencies have occurred and therefore depend on highly idiosyncratic processes of development. Inter-industry externalities, rather than within-industry externalities have become more important in the last decade. The different width and importance of externalities in the IDs surveyed and in various periods of time underscore a difficulty in generalizing a theory of agglomeration (of SMEs). Our results, therefore, may be added to those surveyed by Martin and that led him to sustain that 'This diversity may well limit the ambition and success of constituting an overarching universal model of spatial agglomeration' (1999, p. 80)

As regards the performance of the various typologies, the concentrated ID shows the best overall performance. The increasing role of white-collar workers in these IDs, as both managers and technical supervisors – a trend matched by a reduction in self-employed workers – highlights greater differentiation in the structure of firms, where the entrepreneur is no longer the *factotum* but delegates certain specialist functions. Qualitative information on these IDs also shows that spontaneous or informal relationships with final subcontractors are being replaced by networks or constellations of firms, with some firms having a leading or 'interconnecting' firms. In most of these IDs, technological innovations concerning new products, materials or processes can be observed. A virtuous interaction between tacit and codified knowledge has therefore been realized.

Marginal IDs, mainly located in southern regions, achieve bad social performance matched by a low endowment of infrastructure and amenities – although they fare better than southern Italy on average. These IDs include relatively larger and presumably less efficient firms. There are also very small firms in these areas, but they are few in number and operate either as subcontractors or as final producers, generally for clients or traders located outside the area concerned. Although the southern areas in the sample are among the most industrialized, and thus convey a new image of the south, the wide and serious 'gap' with respect to the north still persists. It is also true, however, that these areas generally began their industrial development on the basis of very different 'initial conditions'.

The areas closest to the 'canonical' model, in particular those exhibiting a fragmented division of labour based on self-employed and ancillary workers, are not the only successful ones. Other typologies have proved viable, with the consequence that the 'canonical' model is far from being normative. In addition, these areas significantly declined in number between 1981 and 1991, which suggests that the properties of the canonical model were more suited to the external demand and technology conditions of past decades than they are to those of the present scenario, with its profound transformation and evolution toward new models.

The wide variety of real IDs resulting from the research also has important policy implications in that it recommends differentiated and 'phase-based' industrial policies. The evidence collected suggests that 'blanket' solutions should be avoided, given that IDs differ greatly as regards the structure of interfirm relationships, the nature of competitive advantage, the patterns of learning, modes of regulation, weaknesses and strengths, and engines of growth. Also, the variety within IDs relating to the emergence of networks of firms or integrated firms suggests that selective policies should seek to identify and foster the most dynamic actors. Providing incentives for innovative actors, at either the organizational or technological level, may trigger pathbreaking events or redirect the trajectory of development in a manner that the self-organized nature of the ID is not able to produce spontaneously (Chapter 5).

6.2. CRITICAL ISSUES IN ITALIAN INDUSTRIAL DISTRICTS

However, notwithstanding the overall good performance of the sample, there are some weaknesses to be highlighted. Transformation processes are underway, and the nature and future prospects of these areas are likely to change, although how they will do so is difficult to predict at this stage. Discussed here are some of the contradictions of IDs that may challenge their future competitiveness and their sustainability as a socio-economic model of industrial development able to combine efficiency and competitiveness with social cohesion.

Firstly, the scale on which IDs – local, national or international – are observed must be analysed before conclusions can be drawn. The decline of an ID in one region may coincide with its growth in another region or country. This has already occurred in Italy, where the development of IDs in the southern regions is apparently indicative of some sort of 'fetch and carry' phenomenon. In the last two decades, the southern regions have 'fetched' – that is, inherited the more traditional specializations of northern regions – outperforming them in export values and employment growth. A national network can be envisaged as a further source of external economies in Italy, but there are already signs that new IDs are arising in Eastern European or – albeit to a lesser extent – in Mediterranean countries, as the offshoots of IDs located in north-eastern, and also south-eastern, Italy.

Some phases of production previously carried out within the boundaries of Italian IDs are now migrating to Romania, Slovenia, Albania and Morocco, where costs are lower and factors more widely available. Cases of delocation concern subcontractors and/or larger sections of the district value chain, and incidentally show that the internationalization of Italian IDs is systemic in its nature, because foreign investment by a leader firm is then imitated by its neighbours. Although this is an aspect that warrants further research, the scattered evidence collected suggests that these investments are motivated either by a search for cheaper labour or land, or lower administrative costs in establishing a factory, or by the prospects of growing demand in the recipient country. The search for cheaper input factors may lead to an improved quality level of products at lower cost, thereby preserving local competitiveness, but it may also coincide with a weakening of IDs. Market-seeking motivations assume that the recipient countries will follow a pattern of consumption similar to Italy's in the post-war period, when consumption goods like footwear, clothing and furniture grew at a high rate. We have already mentioned that Italian IDs are losing their market shares in international trade, because new competitors are emerging and the products achieving the greatest growth are those in which IDs are not specialized (Section 3.2.5). This loss of market share in world trade by IDs may also be indicative of their new positioning in the international division of labour. This, in fact, is one of the major question marks hanging over the future competitiveness of Italian IDs, and the country itself, given its overall model of international specialization. The reasons for delocation are obviously linked to the structural features of IDs analysed in previous chapters.

Among the various changes taking place, to be especially emphasized is the increasing concentration of production into fewer hands. Chapter 3 showed that the replacement of spontaneous or informal relationships by formal subcontracting relations, the creation of networks or constellations of firms, and the increasing role of leading or 'interconnecting' firms do not necessarily widen the gap between social and economic performance. The cluster of 'integrated' IDs exemplifies how restructuring does not necessarily affect the social welfare of the local population adversely. However, these results should be evaluated in the long term, while our research has provided only an initial account.

As explained in more detail in Section 3.4, a well-founded prediction on the viable organizational evolution of IDs is that organizational forms and competitive strategies of the most dynamic actors of the districts will intermingle, a feature that warrants further research.

New organizational forms, like leading firms (generally of a larger size) or groups, may also generate external economies locally. They may introduce radical innovation and thereby stimulate smaller firms to innovate their product/process, something which they would otherwise fail to do without pressure from outside. They may also introduce the better management practices that small firms are unable to develop because they lack the requisite human and financial resources. Large firms or leading firms can also produce public goods that generate externalities for smaller firms (logistical infrastructures, education centres). This, for example, is the case of Matera, where the leader firm, Natuzzi, has sponsored several initiatives to promote best practices and technological capabilities (Belussi, 1999).

Hence, the formation of protagonists (such as larger firms or groups that differ from the local scale of the district, or the increasing frequency of delocation), do not impair overall performance in the areas concerned, at least in the period observed by our research. In these circumstances, the local 'community' becomes more selective, encompassing only some sectors of local society and extending its boundaries towards the global environment. However, these phenomena, according to Becattini, send the ID 'out of scale'; out of the canonical form of the Marshallian ID (Becattini, 1990).

A look at the past history of IDs, also suggests that the process or product innovations have often been introduced by actors not belonging to the ID, rather than by self-organized processes, thereby suggesting that change originates from exogenous sources. In other words, the implicit conclusion – coming back to the questions raised in Chapter 1 – is that change in IDs will not come about through reliance on traditional local resources; instead, it will derive from 'contamination' by or 'hybridization' with new actors: processes that generate new practices and rationalities that may enrich local patterns of learning.

Among the critical weaknesses of IDs we have also identified the lower educational level of local populations, large-scale immigration from eastern Europe or Mediterranean countries, and a widespread shortage of skilled workers (Chapter 5).

The sample of IDs analysed displays levels of higher schooling below the national average and an education profile of the local population concentrated in the lower levels of schooling. The question is whether a more complex internal organization of firms and more sophisticated technologies, or merely the introduction of ICTs, is feasible with these skill levels. To put it another way, will workers (and entrepreneurs) possessing such low levels of schooling be able to cope with a higher degree of complexity in both technologies and organizational practices? And, will they be able to convert tacit into codified knowledge (and the reverse)? We are referring to the need to improve quality and management capabilities, to manage international markets and production relationships, and to innovate products and business organization.

All the areas in the sample suffer from a shortage of qualified labour; a problem that frequently gives rise to 'labour poaching', the practice whereby firms offer higher wages to the most highly qualified workers employed by their rivals. Such poaching is an unfair form of competition which tends to vitiate the 'good' competition that should characterize a canonical ID and represents one of the most pernicious kinds of non-cooperative behaviour. The phenomenon of labour shortage is due to the unsuitability of local training provision, which should consequently be overhauled (Chapter 5).

Some of the most industrialized areas in the sample also manifest unsatisfied demand for unskilled workers to undertake the most fatiguing and health-threatening job tasks. This problem is generally resolved by 'spontaneous' mechanisms that attract immigrants from less-developed countries.

The increasing inflow of immigrants into IDs may have ambiguous consequences for their competitiveness and social cohesion. On the one hand, immigrants may inject new competencies and practices into manufacturing, or just continue old specializations – presently abandoned by young natives – and revitalize local production by offering a new basis for local reputation and competitive advantage. On the other hand, migrants may create, in Italy as in other countries, downward pressure on wages in ID labour markets by impeding the technological upgrading of local production and related worker-education levels. Social integration would also be undermined, which would require new mechanisms for the local regulation of informal work practices and tax evasion, or the provision of social services specifically for immigrants. Mediation of these contrasting tendencies, and the ability of local populations not only to integrate migrants but also to reactivate the endogenous formation of new skills and knowledge, will determine the future viability of IDs as an enduring example of places able to preserve their local identity while achieving competitiveness.

The weaknesses listed thus far – namely, the declining effectiveness of the traditional mechanisms of skills' transmission, the continuation of marginal or even standardized productions in IDs, often performed by communities of immigrants, and a shortage of qualified workers – with the labour poaching consequent upon it – are all phenomena that impede adoption of more sophisticated production methods and vitiate a climate of fair competition.

These internal circumstances occur in a competitive scenario characterized by more intense competitive pressure, shorter lead times and highly customized products, and a change in distribution markets brought about by the spread of integrated department stores; all factors that jointly render inappropriate the traditional methods used by small firms to tackle markets.

Forms of social dumping (prices lower than the 'sustainable' level for the ID) or tighter competition, risk reducing the surplus that allegedly ensured continuous investments in tangible and intangible assets. Moreover, there are also some cognitive restraints – related to the typical entrepreneurial pattern of IDs – that impede more successful strategies. One of the most noticeable weaknesses of the typical entrepreneurial class in canonical and 'craft-based' IDs in particular (largely based on the self-employed worker), is the difficulties its members have in adopting more sophisticated and updated certification procedures.

It has been mentioned that increasing numbers of local firms are adopting more advanced forms of coordination to exchange goods, information and technologies among a relatively stable group of firms according to a more uniform standard of communication, generally represented by certification procedures or CWCQ methods. The internal functioning of IDs – according to the evidence provided by primary or secondary sources – rests on co-ordination mechanisms with different cognitive foundations. In this case, firms need to develop not a common abstract language but a universal protocol that enables linkages to be established even among actors who, although they belong to different regional or even national contexts, share a common technical culture.

The strategies just mentioned enhance firms' learning capabilities and competitiveness but they are not adopted by all local firms. Most of the firms in (quasi) canonical or craft-based IDs do not always react appropriately to new trends; rather, they seem to prefer niche strategies. Local entrepreneurs fear that the formalization of procedures implied by the adoption of certification procedures or CWCQ methods may impair the flexibility that ensured their success in past decades. This attitude is also apparent in the adoption of ITCs. According to a very recent survey (FEDERCOMIN, 2001) out of 51 Italian IDs, half of which coincide with those examined here, digital technologies have been introduced by only a small fraction of firms within a few IDs. Among the latter, in Prato, Arzignano, Fermo and Pesaro an estimated proportion of 8 per cent of local sales has been invested in digital innovations: mostly e-mail systems or websites shared by several firms, while 'discussion groups' are rarer. On browsing the Web, one finds that some associations in the larger IDs have developed portal shop windows for local firms and the ID as a whole, the intention being to promote the area's reputation or to offer information or e-procurement services. In some cases, these initiatives are larger than the district in scale and are, for example, fostered by a regional agency for local development (like ASTER in Emilia Romagna). However, in these cases too, only very restricted use is made of such new methods of communicating or approaching upstream or downstream markets. On average, small entrepreneurs are reluctant to master new technologies, whether electronics or ICTs.

This evidence suggests that there is a need to reconsider the factors typically cited in the literature to explain IDs' success, and to draw some theoretical implications.

6.3. SOME THEORETICAL AND RESEARCH IMPLICATIONS OF THE FINDINGS

6.3.1. Reassessing the Role of Trust and Cooperation in Industrial Districts

As discussed in Chapter 1, cooperation supposedly regulates interfirm relationships along vertical lines as well as relationships among peers for the regulation of competition and the provision of 'public' goods. The research described in this book was not specifically concerned with analysis of cooperative behaviours. However, it collected enough evidence to support the idea that cooperation is not an invariant feature of IDs, and this suggests that some of the theoretical hypotheses put forward in the literature on IDs should be reformulated.

As regards 'fair' rules of cooperation, and cooperation among peers in the provision of public goods, mention has already been made of cases of labour poaching and other forms of non cooperative behaviour (Chapter 3). The point to emphasize here, however, concerns the inability of inter-entrepreneur traditions of solidarity or cooperative attitudes to cope with new challenges.

In Bassano, a long tradition of solidarity – which gave rise, for example, to the creation of a compensation fund for artisan employers – proved fragile in the 1990s when a structural decline in demand combined with a shortage of a crucial raw material: wood. An effective response in this situation would have been the creation of a purchasing consortium, which might, for example, have bought wood from the nearby Eastern Europe markets. However, none of the local industrial associations was able to promote any such form of cooperation. In addition, many 'market-spoiling' forms of behaviour ensued. Competition grew fierce, and there was a risk that the imitation strategies adopted would destroy the reputation of local production. Also, the case of Marostica provides an object lesson in this regard. Here the 'collaboration group' set up by a dozen local firms does not constitute a strategic alliance and goes no further than the occasional exchange of orders, thus jeopardizing the competitive survival of the area.

Associationism has also been cited as one of the main resources of IDs, as the basis for their efficacious regulation of economic relationships. Diseconomies of firms, mainly related to the small scale of production, have been remedied by the pooling of services through mobilization of a 'sense of belonging' and local values. Most of these initiatives have been effective, although some evidence shows that export or purchasing consortia have often been unstable (Grandori and Soda, 1995; Paniccia, 1998). In the cases of consortia and service centres – which often comprise competing firms – the sharing of the same facility and the use of the same service did not previously prejudice their competitiveness because they concerned non-core activities (export assistance, bookkeeping, and so on) and therefore cooperation was easier. However, in the new competitive scenario, the diseconomies of small firms are no longer due to their size alone but are capability related. As a consequence, the pooling of resources in a consortium or a service centre is no longer sufficient.

The kind of cooperation, and therefore the amount of coordination (the codes of communication and, more generally, the cognitive and moral resources), needed to establish purchasing or credit consortia, or to share common services or to facilitate access to production factors (credit, business services, labour, and so on) is not as close as that required to conduct a joint project to search out a new market, to develop a new technology or product or to organize a logistic chain.

The entrepreneur is called upon to abandon the routines and patterns of action that have ensured his/her success in the past (past-experience 'lock-in'). The phenomenon of IDs in Italy is historically tied to a specific model of entrepreneurship, whether with a rural, artisan or industrial background. Pride in one's profession and ability explains many cases of non-collaboration, rather than the reverse – as Piore proposed when he drew the distinction between 'work' and 'labour' (1990). Attachment to one's work and pride in one's expertise may be factors that make the maximization of profit of secondary importance – according to Piore – but they are also obstacles against cooperation. It is the conviction of being smarter than one's rival that impedes collaboration or prevents the revealing of alleged secrets. The most noteworthy cases of cooperation, in fact, are to be found in the mechanical engineering industry, where a user–producer pattern of innovation exists. The systemic nature of innovation in this industry fosters joint agreements and common projects among small specialist producers (but not between large manufacturers and small subcontractors).

It emerges from the description of the cooperative and non cooperative behaviours that IDs are a strong expression of a highly specific entrepreneurial culture in which the individual ethos is very solid and a recursive calculative ability constitutes the dominant cognitive approach.

A basic and usually technical education matched with a craft background and/or on-the-job-training has been the typical feature of the first- or second-generation entrepreneurial class in most of the areas examined. This technical culture seems to be characteristic of dominant local cognitive mechanisms, as well as of the process of learning and problem solving.

Parochialism may inhibit technological or technical spillovers, and therefore the diffusion of an industry. Whilst these factors play a positive role in stimulating competition with the unconscious aim of defeating a rival 'foreigner', on the other hand they make entrepreneurs too self-reliant and unwilling to seek out new methods and routines, and they also prevent the diffusion and spillover of critical skills. They affect expectations about other people's qualities and aims, and thus affect the mechanisms of trust generation.

The factors cited in the literature – like 'common belonging', a similar cultural context and the sharing of a common system of values (Chapter 1) – as factors explanatory of trust and cooperation, underlie different and often conflicting behaviours taken by firms. Actually, the firms' or institutions' behaviours appear in most of the cases as context-driven (dependent on the balance of rewards and penalties, number of actors, type of uncertainty, and so on) or path dependent. The nature of cooperation is intrinsically dynamic, and history plays an important role in its evolution (Axelrod, 1984). Indeed, we have gathered cases where even two contiguous areas (namely, Ascoli Piceno and Giulianova) exhibit different cooperative attitudes as a consequence of their very recent history. IDs, as well as networks, are very real 'hybrid institutions' governed by often conflicting rules. This view of IDs points to a possible redirection of research towards comparative studies within the multifaceted world of IDs, which overcomes a misleading divide between cooperative and non-cooperative systems, IDs and markets, and IDs and hierarchies. Rather than insisting on the assumption of trust to explain inter-company and peer relationships within IDs or networks, this book has illustrated cases in which trust may be one of the many possible outcomes of interactions, depending on structural context-related features. However, whilst cooperation ensured the success of IDs in the 1990s, what is needed now is the injection of new techniques, managerial practices, routines, and specializations obtained by means of closer interaction between local and non-local resources and skills.

Moreover a common cultural allegiance may not be necessary when new organizational principles are adopted. The example of the Natuzzi company in the southern area of Matera illustrates the case. Team working, and problem-solving procedures adopted internally, have formed a trust climate within the integrated firm. The alleged personal characteristics of the local population, such as honesty, attachment to work, and a certain artisan tradition in the same specialized industry as the leader firm, have facilitated this kind of organization, as well as spin-offs of new suppliers or subcontractors in the area, but they have not driven its industrial development, which has instead been spurred by the location of a dynamic large firm.

On the one hand, cooperation is not an invariant or pervasive feature of all the types of IDs or all their phases of development. On the other hand, it may be produced by means of mechanisms or institutions different from those underlined in the canonical literature. However, looking at the weaknesses of existing IDs, a doubt arises whether cooperation – if not further qualified – is a necessary condition for their sustainability. It therefore appears that the critical resource for competitiveness and growth is no longer cooperation, as suggested by the 'canonical' literature, but hybridization or contamination: the ability to learn and adapt new codes and practices.

The challenges now facing IDs require entrepreneurial skills that cannot be produced by reliance on craft experience, personal savings, basic schooling, personal contacts, work ethics and family support alone; a point also made by Amin (1997). The cognitive abilities necessary to understand new technologies and new markets or to organize the exchange of goods in a network of suppliers and distributors are rarely acquired in technical schools, even less through compulsory schooling. Indeed, the 'embeddedness' of traditional institutions may reveal a factor of inertia.

This also means that the integration of execution and conception at a firm level or the autonomy and entrepreneurialism of the nodes in the ID network are not in themselves sufficient to foster competitiveness, as implied in Piore and Sabel's *Second Industrial Divide* (1984) or in networks' literature.

Certification procedures not only require higher cognitive capabilities but also create a different and upgraded basis for mutual understanding and communication that does not merely coincide with trust.

Paradoxically, we may conclude with the words of one of the most convinced proponents of the canonical approach, who more recently has conducted critical appraisal of the virtues of the craft-based ID model by contrasting it with goal-oriented coordination among Japanese decentralized firms:

> [F]orms of coordination, derived from Japanese experience, that encourage deliberate, experimental revision of the definition and distribution of tasks within and among economic institutions outperform those based on notions of craft or entrepreneurship, that pursue the reintegration of conception and execution of tasks within a division of labour assumed to be natural and beyond reflection. This system of coordination I will call learning by monitoring because of the way it links evaluation of performance to reassessment of goals. (Sabel, 1995, p. 4)

6.3.2.   A New Wave of Research on Industrial Districts

A rejection of determinism in the assessment of cooperation in IDs is an indirect implication of the foregoing discussion. Cooperation has always been assumed when the literature has summarily declared an area to be an ID, without close scrutiny of its real correspondence to an ID framework. The same goes for innovation. Even more hastily, IDs are deemed to be innovative merely because some more successful cases appear to be so. It is the lack of controllable criteria that generates the risk of determinism and the facile extension of features valid only on theoretical grounds to the empirical phenomenon on the mere basis of analogy.

At the time of writing the conclusions to the book, the prestigious Bank of Italy research department has published a collection of essays that espouse a quantitative approach to IDs (Signorini, 2001). This bears out the methodological choice underlying this study. Indeed we claim that the literature has now achieved a maturity that parallels that of real IDs, and it has moved beyond the phase of case studies to explaining the inner workings of IDs. The present 'new wave', as we may call it, relies more closely on quantitative and comparative studies among Italian and international IDs. More precisely, we have here encouraged a combination of a qualitative and quantitative approach that may reconcile richness of analysis with rigour and controllability of results. Case studies could be selected among and between types of IDs, resulting from multivariate analysis, this avoiding the subjectivity often implicit in the choice of case studies. Moreover, the data-set underlying this book can be implemented, enriched and updated (for example, with the 2001 Census data) for the purposes of further and more refined research.

Comparative analysis using different counterfactuals – for example firms that do not belong to IDs – would have been desirable, but constructing a sample of this kind is difficult in Italy. Most of the industries in which IDs are specialized, in particular tannery and footwear, are very localized and it is consequently hard to find an LLMA that is not an ID for each of the macro-regions of Italy specialized in the same industry. However, we have already shown the wide variety of forms that fall under the umbrella term of 'ID'.

On the one hand, theoretical frameworks applied to IDs must be refined so that they yield testable hypotheses. A consistent model of IDs is not provided in this book. Work in progress by the author is addressing the issue of combining different strands of the literature and determining the performance of IDs as resulting from the interplay of their different markets: the labour market, the intermediate-inputs market, and the institutional supply of services. It should, however, be borne in mind that even if theory makes advances, the testing of hypotheses is severely impaired by the scant availability of data at the break-down level suitable for IDs. The recent commitment by ISTAT to provide more timely data at the municipal level on firms, employees, added value, sales and exports may facilitate more in-depth analyses of LLMA performance.

Promising areas of research lie in both the sociological and economic domains. The new social institutions that may replace the traditional ones, and the viability of a localized system of firms, warrant special attention. Careful monitoring of attitudes to work among young people (the offspring of first- or second-generation district entrepreneurs), on the one hand, and among immigrants on the other, and an assessment of the obvious patterns of integration of both may yield critical insights into the evolution of IDs. Longer time-series data would also enable verification of whether there exist historical cycles or patterns of development. An international comparative work may highlight the functional equivalents for the emergence of IDs. The main sources of the data used for this work – population and industry censuses – are relatively standardized and therefore allow replication of the research design in other countries.

As mentioned in Chapter 3, analysis that focuses on individual leading companies or groups of coordinators, and then examines their linkages with other firms and their ability to upgrade a large set of connected firms would be more predictive of ID performances. A comparison among the roles performed by these coordinators in IDs with similar socio-economic conditions such as those identified by our multivariate analysis – and therefore within each typology – would permit better assessment of the viability of IDs in the future.

A systematic study of the impact of new technologies or the diffusion of ICTs on the nature of interfirm and intrafirm relationships may also provide important findings with which to describe the evolutionary pattern of IDs.

More profound analysis of ID performance could also be accomplished by inspecting the performance of two matched samples of firms located in two similar LLMAs (ones belonging to the same type, for example). In this case balance sheets could provide reliable data on efficiency, profitability and financial structure.

Case studies should be based on interviews administered to a sample of firms and covering various aspects of the cultural backgrounds of entrepreneurs and managers/workers, organizational features, and relationship with other institutions.

The interaction between service and manufacturing activities within IDs is another area that deserves further attention. Our results did not permit to draw firm conclusions on this issue, since we observed a general increase of the specialization in service industries and a higher tertiarization within firms, without being able to estimate which trend is predominant. This also derives from the choice of the LLMA as our unit of analysis that may represent a geographical scale not adequate for the location of service activities. As already mentioned, professionals and services' workers generally prefer to locate in non-peripheral areas provided with the necessary business infrastructures and amenities. The methodological question of the appropriateness of the notion of LLMAs also arises when considering the increasing degree of openness of IDs. We find that it is still adequate in relation to the years analysed and in most of the areas. One exception is those cases where there are functional linkages between different LLMAs, since the notion fails to grasp the interdependencies and interactions among more peripheral municipalities specialized in industrial activities and the main urban centres more specialized in service industries, which are generally located in different LLMAs. Another exception is those cases where the degree of self-containment is low, due either to a high reliance on external commissioning firms, as in most of the 'marginal' IDs, or on external suppliers or subcontractors, as could be predicted for some 'quasi-canonical' or concentrated IDs. For further research on IDs and agglomeration phenomena we suggest a multi-step methodology departing from the notion of LLMA and then moving to larger aggregations in the so-called 'functional areas'.

Appendix

LIST OF INDICATORS

The source of data is ISTAT, Census of Industry and Population, various years, unless otherwise specified.

No	Label of the variable	Description (algorithm)

Demographic Ratios

1	*Rpop*	Resident population (thousands).
2	*Emi*	Emigration rate: absent population over resident population.
3	*Po65*	Population aged 65 and more; calculated in 1991 only.
4	*Po14*	Population aged 14 and under; calculated in 1991 only.
5	*immi*	Resident and transient foreign population over resident population*1000 (year 1991).
6	*immi99*	Resident and transient foreign population over resident population*1 000 (year 1999).

Indicators of Social Structure

Structure of the family

7	*famy*	Percentage of 'extended' families over all types of families. 'Extended' families correspond to type D of ISTAT classification (1995a).

Education ratios

8	*laur*	Percentage of population with a bachelor degree ('laurea') over population aged six and over.
9	*dipl*	Percentage of population with a senior-secondary school degree ('diploma') over population aged six and over.

10	*high*	rate of higher education; variable *laur* and variable *dipl*.
11	*seco*	Percentage of population with junior secondary-school certificate ('Licenza Media').
12	*prim*	Percentage of Population with primary-school certificate ('Licenza elementare') over population aged six and more.
13	*comp*	Rate of compulsory schooling; = variable *prim* and variable *seco*.
14	*illi*	Rate of illiteracy: literate population without qualification and illiterate individuals across population aged six and over.
15	*drop*	Schooling drop out in the group aged 19–42.
16	*qual34*	Diploma qualification in the group aged 19–34.
17	*qual44*	Diploma qualification in the group aged 35–44.
18	*qual19*	Diploma qualification in the group aged 19 and over.

Inclusiveness of local business community and work attitudes

19	*apop*	People economically active across population aged six and over.
20	*unem*	Rate of unemployment (including people seeking a first job and a second employment/occupation).
21	*inac*	Rate of inactivity: population economically inactive across total population aged six and over.
22	*hous*	Rate of housekeeping (housekeepers across female population aged 14 and over).
23	*apyo*	rate of activity of young generation aged 19–29; Economically active individuals aged 19–29 across total population.

Social Structure Indicators in Industry Sector

Population with a professional status in industry by employment status

24	*ient*	Percentage of employers (entrepreneurs) and professional workers in industrial activities.
25	*enti*	*ient* and *coop*
26	*iman*	Percentage of managers in industrial activities (available in 1991 only).
27	*isem*	Percentage of self-employed workers in industrial activities.
28	*icle*	Percentage of employees (low-level clerks and industry workers) in industrial activities.

29	*clei*	*icle* and *mana*.
30	*ianc*	Percentage of ancillary workers in industrial activities.
31	*iwor*	Percentage of workers in industrial activities.
32	*coop*	Percentage of members of co-operatives in industrial activities (available in 1991 only).

Indicators of Economies of Urbanization and Well-being

| 33 | *infr* | Rate of infrastructure. (ISTAT, 1996) (Italy = 100). The indicator, as provided by ISTAT, is calculated at provincial level. |

Indicators of Civicness and Political Participation

34	*unio*	Rate of unionization: number of workers associated to main trade unions (local branches of CGIL and CISL) over total workers (approximated values obtained from a mailed questionnaire and interviews).
35	*poli*	Presence of a dominant political subculture (measured by the percentage of votes taken by the first political party or coalition in 1992 national polls (ISTAT, 1994 and interviews to local branches of national parties).
36	*asso*	Rate of associationism: number of voluntary associations over inhabitants*10000. Available in 1981 only (Mortara, 1985).

Industrial Structure and Economic Indicators

37	*mane*	Percentage of manufacturing employees over all employees in all activities.
38	*finh*	Rate of entrepreneurship: percentage of firms (establishments) in the leading (or 'key') industrial sector over inhabitants.
39	*einh*	Number of employees in the leading industry by inhabitants.
40	*einhi*	Number of employees in the leading and 'secondary' industries by inhabitants.
41	*firm*	Number of firms (establishments) in the 'leading' industry (thousands).
42	*empl*	Number of employees (establishments) in the leading industry (thousands).
43	*spcf*	Index of specialization by number of firms: percentage of firms (establishments) in the 'key' industry over all firms in manufacturing.

44	*spce*	Index of specialization by number of employees: percentage of employees in the leading industry over all employees in manufacturing.
45	*spec1*	Rate of specialization by number of firms: percentage of firms (establishments) in the 'key' industry over all firms in manufacturing (normalized by the corresponding indicator at regional level).
46	*spec2*	Rate of specialization by number of employees: percentage of employees in the leading industry over all employees in manufacturing (normalized by the corresponding rate at regional level).
47	*secf*	Index of specialization in the first 'ancillary' industry by number of firms: percentage of firms (establishments) in the 'ancillary' industry over all firms in manufacturing.
48	*sece*	Index of specialization in the first 'ancillary' industry by number of employees: percentage of employees in the 'ancillary' industry over all employees in manufacturing.
49	*mechf*	Index of specialization in the mechanical engineering industry by the number of firms: percentage of firms (establishments) in the 'ancillary' industry over all firms in manufacturing.
50	*meche*	Index of specialization in the mechanical engineering industry by the number of employees: percentage of employees in the mechanical industry over all employees in manufacturing.
51	*arti*	Proportion of craft firms over total firms in the leading industry.
52	*auto*	Proportion of turnover accounted by independent terminal firms in the leading industry. See Section 2.5.3 for the description of the variable and Section 3.3 for qualitative sources. For the source of data on turnover, see variable n. 71.
53	*isef*	Index of specialization in 'business services': percentage of firms (local units) in 'business services' over firms (establishments) in all activities.
54	*sosf*	Index of specialization in 'social services' by the number of firms (establishments): percentage of firms in 'social services' across inhabitants.
55	*bankf*	Index of specialization in 'financial services' by number of firms (establishments): percentage of firms

		in 'financial services' over firms (establishments) in all activities.
56	*serve*	Index of specialization in 'service industries': percentage of employees in 'services' over total employment.
57	*RDsp*	Index of specialization in R&D activities: percentage of employees in R&D activities over employment in all industries.
58	*C1*	Number of employees in establishments with fewer than ten employees in the leading industry.
59	*C2*	Number of employees in establishments having between 10 and 50 employees in the leading industry.
60	*C3*	Number of employees in establishments with more than 50 employees in the leading industry.
61	*HH*	Index of manufacturing diversification.

$$HH_{id},t = \_{jt \neq I} \ E^2_{jd}$$

where:

t = census year: 1951, 1961, ... , 1996 ;

I = manufacturing industry less industry i;

d = industrial district: 1, 2, ..., 39;

E = proportion of employment in industry i in ID d over total manufacturing industry in the same d;

62	*size*	Average size of firms (establishments) in leading industry.
63	*C5*	Degree of concentration of production: market share of the first largest five firms (source: estimated values and CENSIS, 1997; Regione Emilia Romagna et al., 1998; CREI, 1995).

Indicators of employment growth

64	*vafi*	Percentage variation of firms in i leading industry (t = 1951, 1961, 1971, 1981, 1991 and 1996).
65	*Lnvafi*	Rate of firms variation in logarithm (ln) = $\ln(firm_{it}) - \ln(firm_{it-1})$.
66	*vale*	Variation of employees in i leading industry (t = 1951, 1961, 1971, 1981, 1991 and 1996).
67	*Lnvale*	Logarithm of vale: $\ln(vale_{it}) - \ln(empl_{it-1})$.

Indicators of performance

68	*inco81*	Indicator of richness: income per capita, 1981 (Banco di Santo Spirito, 1982).
69	*inco91*	Indicator of richness: income per capita, 1991 (Banco di Santo Spirito, 1987)
70	*inco96*	Indicator of richness: income per capita, 1996 (estimates on Istituto Tagliacarne, 2000).
71	*exp1*	Variation of export in leading industry between 1986 and 1991 (data at provincial level) standardized by the variation of the same industry at national level (data at provincial level provided by ISTAT, 1999a).
72	*exp6*	Variation of export in leading industry between 1991 and 1996 standardized by the variation of the same industry at national level (data at provincial level).
73	*sale*	Sales per capita (millions of lira): total sales in value of the leading industry i over total employment in industry I (estimated values on different sources: Associazione Industriale della provincia di Vicenza, 1998; CENSIS, 1997; CREI, 1995; Moussanet and Paolazzi, 1992; OSEM, 1995/6; Regione Emilia Romagna et al., 1998; Unione Industriale Pratese, 1998; Viesti, 2000 and interviews).
74	*saled*	Sales per capita standardized by the corresponding ratio at the national average: average sales in district d in industry i over average sales in industry i at national level (source of data on national values: ISTAT, 1999b).

Indicators of Dwellings' Facilities

75	*M2av*	Households' average size in square metres.
76	*M2in*	Square metres by inhabitants: total surface of dwellings divided by inhabitants.
77	*room*	Number of rooms per households.

References

Adelman, M. (1958), 'Concepts and statistical measurement of vertical integration', in G.J. Stigler (ed.), *Business Concentration and Price Policy*. Princeton, NJ: Princeton University Press, pp. 318–20.

Aeeg (Autorità per l'energia elettrica e il gas) (2001), 'Confronti internazionali di prezzo', www.autorita.energia.it/Documentazione.

Amin, A. (1988), 'Specialisation without growth: small firms in an inner-city area of Naples', mimeo, University of Newcastle.

Amin, A. (1993), 'The globalization of the economy: an erosion of regional networks?' in G. Grabher (ed.), *The Embedded Firm. On Socioeconomics of Industrial Networks*, London: Routledge.

Amin, A. (1997), 'Institutional foundations and problems of adaptation in entrepreneurial regions: illustrations from Emilia-Romagna', mimeo, Durham: University of Durham.

Amin, A. and K. Robins (1990), 'Industrial Districts and Regional Development: Limits and Possibilities', in F. Pyke, G. Becattini and W. Sengenberger (eds), *Industrial Districts and Inter-firm Co-operation in Italy*, pp. 185–217.

Amin, A. and N. Thrift (1992), 'Neo-Marshallian nodes in global networks', *International Journal of Urban and Social Research*, **16**, 571–87.

Antonelli, C. (2000), 'Collective knowledge, communication and innovation', *Regional Policy*, **34** (6), 535–47.

Archibugi, D. (1992), 'Patenting as an indicator of technological innovation: a review', *Science and Public Policy*, **19** (1), 357–68.

Arrighetti, A.and G. Seravalli (eds) (1999), *Istituzioni intermedie e sviluppo locale*, Roma: Donzelli.

Arrow, K.J. (1962), 'The economic implications of learning by doing', *Review of Economic Studies*, **29**, pp. 155–73.

Arthur, W.B. (1994), *Increasing Returns and Path Dependence in the Economy*, Michigan: Michigan University Press.

Asheim, B.T. (1994), 'Industrial districts, inter-firm co-operation and endogenous technological development: the experience of developed countries', in M.P. Van Dijk et al. (eds), *Technological Dynamism in Industrial Districts: an Alternative Approach to Industrialisation in Developing Countries?*, New York and Geneva: Unctad, United Nations,

Asheim, B.T. (1996), 'Industrial districts as "learning regions": a condition for prosperity', *European Planning Studies*, **4** (4), 379–400.

Ashworth, G.J. and H. Voogd (1990), *Selling the City: Marketing Approaches in Public Sector Urban Planning*, London: Belhaven Press.

Associazione Industriali della provincia di Vicenza (1998), *Indicatori economici dell'industria vicentina* (Annual Report on production, sales, employment, export, firms), Vicenza: Associazione Industriali di Vicenza.

Assopiastrelle (1997), *Relazione annuale*, Modena: Assopiastrelle.

Axelrod, Robert (1984), *The Evolution of Co-operation*, New York: Norton.

Axelsson, B. and G. Easton (eds) (1992), *Industrial Networks: a New View of Reality*, London: Routledge.

Aydalot, P. (ed.) (1986), *Milieux Innovateurs in Europe*, Paris: Gremi.

Baculo, L. (ed.) (1996), *Impresa forte politica debole*, Napoli: Edizioni Scientifiche Italiane.

Baffigi, A., M. Pagnini and F. Quintiliani (1999), 'Industrial districts and local banks: do the twins ever meet?', Rome: Bank of Italy, *Temi di discussione del Servizio Studi*, No 147.

Bagnasco, A. (1977), *Tre Italie. Problematiche dello sviluppo italiano*, Bologna: Il Mulino.

Bagnasco, A. (1988), *La costruzione sociale del mercato*, Bologna: Il Mulino.

Bagnasco, A. and C. Trigilia (1984), *Società e politica nelle aree di piccola impresa*, Venezia: Edizioni Arsenale.

Balestri, A. (1993),'Il distretto tessile di Prato', in L. Boscarelli (ed.), *Il successo con le 'operations'. Produzione e mercato. La via italiana all'eccellenza*, Torino: Isedi.

Balestri, A. and D. Toccafondi (1994), *Imprenditori e distretti industriali*, Prato: Edizioni Pratofutura.

Bambi, G. (1998), 'The Evolution of a Furniture Industrial District: the Case of Poggibonsi in Tuscany', in M. Lorenzen (ed.), *Specialization and Localised Learning*, Handelshøjskolens Forlag, Copenhagen Business School Press.

Banco di S. Spirito (1982), *Il reddito dei comuni italiani*, Rome: Banco di S. Spirito.

Banco di S. Spirito (1987), *Il reddito dei comuni italiani*, Rome: Banco di S. Spirito.

Banfield, E.C. (1958), *The Moral Basis of a Backward Society*, Chicago: The Free Press, quoted in Putnam (1993).

Baptista, R. (2000), 'Clusters, Innovation and Growth: a Survey of the Literature', in G.M.P. Swann, M. Prevezer and D. Stout, *The Dynamics of Industrial Clustering*, Oxford: Oxford University Press, pp. 13–51.

Barca, F. (ed.) (1994), *Proprietà, modelli di controllo e riallocazione nelle*

212 Industrial Districts: Evolution and Competitiveness in Italian Firms

imprese industriali italiane, Vol. I. Bologna: Il Mulino.

Barca, F. (2000), La nuova programmazione economica, paper presented at the XLI meeting of the Italian society of economists (SIE), 26–28 October 2000.

Barca, F. and M. Magnani (1989), *L'industria tra capitale e lavoro*, Bologna: Il Mulino.

Baumol, W.J., J. Panzar and R. Willig (1982), *Contestable Market and the Theory of Industrial Structure*, New York: Harcourt Brace Jovanovich.

Becattini, G. (1979), 'Dal "settore industriale" al "distretto industriale". Alcune riflessioni sull'unità di indagine nell'economia industriale', *Rivista di Economia e Politica Industriale*, I (1) (reprinted as G. Becattini (1989), 'Sectors and/or Districts: Some Remarks on the Conceptual Foundations of Industrial Economics', in E. Goodman and J. Bamford (eds), *Small Firms and Industrial Districts in Italy*, London: Routledge, pp. 123–35.

Becattini, G. (ed.) (1987), *Mercato e forze locali: il distretto industriale*, Bologna: Il Mulino.

Becattini, G. (ed.) (1989), *Modelli locali di sviluppo*, Bologna: Il Mulino.

Becattini, G. (1990), 'The Marshallian industrial district as a socio-economic notion', in F. Pyke, G. Becattini and W. Sengenberger (eds), *Industrial Districts and Inter-firm Co-operation in Italy*, International Institute for Labour Studies, Geneva, pp. 37–51.

Becattini G. (1997), 'Totalità e cambiamento: il paradigma dei distretti industriali, (intervista a cura di T. Maccabelli)', *Sviluppo Locale*, IV (6), 75–94.

Becattini, G. and S. Menghinello (1998), 'Contributo e ruolo del made in Italy "distrettuale" nelle esportazioni nazionali di manufatti', *Sviluppo Locale*, V (2), 5–41.

Becattini, G. and E. Rullani (1993), 'Sistema locale e mercato globale', *Economia e Politica Industriale*, XX (80), 25–48.

Bellandi, M. (1989), 'The industrial district in Marshall', in E. Goodman and J. Bamford (eds), *Small Firms and Industrial Districts in Italy*, London: Routledge, pp. 135–52.

Bellandi, M. (1992), 'The incentives to decentralized industrial creativity in local systems of small firms', *Revue d'Economie Industrielle*, (59), 99–110.

Bellandi, M. and M. Romagnoli (1993), 'Prato e l'industria tessile', in R. Leonardi and R.Y. Nanetti (eds), *Lo sviluppo regionale dell'economia europea integrata: Il caso toscano*, Venezia: Marsilio, pp. 183–211.

Belussi, F. (1999), 'Path-dependency vs. industrial dynamics: the analysis of two heterogeneous Italian districts specialised in leather upholstery', *Human System Management*, 18 (2), pp.161–74.

Belussi, F. and F. Arcangeli (1998), 'A typology of networks: flexible and evolutionary firms', *Research Policy*, **27** (2), 415–28.

Belussi, F. and S. Gottardi (2000), *Evolutionary Patterns of Local Industrial Systems*, Aldershot: Ashgate.

Belussi, F. and L. Pilotti (2000), 'Knowledge creation and collective learning in the Italian local production systems', Discussion Paper, Dipartimento di Scienze economiche 'Marco Fanno', University of Padua.

Benko, G., M. Dunford and J. Heurley (1997), 'Districts industriels: vingt ans de recherches', *Espaces et Sociétés*, 88/89, pp. 305–27.

Benton, L. (1992), 'The Emergence of Industrial Districts in Spain: Industrial Restructuring and Diverging Regional Responses', in W. Sengenberger and F. Pyke (eds), *Industrial Districts and Local Economic Regeneration*, Geneva: International Institute for Labour Studies.

Best, M. (1990), *The New Competition: Institutions of Industrial Restructuring*, Cambridge MA: Harvard University Press.

Bianchi, P. (1989), 'Concorrenza dinamica, distretti industriali e interventi locali', in F. Gobbo (ed.), *Distretti e sistemi produttivi alla soglia degli anni '90*, Milano: F. Angeli, pp. 47–60.

Bigarelli, D. and P. Crestanello (1994a), 'An analysis of the changes in the knitwear/clothing district of Carpi during the 1980s, *Entrepreneurship and Regional Development*, **6**, 127–44.

Bigarelli, D. and P. Crestanello (1994b), 'Strategie di diversificazione e di riorganizzazione produttiva a Carpi negli anni Ottanta', in M. Bellandi and M. Russo (eds), *Distretti industriali e cambiamento economico locale*, Torino: Rosenberg & Sellier.

Biggiero, L. (1998), 'Italian industrial districts: the triple helix of problem–solving', *Industry and Higher Education*, **12** (4), 227–34.

Biggiero, L. (1999), 'Markets, hierarchies, districts: a cybernetic approach', *Human System Management*, **18** (2), 71–86.

Biggiero, L. and A. Sammarra (2001), 'Identity and identification in industrial districts', *Journal of Corporate Governance*, (5), 61–82.

Birkinshaw, J. and N. Hood (1995), 'An empirical study of development processes in foreign owned subsidiaries in Canada and Scotland', Proceedings of the EIBA conference 'New challenges for European and International Business', edited by R. Schiattarella, Urbino: Facoltà di Economia.

Borjas, G., R. Freeman, and L.F. Katz (1992), 'On the Labor Market Effects of Immigration and Trade', in G. Borjas and R. Freeman (eds), *Immigration and the Workforce*, NBER, Chicago: University of Chicago Press.

Bradach, J.L. and R.G. Eccles (1989), 'Markets versus Hierarchies: from ideal types to plural forms', *Annual Review of Sociology*, **15** (1), 97–118.

Bramanti, A. and A.M. Maggioni (eds) (1997), *La dinamica dei sistemi produttivi territoriali: teorie, tecniche, politiche*, Milano: F. Angeli.

Brusco, S. (1982), 'The Emilian model: productive decentralisation and social integration', *Cambridge Journal of Economics*, **6**, 167–84.

Brusco, S. (1986), 'Small Firms and Industrial Districts: the Experience of Italy', in D. Keeble and E. Wever (eds), *New Firms and Regional Development*, London: Croom Helm.

Brusco, S. (1989), *Piccole imprese e distretti industriali: una raccolta di saggi*, Torino: Rosenberg & Sellier.

Brusco, S. (1990), 'The Idea of the Industrial District: its Genesis', in F. Pyke, G. Becattini and W. Sengenberger (eds), *Industrial Districts and Inter-firm Co-operation in Italy*, Geneva: International Institute for Labour Studies, pp. 10–19.

Brusco, S. and S. Paba (1997), 'Per una storia dei distretti industriali dal secondo dopoguerra agli anni Novanta', in F. Barca (ed.), *Storia del capitalismo italiano*, Roma: Donzelli, pp. 265–333.

Brutti, P. and G. Ricoveri (eds) (1988), *La quarta Italia. Il lavoro e la politica industriale nei distretti e nelle aree integrate*, Roma: Ediesse.

Bursi, T. (1997), *Strategie di crescita ed acquisizioni nell'industria ceramica italiana*, Torino: Giappichelli.

Cadene, P. and M. Holstrom (eds) (1992), *Decentralized Production in India*, New Delhi: Sage.

Caillez, F. and J.P. Pages (1976), *Introduction à l'analyse des données*, Paris: SMASII.

Cainelli, G. and R. Leoncini (1999), 'Esternalità e sviluppo industriale di lungo periodo in Italia. Un'analisi a livello provinciale', *L'Industria*, **XX** (1), 147–66.

Calza-Bini, P., M.C. Bosco, C. Oteri and D. Pieri (1996), *Sistema locale e distretto industriale: il caso di Civita Castellana*, Civita Castellana: Edizioni Biblioteca Comunale.

Camagni, R. (1991), 'Introduction: From the Local "Milieu" to Innovation through Cooperation Networks', in R. Camagni (ed.), *Innovation Networks: Spatial Perspectives*, London: Belhaven Press, pp. 1–9.

Cantwell, J.A. (1989), *Technological Innovation and Multinational Corporation*, Oxford: Basil Blackwell.

Cantwell, J.A. (1992), 'The Effects of Integration on the Structure of Multinational Corporation Activity in the EC', in M.W. Klein and P.J.J. Welfens (eds), *Multinationals in the New Europe and Global Trade*, Berlin: Springer-Verlag.

Cantwell, J.A. (ed.) (1994), *Transnational Corporations and Innovatory Activities*, London: Routledge.

Capecchi, V. (1990), 'Flexible specialization and industrial districts in Emilia-Romagna', in F. Pyke, G. Becattini and W. Sengenberger (eds),

Industrial Districts and Inter-firm Co-operation in Italy, Geneva: International Institute for Labor Studies, pp. 20–36.

Carroll, G.R. (1997), 'Long-term evolutionary change in organizational populations: theory, models and empirical findings in industrial demography', *Industrial and Corporate Change*, **6** (1), 120–43.

Casson, M.C. (1995), *Entrepreneurship and Business Culture*, Aldershot, UK and Brookfield, US: Edward Elgar.

Cavalieri, A. and H. Liberanome (eds) (1989), *L'organizzazione commerciale delle esportazioni nei distretti industriali della Toscana Centrale*, Milano: F. Angeli.

CENSIS (1984), *Dal sommerso al post-industriale*, Milano: F. Angeli.

CENSIS (1997), *Forum sulle economie locali*, Roma: CENSIS.

CENSIS – Unioncamere (1995), *Da protagonisti a leader: imprese e istituzioni nei distretti industriali che cambiano*, Milano: F. Angeli.

Cersosimo, D. (2000), 'Sulle tracce dei distretti', in D. Cersosimo and C. Donzelli, *Mezzo Giorno*, Roma: Donzelli, pp. 187–208.

Chipman, J.S. (1965), 'External economies of scale and competitive equilibrium', *Quarterly Journal of Economics*, (84), 347–85.

CITER (1990), *Struttura e strategia delle imprese del tessile abbigliamento in Emilia Romagna*, Nomisma and Dipartimento di economia aziendale dell'Università di Modena.

Coase, R. (1937), 'The nature of the firm', *Economica*, **4**, 386–405.

Coleman, J.S. (1988), 'Social capital in the creation of human capital', *Academic Journal of Sociology*, (94), 95–120.

Comei, M. (2000), 'Percorsi di industrializzazione leggera: piccole imprese dell'area barese tra marginalità e nuove opportunità (1911–1981)', in *Annali di storia dell'impresa*, Assi, Bologna: Il Mulino, pp. 151–95.

Cooke, P. and K. Morgan (1998), *The Associational Economy. Firms, Regions, and Innovation*, Oxford: Oxford University Press.

Coombes, M.G., A.E. Green and S. Openshaw (1986), 'An efficient algorithm to generate official statistical reporting areas: the case of 1984 Travel-To-Work areas revision in Britain', *Journal of the Operational Research Society*, (10), 943–53.

Corò, G., P. Gurisatti and A. Rossi (1998), 'Il distretto sport system di Montebelluna', in G. Corò and E. Rullani (eds), *Percorsi locali di internazionalizzazione. Competenze e autorganizzazione nei distretti industriali del nord-est*, Milano: F. Angeli.

Corò, G. and E. Rullani (eds) (1998), *Percorsi locali di internazionalizzazione. Competenze e autorganizzazione nei distretti industriali del nord-est*, Milano: F. Angeli.

Corvino, A. (1988), *Lo sviluppo del settore calzaturiero in un'area periferica*, Napoli: ESI.

CREI (1995), *Industrial Districts Survey*, Vicenza. CREI.

Dei, A. (1998), 'Gli accordi collettivi sulle tariffe di fornitura per conto terzi nel distretto tessile pratese', *Sviluppo Locale*, **V** (9), 74–98.

Dei Ottati, G. (1987), 'Il mercato comunitario', in G. Becattini (ed.), *Mercato e forze locali: il distretto industriale*. Bologna: Il Mulino, pp. 117–42.

Dei Ottati, G. (1994), 'Trust, inter-linking transactions and credit in the industrial district', *Cambridge Journal of Economics*, **18** (6), 529–46.

Dematteis, G. (1994), 'Possibilità e limiti dello sviluppo industriale', *Sviluppo Locale*, **1** (1), 10–30.

D'Ercole, M. (1992), 'Il distretto di Casarano', in F. Onida, G. Viesti and A.M. Falzoni, *I distretti industriali: Crisi o evoluzione?* Milano: EGEA, pp. 169–87.

Di Bernardo, B. and E. Rullani (1988), *Il management e le macchine*, Bologna: Il Mulino.

Dicken, P. and P.E. Lloyd (1990), *Location in Space. A theoretical Approach to Economic Geography*, New York: Harper & Row.

Di Tommaso, M. and R. Rabellotti (eds) (1999), *Efficienza collettiva e sistemi d'impresa*, Bologna: Il Mulino.

Dunning, J.H. (1988), *Explaining International Production*, London: Unwin Hyman.

Dunning, J.H. (1992), 'Re-evaluating the benefits of foreign direct investment', *DP in International Investment and Business Studies*, 188.

Dunning, J.H (1993), *Multinational Enterprises and The Global Economy*, Wokingham: Addison-Wesley.

Esposito, G.F. (1994), 'Impresa e mercato: alcune ipotesi interpretative sulle dinamiche evolutive dei distretti industriali', Istituto G. Tagliacarne, Working Paper No. 37.

Esposito, G.F. and M. Labia (1993), 'I distretti industriali tra conservazione e mutamento strategico', *Studi e Informazioni*, Banca Toscana, **16** (1), 123–39.

Everitt, B. (1981), *Cluster Analysis*, (2nd ed), New York: Halsted Press.

Fabiani, S. and G. Pellegrini (1998), 'Un'analisi quantitativa delle imprese nei distretti industriali italiani: redditività, produttività e costo del lavoro', *L'Industria*, **XIX** (4), 811–31.

Fabbrini, A. and R. Olivieri (1999), 'Il distretto industriale di Ascoli Piceno', *Economia Marche*, **XVIII** (2), 113–29.

FEDERCOMIN (2001), *I distretti produttivi digitali*, Roma (www.federcomin.it).

Ferrucci, L. and R. Varaldo (1993), 'La natura e la dinamica dell'impresa distrettuale', *Economia e Politica Industriale*, **XX** (80), 73–91.

Floridia, A. (1994), 'Continuità e mutamento nel distretto conciario di Santa Croce', in A. Floridia, L. Parri and F. Quaglia, *Regolazione sociale ed economie locali: attori, strategie, risorse*, Milano: Irpet-F. Angeli, pp. 106–208.

Forni, M. and S. Paba (1997), 'Esternalità tecnologiche e crescita delle industrie locali. L'evidenza italiana: 1971–1991', mimeo.

Franchi, M. and V. Rieser (1991), 'Le categorie sociologiche nell'analisi del distretto industriale', *Stato e Mercato*, (33), 451–76.

Freschi, C. (1992), *I centri di servizi alle imprese in Toscana*, Firenze: Regione Toscana.

Freschi, C. (1994), 'Istituzioni politiche e sviluppo locale nella terza Italia', *Sviluppo locale*, **I** (1), 71–118.

Fuà, G. (1983), 'L'industrializzazione nel Nord est e nel Centro', in G. Fuà and C. Zacchia (eds), *Industrializzazione senza fratture*, Bologna: Il Mulino.

Gambetta, D. (1988), 'Can We Trust Trust?', in D. Gambetta (ed.), *Trust: Making and Breaking Co-operative Relations*, New York: Blackwell, pp. 213–37.

Gandolfi, V. (1988), *Aree sistema: internazionalizzazione e reti telematiche*, Milano: F. Angeli.

Garofoli, G. (1983), *Industrializzazione diffusa in Lombardia*, Milano: Irer-F. Angeli.

Garofoli, G. (1991a), *Modelli locali di sviluppo*, Milano, Progetto finalizzato CNR-F. Angeli.

Garofoli, G. (1991b), 'Local Networks, Innovation and Policy in Italian Industrial Districts', in Bergman et al. (eds), *Regions Reconsidered. Economic Networks, Innovation and Local Development in Industrialized Countries*, London: Mansell.

Garofoli, G. (1992), 'Industrial Districts: Structure and Transformation', in G. Garofoli (ed.), *Endogeneous Development and Southern Europe*, Avebury: Aldershot, pp. 49–60.

Ginsborg, P. and F. Ramella (eds) (1999), *Un'Italia Minore: Famiglia, istruzione e tradizioni civiche in Valdelsa*, Firenze, Regione Toscana: Giunti Editore.

Glaeser, E.L., D.I. Laibson, J.A. Scheinkman and C.L. Soutter (2000), 'Measuring trust', *The Quarterly Journal of Economics*, **115** (3), 811–46.

Glaeser, E.L., H.D. Kallal, J.A. Scheinkman and A. Shleifer (1992), 'Growth in cities', *Journal of Political Economy*, **100** (6), 1126–52.

Gobbo, F. (ed.) (1989), *Distretti e sistemi produttivi alla soglia degli anni '90*, Milano: F. Angeli.

Good, D. (1988), 'Individuals, Interpersonal Relations, and Trust', in D. Gambetta (ed.), *Trust: Making and Breaking Co-operative Relations*, New York: Blackwell, pp. 31–48.

Grabher, G. (ed.) (1993), *The Embedded Firm. On Socioeconomics of*

Industrial Networks, London: Routledge.

Grandori, A. (1990), 'Epistemologia ed economia aziendale: note per un dibattito', *L'Industria*, **XI** (4), 76–103.

Grandori, A. (1997), 'An organizational assessment of interfirm co-ordination modes', *Organization Studies*, **18** (6), 897–925.

Grandori, A. and G. Soda (1995), 'Inter-firm networks: antecedents, mechanisms and forms', *Organization Studies*, **16** (2), 183–214.

Granovetter, M. (1985), 'Economic action and social structure: the problem of embeddedness', *American Journal of Sociology*, **91** (3), 481–510.

Granovetter, M. (1992), 'Problems of Explanation in Economic Sociology', in N. Nohria and R.G. Eccles (eds), *Networks and Organizations: Structure, Form, and Action*, Boston, Massachusetts: Harvard Business School Press.

Grotz, R. and B. Braun (1997), 'Territorial or trans-territorial networking: spatial aspects of technology-oriented co-operation within the German mechanical engineering industry', *Regional Studies*, **31** (6), 545–57.

Guerra, P. (1988), 'I sistemi produttivi mobilieri del Livenza e del Quartier del Piave', in G. Corò and E. Rullani, *Percorsi locali di internazionalizzazione: Competenze e autorganizzazione nei distretti industriali del nord-est*, Milano: F. Angeli.

Gurisatti, P. and C. Vedù (eds) (1993), *Analisi e prospettive della ceramica artistica vicentina*, Vicenza: Camera di Commercio di Vicenza.

Hannan, M. and J. Freeman (1989), *Organizational Ecology*, Cambridge: Cambridge University Press.

Harrison, B. and M. Storper (1991), 'Flexibility, hierarchy and regional development: the changing structure of industrial production systems and their forms of governance in the 1990s', *Research Policy*, **20** (5), 343–73.

Henderson, V. (1996), *Externalities and Industrial development*, Providence (USA), Brown University, mimeo.

Henderson, V., A. Kuncoro and M. Turner (1995), 'Industrial development in cities', *Journal of Political Economy*, **CIII** (5), 1067–90.

Herrigel, G. (1996), *Industrial Constructions: the Sources of German Industrial Power*, Cambridge: Cambridge University Press.

Hofstede, G. (1991), *Cultures and Organizations: Software of the Mind*, London: McGraw-Hill.

Hutter, M. and G. Teubner (1993), 'The parasitic role of hybrids', *Journal of Institutional and Theoretical Economics*, **149** (4), 706–15.

Iannuzzi, E. (1995), 'Verso una ridefinizione dei caratteri del distretto conciario di Solofra', *Rassegna Economica*, **LVII** (3/4), 863–92.

ISFOL (1995), *Rapporto Isfol 1995. Formazione, orientamento, occupazione, nuove tecnologie, professionalità*, Milano: F. Angeli.

ISTAT (1994), *Elezioni della Camera dei deputati e del Senato della*

Repubblica: 5 aprile 1992, Roma: ISTAT.

ISTAT (1995a), Census of population: *7° Censimento generale della popolazione e delle abitazioni*, 25 October 1991, Roma: ISTAT.

ISTAT (1995b), Census of industry: *7° Censimento generale dell'Industria, del Commercio e dell'Artigianato*, 26 October, 1991, Roma: ISTAT.

ISTAT (1996), *Rapporto Annuale 1995*, Roma: ISTAT.

ISTAT (1997), *I sistemi locali del lavoro*, F. Sforzi (ed.), Roma: ISTAT.

ISTAT (1998), *I censimenti delle attività produttive dal 1951 al 1991. Dati comunali*, Roma: ISTAT.

ISTAT (1999a), *Il commercio internazionale italiano per province*, Roma: ISTAT.

ISTAT (1999b), *Indagine sui conti delle imprese con 10 addetti e oltre*, Roma: ISTAT

ISTAT (2000), *Censimento intermedio dell'industria, 1996*, Roma: ISTAT.

ISTAT (2001), *I cittadini stranieri in Italia*, Roma: ISTAT (www./demo/ Istat.it).

ISTAT-Irpet (1989), *I mercati locali del lavoro*, Milano: F. Angeli.

Istituto Tagliacarne (2000), *Il reddito delle province italiane*, Milano: F. Angeli.

Jacobs, J. (1969), *The Economics of Cities*, New York: Random House.

Jarillo, J.C. (1988), 'On strategic networks', *Strategic Management Journal*, **9** (1), 31–41.

Keeble, D. and F. Wilkinson (1999), 'Collective learning and knowledge development in the evolution of regional clusters of high technology SMEs in Europe', *Regional Studies*, **33** (4), 295–303.

Kristensen, P.H. (1992), 'Industrial Districts in West Jutland', in F. Pyke and W. Sengenberger (eds), *Industrial Districts and Local Economic Regeneration*, Geneva: ILO.

Krugman, P. (1991a), *Geography and Trade*, Cambridge MA: MIT Press.

Krugman, P. (1991b), 'Increasing returns and economic geography', *Journal of Political Economy*, **99** (33), 483–99.

Krugman, P. (1996), *The Self-Organising Economy*, Oxford: Blackwell.

Langlois, R.N. (1988), 'Economic change and the boundaries of the firm', *Journal of Institutions and Theoretical Economics*, **144** (4), 635–57.

Langlois, R.N. and P.L. Robertson (1995), *Firms, Markets and Economic Change*, London & New York: Routledge.

Lazerson, M.H. (1990), 'Subcontracting in the Modena knitwear industry', in F. Pyke, G. Becattini and W. Sengenberger, *Industrial Districts and Inter-firm Co-operation in Italy*, Geneva: International Institute for Labour Studies, pp. 108–33.

Lazerson, M. (1995), 'A new Phoenix? Modern Putting-Out in the Modena knitwear industry,' *Administrative Science Quarterly*, (40), 34–59.

Lazzeretti, L. and D. Storai (1999), 'An Ecology-Based Interpretation of District "Complexification": the Prato district evolution from 1946 to 1993', in E. Rullani, F. Belussi and G. Gottardi (eds), *Knowledge Creation, Collective Learning and Variety of Institutional Arrangements*, forthcominig, London: Kluwer, first published in *Sviluppo Locale*, **VII** (13), 2000, 5–32.

Lawson C. (1998), 'Towards a competence theory of the region', *Cambridge Journal of Economics*, **23**, 151–66

Lecoq, B. (1989), 'Réseaux et système productif régional. Contenu, portée et fondements théoriques du concept de réseaux', *Dossiers de l'IRER*, **23** (53), Université de Neuchâtel.

Leijonhufvud, A. (1986), 'Capitalism and the Factor System', in R. Langlois (ed.), *Economics as a Process: Essays on the New Institutional Economics*, New York: Cambridge University Press.

Locke, R.M. (1995), 'Una economia differenziata: politica locale e cambiamento industriale', *Stato e Mercato*, (43), 27–64.

Lorenz, E.H (1992), 'Trust, community, and cooperation. Toward a theory of industrial districts', in M. Storper and A.J. Scott, *Pathways to Industrialization and Regional Development*, London: Routledge, pp. 195–204.

Lorenz, E.H. (1993), 'Flexible production Systems and the Social Construction of Trust', *Politics and Society*, **21** (3), 307–24.

Lorenzoni, G. (1990), *L'architettura di sviluppo delle imprese minori. Costellazioni e gruppi*, Bologna: Il Mulino.

Lorenzoni, G. and O. Ornati (1988), 'Constellation of firms and new ventures', *Journal of Business Venturing*, (3), 41–57.

Luhman, N. (1988), 'Familiarity, Confidence, Trust: Problems and Alternatives', in D. Gambetta (ed.), *Trust: Making and Breaking Cooperative Relations*, New York: Blackwell, pp. 94–107.

Lundvall, B.Å. (1988), 'Innovation as an Interactive Process: From User-Producer Interaction to the National System of Innovation', in G. Dosi, C. Freeman, R. Nelson, G. Silverberg and L. Soete (eds), *Technical Change and Economic Theory*, London: Pinter Publishers.

Lundvall, B.Å. (ed.) (1992), *National Systems of Innovation*, London: Pinter Publishers.

Maillat, D. (1995), 'Territorial dynamics, innovative milieux and regional policy', *Entrepreneurship and Regional Development*, **7**, 157–65.

Maillat, D. and B. Lecoq (1992), 'New technologies and transformation of regional structures in Europe: The role of the milieu', *Entrepreneurship & Regional Development*, **4**, 1–20.

Manacorda, P.M. and M. Pattarozzi (1990), 'Informazione e comunicazione nei distretti industriali delle calzature e del mobile nelle Marche', **IX** (1),

5–36.

Markusen, A. (1996), 'Sticky Places in Slippery Space: A Typology of Industrial Districts', *Economic Geography*, **72** (3), 293–313.

Marshall, A. (1920), *Industry and Trade*, London & New York: Macmillan.

Marshall, A. (1950), *Principles of Economics*, (8th edn) London and New York: Macmillan.

Martin, R. (1999), 'The new "geographical turn" in economics: some critical reflections', *Cambridge Journal of Economics*, **23 (2)**, 65–91.

Maselli, M. (1993), 'Mercato terzisti e tariffe', *Pratofutura*, (51), 1–3.

Maskell, P. (1999), 'Globalisation and Industrial Competitiveness: the Process and Consequences of Ubiquitification', in E. Malecki and P. Oinas (eds), *Making Connections: Technological Learning and Regional Economic Change*, Aldershot: Ashgate, pp. 35–59.

Maskell, P. and A. Malmberg (1999), 'Localised learning and industrial competitiveness', *Cambridge Journal of Economics*, **23** (2), 167–86.

Meldolesi, L. (1995), 'Il Mezzogiorno perduto e ritrovato', *Sviluppo locale*, **II** (2/3), 43–73.

Meldolesi, L. (1998), *Dalla parte del Sud*, Bari: Laterza.

Messina, P. (2001), *Nuovi modelli di regolazione sociale*, Padova: Utet.

Mezzino, A. (1985), 'Sviluppo settoriale e organizzazione territoriale di un'area di piccola impresa: il distretto di Pesaro', in R. Innocenti (ed.), *Piccola città e piccola impresa*, Milano: Angeli.

Micucci, G. (1999), 'Il distretto calzaturiero di Civitanova Marche', *Economia Marche*, **XIX** (2), 85–111.

Mistri, M. (1997), 'Distretti industriali e "competenza comunicativa" come processo autopoietico', in E. Benedetti, M. Mistri and S. Solari (eds), *Teorie evolutive e trasformazioni economiche*, Padova: Cedam.

Molinari, G. (1996), 'L'area sistema dei salotti della Murgia', in L. Baculo (ed.), *Impresa forte politica debole*, Napoli: Edizioni Scientifiche Italiane.

Morgan, K. (1997), 'The learning region: institutions, innovation and regional renewal', *Regional Studies*, **31** (5), 491–503.

Mortara, A. (1985), *Le associazioni italiane*, Collana Ciriec, Milano: F. Angeli.

Moussanet, M. and L. Paolazzi (eds) (1992), *Gioielli, bambole, coltelli*, Milano: Il Sole 24Ore.

Nohria, N. and R.G. Eccles (eds) (1992), *Networks and Organizations*, Boston, Massachusetts: Harvard Business School Press.

Nonaka, I. (1994), 'A dynamic theory of organizational knowledge creation', *Organization Science*, **5** (1), 14–37.

Nuti, F. (1989), 'Sistemi articolati di produzione e rapporti tra imprese', in F. Gobbo (ed.), *Distretti e sistemi produttivi alla soglia degli anni '90*, Milano: F. Angeli.

Nuti, F. (ed.) (1992), *I distretti dell'industria manifatturiera in Italia*, Vol. II., Milano: F. Angeli.

OECD (1996), *Networks of Enterprises and Local Development, Territorial Development*, Paris: OECD.

Omiccioli, M. and P. Tamburini (1999), 'Il distretto del mobile di Pesaro', *Economia Marche*, **XIX** (2), 67–83.

Onida, F., G. Viesti and A.M. Falzoni. (1992), *I distretti industriali: Crisi o evoluzione?*, Milano: EGEA.

Origo, I. (1957), *The Merchant of Prato*, London: Jonathan Cape.

OSEM (1995/6), *Osservatorio sulle dinamiche del distretto di Montebelluna*, Montebelluna: Museo dello scarpone.

Paci, M. (1982), *La struttura sociale italiana*, Bologna: Il Mulino.

Paloscia, R. (1987), 'Nuova geografia industriale e aree a economia diffusa del centro-sud: il caso di Barletta', in R. Innocenti (ed.), *Piccola città e piccola impresa*, Milano: Franco Angeli.

Paniccia, I. (1998), 'One, a hundred, thousands industrial districts. Organizational variety in local networks of small and medium sized enterprises', *Organization Studies*, **19** (4), 677–99.

Paniccia, I. (1999), *Italian Industrial Districts. Results of a comparative study*, PhD dissertation, University of Reading.

Parri, L. (1994), 'Alleanze aziendali, associazionismo imprenditoriale e intervento pubblico nel distretto conciario di Arzignano', in A. Floridia, L. Parri and F. Quaglia, *Regolazione sociale ed economie locali: attori, strategie, risorse*, Milano: Irpet – F. Angeli, pp. 209–43.

Passaro, R. (1994), 'Le strategie competitive delle piccole imprese di un'area interna del mezzogiorno: il caso del settore conciario a Solofra', *Piccola Impresa/Small Business*, (3), 85–112.

Pavan, M. (1992), 'Il distretto ceramico di Sassuolo-Scandiano', in F. Onida, G. Viesti and A.M. Falzoni, *I Distretti Industriali: Crisi o Evoluzione?*, Milano: EGEA, pp. 303–41.

Pavitt, K. (1984), 'Sectoral patterns of technological change: toward a taxonomy and a theory', *Research Policy*, **13**, 343–73.

Perroux, F. (1955), 'Note sur la notion de pole de croissance', *Économie Appliqée*, (1/2), 307–20.

Perrow, C. (1992), 'Small-firms networks', in N. Nohria and R.G. Eccles (eds), *Networks and Organizations*, Boston, MA: Harvard Business School Press, pp. 445–70.

Perulli, P. (ed.) (1998), *Neoregionalismo. L'economia-arcipelago*, Torino: Bollati Boringhieri.

Pietrobelli, C. (2000), 'Competitiveness and its Socio-economic Foundations: Empirical Evidence on the Italian Industrial Districts', in M. Bagella and L. Becchetti (eds), *Evolutionary Patterns of Industrial Districts.*

Theoretical and Empirical Analysis, Heidelberg: Physica Verlag, pp. 3–20.

Pilotti, L. (1997), 'I sistemi locali industriali del nordest: apprendimento, conoscenza, istituzioni', *Sviluppo Locale*, **IV** (5), 64–122.

Piore, M.J. (1990), 'Work, Labour and Action: Work experience in a system of flexible production', in F. Pyke, G. Becattini and W. Sengenberger, *Industrial Districts and Inter-firm co-operation in Italy*, Geneva: International Institute for Labour Studies, pp. 52–74.

Piore, M.J. (1992), 'Fragments of a Cognitive Theory of Technological Change and Organizational Structure', in N. Nohria and R.G. Eccles (eds), *Networks and Organizations: Structure, Form, and Action*, Boston, MA: Harvard Business School Press, pp. 430–44.

Piore, M.J. and C.F. Sabel (1984), *The Second Industrial Divide*, New York: Basic Books.

Pizzi, P. (1998), 'Il distretto tessile di Teramo', *Economia Marche*, **XVII** (3), 101–12.

Polanyi, M. (1962), *Personal Knowledge. Towards a post-Critical Philosophy*, London: Routledge and Kegan.

Porter, M.E. (1990), *The Competitive Advantage of Nations*, New York: The Free Press.

Prahalad, C. and G. Hamel (1990), 'The core competence of the corporation', *Harvard Business Review*, **3** (1), 79–91.

Putnam, R.D. (1993), *Making democracy work. Civic traditions in modern Italy*, Princeton: Princeton University Press.

Pyke, F. and W. Sengernberger (1990), Introduction, in F. Pyke, G. Becattini and W. Sengenberger (eds) (1990), *Industrial Districts and Inter-firm Co-operation in Italy*, Geneva: International Institute for Labour Studies, ILO, pp. 1–9.

Powell, W.W. (1990), 'Neither market nor hierarchy: network forms of organization', in G. Thompson, J. Frances, R. Levacic and J. Mitchell (1991), *Markets, Hierarchies and Networks*, London: Sage Publications-The Open University, pp. 265–76.

Quaglia, F. (1995), 'Nuove stilizzazioni nell'organizzazione industriale delle Marche', *Economia Marche*, **XIV** (3), pp. 357–403.

Rabellotti, R. (1997), *External Economies and Cooperation in Industrial Districts: a Comparison of Italy and Mexico*, New York: MacMillan.

Regione Emilia Romagna, Comune di Carpi and Ricerche e Interventi (1998), *Osservatorio del distretto tessile abbigliamento nel distretto di Carpi. Quarto Rapporto*, Carpi.

Ring, P.S. (1993) 'Processes facilitating reliance on trust in inter-organizational networks', paper prepared at the EMOT conference, Berlin, September 1993.

Romer, P.M. (1986), 'Increasing returns and long-run growth', *Journal of Political Economy*, (94), 1002–37.

Russo, M. (1985), 'Technical change and the industrial district: The role of interfirm relations in the growth and transformation of ceramic tile production in Italy', *Research Policy*, **14**, 329–43.

Russo, M., G. Allari, S. Bertini, P. Bonaretti, E. De Leo, G. Fiorani and G. Rinaldini (2000), 'The challenges for the next decade: notes on the debate on the development of the Emilia-Romagna region', ESCR Working Paper No. 176.

Sabel, C.F. (1995), 'Experimental regionalism and the dilemmas of regional economic policy in Europe', mimeo, MIT, Cambridge, MA.

Sabel, C. and J. Zeitlin (1982), 'Historical alternatives to mass production: Politics, market and technology in nineteenth century industrialisation', *Past and Present*, **108**, 133–76.

Salais, R. and M. Storper (1992), 'The four worlds of contemporary industry', *The Cambridge Journal of Economics*, **16**, 79–98.

Saxenian, A. (1994), *Regional Advantage: Culture and Competition in Silicon Valley and Route 128*, Cambridge, MA: Harvard University Press.

Scitovski, T. (1954), 'Two concepts of external economies', *Journal of Political Economy*, **62**, 143–51.

Scott, A. (1998a), 'Flexible production systems and regional development: The rise of new industrial space in North America and Western Europe', *International Journal of Urban and Regional Research*, **12**, 171–86.

Scott, A. (1998b), *New Industrial Space*, London: Pion.

Scott, A. and M. Storper (1989), 'The Geographical Foundations and Social Regulation of Flexible Production Complexes', in J. Wolch and M. Dean (eds), *The Power of Geography: How Territory Shapes Social Life*, London and Boston: Unwin Hyman, pp. 21–40.

Secchia, P. (1960), *Capitalismo e classe operaia nel centro laniero d'Italia*, Roma: Editori Riuniti.

Sforzi, F. (1987), 'Riflessioni sul distretto industriale: Un'ipotesi di identificazione spaziale', in R. Innocenti (ed.), *Piccola città e piccola impresa*, Milano: F. Angeli.

Sforzi, F . (1990), 'The Quantitative Importance of Marshallian Industrial Districts in the Italian Economy', in F. Pyke, G. Becattini and W. Sengenberger (eds), *Industrial Districts and Inter-firm Co-operation in Italy*, pp. 75–107.

Sforzi, F. (1991), 'Il distretto industriale marshalliano: elementi costitutivi e riscontro empirico nella realtà italiana', in S. Conti and P.A. Julien (eds), *Miti e realtà del 'modello' italiano. Letture sull'economia periferica*, Bologna: Patron, pp. 83–115.

Signorini, L.F. (1994), The price of Prato, or measuring the industrial district effect, *Papers in Regional Science*, **73**, 369–92.

Signorini, L.F. (2001), *Lo sviluppo locale: un'indagine della Banca d'Italia sui distretti industriali*, Roma: Meridiana Libri.

Solinas, G. (1982), 'Labour market segmentation and workers' careers: the case of Italian knitwear industry', *Cambridge Journal of Economics*, **6**, 331–52.

Soubeyran, A. and J. Thisse (1998), 'Learning by doing and the development of industrial districts', FEEM Working Paper, ETA 46.

Spence, N. et al. (1982), *British Cities: an Analysis of Urban Change*, Oxford: Pergamon Press.

Sraffa, P. (1926), 'The laws of returns under competitive conditions', *Economic Journal*, **40**, 79–116.

Staber, U. (1997), 'An ecological perspective on entrepreneurship in industrial districts', *Entrepreneurship and Regional Development*, **9**, 45–64.

Staber, U. (1998), 'Inter-firm co-operation and competition in industrial districts', *Organization Studies*, **19** (4), 701–24.

Stigler, G. (1951), 'The division of labour is limited by the extent of the market', *Journal of Political Economy*, **59** (3), 185–93.

Storey, D.J. (1982), *Entrepreneurship and the New Firm*, London: Croom Helm.

Storper, M. (1992), 'The limits to globalization: technology districts and international trade', *Economic Geography*, **68**, 60–93.

Storper, M. (1993), 'Regional "worlds" of production: learning and innovation in the technology districts of France, Italy and the USA', *Regional Studies*, **27** (5), 433–55.

Swann, G.M.P., M. Prevezer and D. Stout (2000), *The Dynamics of Industrial Clustering*, Oxford: Oxford University Press.

Sylos Labini, P. (1974), *Le classi sociali in Italia*, Bari: Laterza.

Taylor, F. (1989), quoted in Lorenz, 1992.

Thompson, G., J. Frances, R. Levacic and J. Mitchell (1991), *Markets, Hierarchies and Networks*, London: Sage Publications–The Open University.

Thompson, J.D. (1967), *Organizations in Action*, New York: McGraw-Hill.

Thorelli, H.B. (1986), 'Networks: between markets and hierarchies', *Strategic Management Journal*, **7** (1), 37–51.

Toennies, F. (1963), *Gemeinschaft und Gesellschaft*, Leipzig, 1887; It. Transl. *Comunità e società*, Milano: Edizioni Comunità.

Tribalat, M., J.P. Garson, Y. Moulier-Boutang and R. Silberman (1991), *Cent Ans d'Immigration, Etrangers d'hier Français d'Aujourdhui*, Paris: PUF.

Trigilia, C. (1986), *Grandi partiti e piccole imprese*, Bologna: Il Mulino.

Trigilia, C. (1990), 'Work and Politics in the Third Italy's Industrial

Districts', in F. Pyke, G. Becattini and W. Sengenberger, *Industrial Districts and Inter-firm Co-operation in Italy*, Geneva: International Institute for Labour Studies, pp. 160–84.

Trigilia, C. (1989), 'Il distretto industriale di Prato', in M. Regini and C. Sabel (eds), *Strategie di riaggiustamento industriale*, Bologna: Il Mulino, pp. 283–333.

Unione industriale di Prato (1998), *7° rapporto annuale sul sistema economico pratese*, www.ui.po.it.

Unione industriale di Prato (2000), *Relazione Annuale*, www.ui.po.it.

Varela, F.J. (1981), 'Autonomy and Autopoiesis', in G. Roth and H. Schwegler (eds), *Self-organizing Systems: an Interdisciplinary Approach*, Frankfurt and New York: Campus Verlag, pp. 14–23.

Varela, F.J., H.R. Maturana and R. Uribe (1974), 'Autopoiesi: The organization of living systems, its characterization and a model', *Biosystems*, (5), 187–96.

Venables, A. (1996), 'Equilibrium locations of vertically linked industries', *International Economic Review*, **37**, 341–59.

Viesti, G. (1995a), 'Modelli e percorsi di sviluppo: alcune riflessioni intorno al caso della Puglia', *Economia Marche*, **XIV** (2), 321–46.

Viesti, G. (1995b),'Lo sviluppo possibile. Casi di successo internazionale di distretti industriali nel Sud d'Italia', *Rassegna Economica*, **LIX** (1), 119–40.

Viesti, G. (1996), 'Il Mezzogiorno esportatore. Caratteristiche strutturali e dinamiche 1985-1995', Comunicazione presentata alla XXXVII Riunione Scientifica Annuale della SIE, 25-26 ottobre 1996, Università di Bologna.

Viesti, G. (2000), *Come nascono i distretti industriali*, Bari: Editori Laterza.

Ward, J.H.C. (1963), 'Hierarchical grouping to optimize an objective function', *Journal of American Statistical Association*, (58), 236–44.

Wasserman, S. and K. Faust (1994), *Social Network Analysis: Methods and Applications*, Cambridge: Cambridge University Press

Wells, L.T. Jr and A.G. Wint (1990), 'Marketing a Country: Promotion as a Tool for Attracting Foreign Investment', Foreign Investment Advisory Occasional Paper No 1, Washington DC: IFCMGA.

Wernerfeld, B. (1984), 'A resource-based view of the firm', *Strategic Management Journal*, **5** (2), 171–80.

Williamson, O.E. (1975), *Market and Hierarchies: Analysis and Anti-trust implications*, New York: The Free Press.

Williamson, O.E. (1985), *The Economic Institutions of Capitalism*, New York: The Free Press.

Williamson, O.E. (1991), 'Comparative economic organization: the analysis of discrete structural alternatives', *Administrative Science Quarterly*, (36), 3–37.

Williamson, O.E. (1992), 'The Firm as a Nexus of Treaties: an Introduction', in M. Aoki, B. Gustafsson and O.E. Williamson (eds), *The Firm as a Nexus of Treaties*, London: Sage Publications, pp. 1–25.

Index